D1222975

Org Mode 7 Reference Manual

Organize your life with GNU Emacs
Release 7.3

by Carsten Dominik

with contributions by David O'Toole, Bastien Guerry, Philip Rooke, Dan Davison, Eric Schulte, and Thomas Dye.
Edited for publication by Brian Gough and Barry Gidden

Published by Network Theory Ltd

A catalogue record for this book is available from the British Library.

First Printing, November 2010

Published by Network Theory Limited.

Email: info@network-theory.co.uk

ISBN 978-1-906966-08-9

Further information about this book is available from
http://www.network-theory.co.uk/orgmode/

This book has an unconditional guarantee. If you are not fully satisfied with
your purchase for any reason, please contact the publisher at the address above.

This manual is for Org version 7.3.

Table of Contents

Publisher's Preface

This manual describes how to use Org mode, a mode for the Emacs editor for organising notes, project planning, and document authoring.

Org is *free software*. The term "free software" refers to your freedom to run, copy, distribute, study, change and improve the software. With Org you have all these freedoms.

You can support free software by joining the Free Software Foundation, which is dedicated to promoting the right to copy, modify, and redistribute computer programs. It also works to raise awareness of the ethical and political issues of freedom in the use of software. For more information visit the website www.fsf.org.

Donations to fund the development of Org itself can be made online through through the Org mode website at orgmode.org.

Brian Gough
Publisher
November 2010

1 Introduction

1.1 Summary

Org is a mode for keeping notes, maintaining TODO lists, and doing project planning with a fast and effective plain-text system.

Org develops organizational tasks around NOTES files that contain lists or information about projects as plain text. Org is implemented on top of Outline mode, which makes it possible to keep the content of large files well structured. Visibility cycling and structure editing help to work with the tree. Tables are easily created with a built-in table editor. Org supports TODO items, deadlines, timestamps, and scheduling. It dynamically compiles entries into an agenda that utilizes and smoothly integrates much of the Emacs calendar and diary. Plain text URL-like links connect to websites, emails, Usenet messages, BBDB entries, and any files related to the projects. For printing and sharing of notes, an Org file can be exported as a structured ASCII file, as HTML, or (TODO and agenda items only) as an iCalendar file. It can also serve as a publishing tool for a set of linked web pages.

As a project planning environment, Org works by adding metadata to outline nodes. Based on this data, specific entries can be extracted in queries and create dynamic *agenda views*.

Org mode contains the Org Babel environment which allows you to work with embedded source code blocks in a file, to facilitate code evaluation, documentation, and literate programming techniques.

Org's automatic, context-sensitive table editor with spreadsheet capabilities can be integrated into any major mode by activating the minor Orgtbl mode. Using a translation step, it can be used to maintain tables in arbitrary file types, for example in LaTeX. The structure editing and list creation capabilities can be used outside Org with the minor Orgstruct mode.

Org keeps simple things simple. When first fired up, it should feel like a straightforward, easy to use outliner. Complexity is not imposed, but a large amount of functionality is available when you need it. Org is a toolbox and can be used in different ways and for different ends, for example:

- an outline extension with visibility cycling and structure editing
- an ASCII system and table editor for taking structured notes
- a TODO list editor
- a full agenda and planner with deadlines and work scheduling
- an environment in which to implement David Allen's GTD system
- a simple hypertext system, with HTML and LaTeX export
- a publishing tool to create a set of interlinked webpages
- an environment for literate programming

There is a website for Org which provides links to the newest version of Org, as well as additional information, frequently asked questions (FAQ), links to tutorials, etc. This page is located at http://orgmode.org.

1.2 Installation

Important: *If you are using a version of Org that is part of the Emacs distribution or an XEmacs package, please skip this section and go directly to Section 1.3 [Activation], page 5. To see what version of Org (if any) is part of your Emacs distribution, type* `M-x load-library RET org` *and then* `M-x org-version`.

If you have downloaded Org from the Web, either as a distribution '.zip' or '.tar' file, or as a Git archive, you must take the following steps to install it: go into the unpacked Org distribution directory and edit the top section of the file 'Makefile'. You must set the name of the Emacs binary (likely either 'emacs' or 'xemacs'), and the paths to the directories where local Lisp and Info files are kept. If you don't have access to the system-wide directories, you can simply run Org directly from the distribution directory by adding the 'lisp' subdirectory to the Emacs load path. To do this, add the following line to '.emacs':

```
(setq load-path (cons "~/path/to/orgdir/lisp" load-path))
```

If you plan to use code from the 'contrib' subdirectory, do a similar step for this directory:

```
(setq load-path (cons "~/path/to/orgdir/contrib/lisp" load-path))
```

Now byte-compile the Lisp files with the shell command:

```
make
```

If you are running Org from the distribution directory, this is all. If you want to install Org into the system directories, use (as administrator)

```
make install
```

Installing Info files is system dependent, because of differences in the 'install-info' program. In Debian it copies the info files into the correct directory and modifies the info directory file. In many other systems, the files need to be copied to the correct directory separately, and 'install-info' then only modifies the directory file. Check your system documentation to find out which of the following commands you need:

```
make install-info
make install-info-debian
```

Then add the following line to '.emacs'. It is needed so that Emacs can autoload functions that are located in files not immediately loaded when Org-mode starts.

```
(require 'org-install)
```

Do not forget to activate Org as described in the following section.

1.3 Activation

Add the following lines to your '.emacs' file. The last three lines define *global* keys for the commands org-store-link, org-agenda, and org-iswitchb—please choose suitable keys yourself.

```
;; The following lines are always needed.  Choose your own keys.
(add-to-list 'auto-mode-alist '("\\.org\\'" . org-mode))
(global-set-key "\C-cl" 'org-store-link)
(global-set-key "\C-ca" 'org-agenda)
(global-set-key "\C-cb" 'org-iswitchb)
```

Furthermore, you must activate font-lock-mode in Org buffers, because significant functionality depends on font-locking being active. You can do this with either one of the following two lines (XEmacs users must use the second option):

```
(global-font-lock-mode 1)                                    ; for all buffers
(add-hook 'org-mode-hook 'turn-on-font-lock) ; Org buffers only
```

With this setup, all files with extension '.org' will be put into Org-mode. As an alternative, make the first line of a file look like this:

```
MY PROJECTS      -*- mode: org; -*-
```

which will select Org-mode for this buffer no matter what the file's name is. See also the variable org-insert-mode-line-in-empty-file.

Many commands in Org work on the region if the region is *active*. To make use of this, you need to have transient-mark-mode (zmacs-regions in XEmacs) turned on. In Emacs 23 this is the default, in Emacs 22 you need to do this yourself with

```
(transient-mark-mode 1)
```

If you do not like transient-mark-mode, you can create an active region by using the mouse to select a region, or pressing C-(SPC) twice before moving the cursor.

1.4 Feedback

If you find problems with Org, or if you have questions, remarks, or ideas about it, please mail to the Org mailing list emacs-orgmode@gnu.org. If you are not a member of the mailing list, your mail will be passed to the list after a moderator has approved it.[1]

For bug reports, please first try to reproduce the bug with the latest version of Org available—if you are running an outdated version, it is quite possible that the bug has been fixed already. If the bug persists, prepare a report and provide as much information as possible, including the version information of Emacs (M-x emacs-version (RET)) and Org (M-x org-version (RET)), as well as the Org related setup in '.emacs'. The easiest way to do this is to use the command

---

[1] Please consider subscribing to the mailing list, in order to minimize the work the mailing list moderators have to do.

```
M-x org-submit-bug-report
```

which will put all this information into an Emacs mail buffer so that you only need to add your description. If you re not sending the Email from within Emacs, please copy and paste the content into your Email program.

If an error occurs, a backtrace can be very useful (see below on how to create one). Often a small example file helps, along with clear information about:

1. What exactly did you do?
2. What did you expect to happen?
3. What happened instead?

Thank you for helping to improve this program.

How to create a useful backtrace

If working with Org produces an error with a message you don't understand, you may have hit a bug. The best way to report this is by providing, in addition to what was mentioned above, a *backtrace*. This is information from the built-in debugger about where and how the error occurred. Here is how to produce a useful backtrace:

1. Reload uncompiled versions of all Org-mode Lisp files. The backtrace contains much more information if it is produced with uncompiled code. To do this, use

   ```
   C-u M-x org-reload RET
   ```

   or select `Org -> Refresh/Reload -> Reload Org` uncompiled from the menu.

2. Go to the `Options` menu and select `Enter Debugger on Error` (XEmacs has this option in the `Troubleshooting` sub-menu).

3. Do whatever you have to do to hit the error. Don't forget to document the steps you take.

4. When you hit the error, a '`*Backtrace*`' buffer will appear on the screen. Save this buffer to a file (for example using `C-x C-w`) and attach it to your bug report.

1.5 Typesetting conventions used in this manual

Org uses three types of keywords: TODO keywords, tags, and property names. In this manual we use the following conventions:

TODO
WAITING
: TODO keywords are written with all capitals, even if they are user-defined.

boss
ARCHIVE
: User-defined tags are written in lowercase; built-in tags with special meaning are written with all capitals.

Release

PRIORITY

> User-defined properties are capitalized; built-in properties with special meaning are written with all capitals.

2 Document structure

Org is based on Outline mode and provides flexible commands to edit the structure of the document.

2.1 Outlines

Org is implemented on top of Outline mode. Outlines allow a document to be organized in a hierarchical structure, which (at least for me) is the best representation of notes and thoughts. An overview of this structure is achieved by folding (hiding) large parts of the document to show only the general document structure and the parts currently being worked on. Org greatly simplifies the use of outlines by compressing the entire show/hide functionality into a single command, `org-cycle`, which is bound to the `TAB` key.

2.2 Headlines

Headlines define the structure of an outline tree. The headlines in Org start with one or more stars, on the left margin.[1] For example:

```
* Top level headline
** Second level
*** 3rd level
    some text
*** 3rd level
    more text


* Another top level headline
```

Some people find the many stars too noisy and would prefer an outline that has whitespace followed by a single star as headline starters. Section 16.8 [Clean view], page 204, describes a setup to realize this.

An empty line after the end of a subtree is considered part of it and will be hidden when the subtree is folded. However, if you leave at least two empty lines, one empty line will remain visible after folding the subtree, in order to structure the collapsed view. See the variable `org-cycle-separator-lines` to modify this behavior.

---

[1] See the variables `org-special-ctrl-a/e`, `org-special-ctrl-k`, and `org-ctrl-k-protect-subtree` to configure special behavior of C-a, C-e, and C-k in headlines.

2.3 Visibility cycling

Outlines make it possible to hide parts of the text in the buffer. Org uses just two commands, bound to `TAB` and S-`TAB` to change the visibility in the buffer.

`TAB`   org-cycle

    Subtree cycling: Rotate current subtree among the states

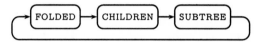

The cursor must be on a headline for this to work.[2] When the cursor is at the beginning of the buffer and the first line is not a headline, then `TAB` actually runs global cycling (see below).[3] Also when called with a prefix argument (C-u `TAB`), global cycling is invoked.

S-`TAB`   org-global-cycle
C-u `TAB`

    Global cycling: Rotate the entire buffer among the states

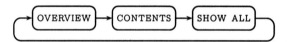

When S-`TAB` is called with a numeric prefix argument N, the CONTENTS view up to headlines of level N will be shown. Note that inside tables, S-`TAB` jumps to the previous field.

C-u C-u C-u `TAB`   show-all

    Show all, including drawers.

C-c C-r   org-reveal

    Reveal context around point, showing the current entry, the following heading and the hierarchy above. Useful for working near a location that has been exposed by a sparse tree command (see Section 2.6 [Sparse trees], page 14) or an agenda command (see Section 10.5 [Agenda commands], page 108). With a prefix argument show, on each level, all sibling headings. With double prefix arg, also show the entire subtree of the parent.

C-c C-k   show-branches

    Expose all the headings of the subtree, CONTENT view for just one subtree.

---

[2] see, however, the option `org-cycle-emulate-tab`.

[3] see the option `org-cycle-global-at-bob`.

C-c C-x b   `org-tree-to-indirect-buffer`
Show the current subtree in an indirect buffer.[4] With a numeric prefix argument N, go up to level N and then take that tree. If N is negative then go up that many levels. With a C-u prefix, do not remove the previously used indirect buffer.

When Emacs first visits an Org file, the global state is set to OVERVIEW, i.e., only the top level headlines are visible. This can be configured through the variable `org-startup-folded`, or on a per-file basis by adding one of the following lines anywhere in the buffer:

```
#+STARTUP: overview
#+STARTUP: content
#+STARTUP: showall
#+STARTUP: showeverything
```

Furthermore, any entries with a 'VISIBILITY' property (see Chapter 7 [Properties and Columns], page 59) will get their visibility adapted accordingly. Allowed values for this property are `folded`, `children`, `content`, and `all`.

C-u C-u (TAB)   `org-set-startup-visibility`
Switch back to the startup visibility of the buffer, i.e., whatever is requested by startup options and 'VISIBILITY' properties in individual entries.

2.4 Motion

The following commands jump to other headlines in the buffer.

C-c C-n   `outline-next-visible-heading`
Next heading.

C-c C-p   `outline-previous-visible-heading`
Previous heading.

C-c C-f   `org-forward-same-level`
Next heading same level.

C-c C-b   `org-backward-same-level`
Previous heading same level.

C-c C-u   `outline-up-heading`
Backward to higher level heading.

C-c C-j   `org-goto`
Jump to a different place without changing the current outline visibility. Shows the document structure in a temporary buffer, where you can use the following keys to find your destination:

(TAB)   Cycle visibility.

---

[4] The indirect buffer (see the Emacs manual for more information about indirect buffers) will contain the entire buffer, but will be narrowed to the current tree. Editing the indirect buffer will also change the original buffer, but without affecting visibility in that buffer.

(down) / (up)	Next/previous visible headline.
(RET)	Select this location.
/	Do a Sparse-tree search

The following keys work if you turn off `org-goto-auto-isearch`

n / p	Next/previous visible headline.
f / b	Next/previous headline same level.
u	One level up.
0-9	Digit argument.
q	Quit

See also the variable `org-goto-interface`.

2.5 Structure editing

M-(RET)   org-insert-heading

Insert new heading with same level as current. If the cursor is in a plain list item, a new item is created (see Section 2.7 [Plain lists], page 15). To force creation of a new headline, use a prefix argument, or first press (RET) to get to the beginning of the next line. When this command is used in the middle of a line, the line is split and the rest of the line becomes the new headline.[5] If the command is used at the beginning of a headline, the new headline is created before the current line. If at the beginning of any other line, the content of that line is made the new heading. If the command is used at the end of a folded subtree (i.e., behind the ellipses at the end of a headline), then a headline like the current one will be inserted after the end of the subtree.

C-(RET)   org-insert-heading-respect-content

Just like M-(RET), except when adding a new heading below the current heading, the new heading is placed after the body instead of before it. This command works from anywhere in the entry.

M-S-(RET)   org-insert-todo-heading

Insert new TODO entry with same level as current heading. See also the variable `org-treat-insert-todo-heading-as-state-change`.

C-S-(RET)   org-insert-todo-heading-respect-content

Insert new TODO entry with same level as current heading. Like C-(RET), the new headline will be inserted after the current subtree.

(TAB)   org-cycle

In a new entry with no text yet, the first (TAB) demotes the entry to become a child of the previous one. The next (TAB) makes it a parent, and so on, all the way to top level. Yet another (TAB), and you are back to the initial level.

M-(left)   org-do-promote

Promote current heading by one level.

---

[5] If you do not want the line to be split, customize the variable org-M-RET-may-split-line.

M-(right)   org-do-demote
    Demote current heading by one level.

M-S-(left)   org-promote-subtree
    Promote the current subtree by one level.

M-S-(right)   org-demote-subtree
    Demote the current subtree by one level.

M-S-(up)   org-move-subtree-up
    Move subtree up (swap with previous subtree of same level).

M-S-(down)   org-move-subtree-down
    Move subtree down (swap with next subtree of same level).

C-c C-x C-w   org-cut-subtree
    Kill subtree, i.e., remove it from buffer but save in kill ring. With a numeric
    prefix argument N, kill N sequential subtrees.

C-c C-x M-w   org-copy-subtree
    Copy subtree to kill ring. With a numeric prefix argument N, copy the N
    sequential subtrees.

C-c C-x C-y   org-paste-subtree
    Yank subtree from kill ring. This does modify the level of the subtree to
    make sure the tree fits in nicely at the yank position. The yank level can
    also be specified with a numeric prefix argument, or by yanking after a
    headline marker like '****'.

C-y   org-yank
    Depending on the variables org-yank-adjusted-subtrees and org-yank-
    folded-subtrees, Org's internal yank command will paste subtrees folded
    and in a clever way, using the same command as C-c C-x C-y. With the
    default settings, no level adjustment will take place, but the yanked tree
    will be folded unless doing so would swallow text previously visible. Any
    prefix argument to this command will force a normal yank to be executed,
    with the prefix passed along. A good way to force a normal yank is C-u
    C-y. If you use yank-pop after a yank, it will yank previous kill items
    plainly, without adjustment and folding.

C-c C-x c   org-clone-subtree-with-time-shift
    Clone a subtree by making a number of sibling copies of it. You will be
    prompted for the number of copies to make, and you can also specify if any
    timestamps in the entry should be shifted. This can be useful, for example,
    to create a number of tasks related to a series of lectures to prepare. For
    more details, see the docstring[6] of the command org-clone-subtree-
    with-time-shift.

C-c C-w   org-refile
    Refile entry or region to a different location. See Section 9.5 [Refiling
    notes], page 93.

---

[6] Docstrings for commands can be displayed with M-x describe-function or C-h f.

C-c ^   `org-sort-entries-or-items`
     Sort same-level entries. When there is an active region, all entries in the
     region will be sorted. Otherwise the children of the current headline are
     sorted. The command prompts for the sorting method, which can be al-
     phabetically, numerically, by time (first timestamp with active preferred,
     creation time, scheduled time, deadline time), by priority, by TODO key-
     word (in the sequence the keywords have been defined in the setup) or by
     the value of a property. Reverse sorting is possible as well. You can also
     supply your own function to extract the sorting key. With a C-u prefix,
     sorting will be case-sensitive. With two C-u C-u prefixes, duplicate entries
     will also be removed.

C-x n s   `org-narrow-to-subtree`
     Narrow buffer to current subtree.

C-x n w   `widen`
     Widen buffer to remove narrowing.

C-c *   `org-toggle-heading`
     Turn a normal line or plain list item into a headline (so that it becomes
     a subheading at its location). Also turn a headline into a normal line by
     removing the stars. If there is an active region, turn all lines in the region
     into headlines. If the first line in the region was an item, turn only the
     item lines into headlines. Finally, if the first line is a headline, remove the
     stars from all headlines in the region.

When there is an active region (Transient Mark mode), promotion and demotion work on all headlines in the region. To select a region of headlines, it
is best to place both point and mark at the beginning of a line, mark at the
beginning of the first headline, and point at the line just after the last headline
to change. Note that when the cursor is inside a table (see Chapter 3 [Tables],
page 23), the Meta-Cursor keys have different functionality.

2.6 Sparse trees

An important feature of Org-mode is the ability to construct *sparse trees* for
selected information in an outline tree, so that the entire document is folded as
much as possible, but the selected information is made visible along with the
headline structure above it.[7] Just try it out and you will see immediately how
it works.

Org-mode contains several commands creating such trees, all these commands
can be accessed through a dispatcher:

C-c /   `org-sparse-tree`
     This prompts for an extra key to select a sparse-tree creating command.

---

[7] See also the variables `org-show-hierarchy-above`, `org-show-following-heading`,
    `org-show-siblings`, and `org-show-entry-below` for detailed control on how much
    context is shown around each match.

C-c / r

> Occur. Prompts for a regexp and shows a sparse tree with all matches. If the match is in a headline, the headline is made visible. If the match is in the body of an entry, headline and body are made visible. In order to provide minimal context, also the full hierarchy of headlines above the match is shown, as well as the headline following the match. Each match is also highlighted; the highlights disappear when the buffer is changed by an editing command,[8] or by pressing C-c C-c. When called with a C-u prefix argument, previous highlights are kept, so several calls to this command can be stacked.

For frequently used sparse trees of specific search strings, you can use the variable `org-agenda-custom-commands` to define fast keyboard access to specific sparse trees. These commands will then be accessible through the agenda dispatcher (see Section 10.2 [Agenda dispatcher], page 99). For example:

```
(setq org-agenda-custom-commands
      '(("f" occur-tree "FIXME")))
```

will define the key C-c a f as a shortcut for creating a sparse tree matching the string 'FIXME'.

The other sparse tree commands select headings based on TODO keywords, tags, or properties and will be discussed later in this manual.

To print a sparse tree, you can use the Emacs command `ps-print-buffer-with-faces` which does not print invisible parts of the document.[9] Or you can use the command C-c C-e v to export only the visible part of the document and print the resulting file.

2.7 Plain lists

Within an entry of the outline tree, hand-formatted lists can provide additional structure. They also provide a way to create lists of checkboxes (see Section 5.6 [Checkboxes], page 53). Org supports editing such lists, and every exporter (see Chapter 12 [Exporting], page 133) can parse and format them.

Org knows ordered lists, unordered lists, and description lists.

- *Unordered* list items start with '-', '+', or '*'[10] as bullets.

---

[8] This depends on the option `org-remove-highlights-with-change`

[9] This does not work under XEmacs, because XEmacs uses selective display for outlining, not text properties.

[10] When using '*' as a bullet, lines must be indented or they will be seen as top-level headlines. Also, when you are hiding leading stars to get a clean outline view, plain list items starting with a star are visually indistinguishable from true headlines. In short: even though '*' is supported, it may be better to not use it for plain list items.

- *Ordered* list items start with a numeral followed by either a period or a right parenthesis,[11] such as '1.' or '1)'. If you want a list to start with a different value (e.g., 20), start the text of the item with [@20].[12] Those constructs can be used in any item of the list in order to enforce a particular numbering.

- *Description* list items are unordered list items, and contain the separator ' :: ' to separate the description *term* from the description.

Items belonging to the same list must have the same indentation on the first line. In particular, if an ordered list reaches number '10.', then the 2–digit numbers must be written left-aligned with the other numbers in the list.

Two methods[13] are provided to terminate lists. A list ends before the next line that is indented like the bullet/number or less, or it ends before two blank lines.[14] In both cases, all levels of the list are closed.[15] For finer control, you can end lists with any pattern set in `org-list-end-regexp`. Here is an example:

```
** Lord of the Rings
   My favorite scenes are (in this order)
   1. The attack of the Rohirrim
   2. Eowyn's fight with the witch king
      + this was already my favorite scene in the book
      + I really like Miranda Otto.
   3. Peter Jackson being shot by Legolas
      He makes a really funny face when it happens.
      - on DVD only
   But in the end, no individual scenes matter but the film as
   a whole. Important actors in this film are:
   - Elijah Wood :: He plays Frodo
   - Sean Austin :: He plays Sam, Frodo's friend. I still
     remember him very well from his role as Mikey Walsh in The
     Goonies.
```

Org supports these lists by tuning filling and wrapping commands to deal with them correctly,[16] and by exporting them properly (see Chapter 12 [Exporting], page 133). Since indentation is what governs the structure of these lists, many structural constructs like #+BEGIN_... blocks can be indented to signal that they should be considered as a list item.

---

[11] You can filter out any of them by configuring `org-plain-list-ordered-item-terminator`.

[12] If there's a checkbox in the item, the cookie must be put *before* the checkbox.

[13] To disable either of them, configure `org-list-ending-method`.

[14] See also `org-empty-line-terminates-plain-lists`.

[15] So you cannot have a sublist, some text and then another sublist while still in the same top-level list item. This used to be possible, but it was only supported in the HTML exporter and difficult to manage with automatic indentation.

[16] Org only changes the filling settings for Emacs. For XEmacs, you should use Kyle E. Jones' `filladapt.el`. To turn this on, put into '.emacs': (require 'filladapt)

If you find that using a different bullet for a sub-list (than that used for the current list-level) improves readability, customize the variable `org-list-demote-modify-bullet`.

The following commands act on items when the cursor is in the first line of an item (the line with the bullet or number). Some of them imply the application of automatic rules to keep list structure intact. If some of these actions get in your way, configure `org-list-automatic-rules` to disable them individually.

TAB   org-cycle
> Items can be folded just like headline levels. Normally this works only if the cursor is on a plain list item. For more details, see the variable `org-cycle-include-plain-lists`. If this variable is set to `integrate`, plain list items will be treated like low-level headlines. The level of an item is then given by the indentation of the bullet/number. Items are always subordinate to real headlines, however; the hierarchies remain completely separated.

M-RET   org-insert-heading
> Insert new item at current level. With a prefix argument, force a new heading (see Section 2.5 [Structure editing], page 12). If this command is used in the middle of a line, the line is *split* and the rest of the line becomes the new item.[17] If this command is executed *before an item's body*, the new item is created *before* the current item. If the command is executed in the white space before the text that is part of an item but does not contain the bullet, a bullet is added to the current line.
>
> As a new item cannot be inserted in a structural construct (like an example or source code block) within a list, Org will instead insert it right before the structure, or return an error.

M-S-RET
> Insert a new item with a checkbox (see Section 5.6 [Checkboxes], page 53).

TAB   org-cycle
> In a new item with no text yet, the first TAB demotes the item to become a child of the previous one. Subsequent TABs move the item to meaningful levels in the list and eventually get it back to its initial position.

S-up
S-down
> Jump to the previous/next item in the current list, but only if `org-support-shift-select` is off. If not, you can still use paragraph jumping commands like C-up and C-down to quite similar effect.

M-S-up
M-S-down
> Move the item including subitems up/down (swap with previous/next item of same indentation). If the list is ordered, renumbering is automatic.

---

[17] If you do not want the line to be split, customize the variable `org-M-RET-may-split-line`.

M-⌊left⌋
M-⌊right⌋

> Decrease/increase the indentation of an item, leaving children alone.

M-S-⌊left⌋
M-S-⌊right⌋

> Decrease/increase the indentation of the item, including subitems. Initially, the item tree is selected based on current indentation. When these commands are executed several times in direct succession, the initially selected region is used, even if the new indentation would imply a different hierarchy. To use the new hierarchy, break the command chain with a cursor motion or so.
>
> As a special case, using this command on the very first item of a list will move the whole list. This behavior can be disabled by configuring org-list-automatic-rules. The global indentation of a list has no influence on the text *after* the list.

C-c C-c

> If there is a checkbox (see Section 5.6 [Checkboxes], page 53) in the item line, toggle the state of the checkbox. Also, makes sure that all the items on this list level use the same bullet and that the numbering of list items (if applicable) is correct.

C-c -

> Cycle the entire list level through the different itemize/enumerate bullets ('-', '+', '*', '1.', '1)') or a subset of them, depending on org-plain-list-ordered-item-terminator, the type of list, and its position.[18] With a numeric prefix argument N, select the Nth bullet from this list. If there is an active region when calling this, all lines will be converted to list items. If the first line already was a list item, any item markers will be removed from the list. Finally, even without an active region, a normal line will be converted into a list item.

C-c *

> Turn a plain list item into a headline (so that it becomes a subheading at its location). See Section 2.5 [Structure editing], page 12, for a detailed explanation.

S-⌊left⌋/⌊right⌋

> This command also cycles bullet styles when the cursor in on the bullet or anywhere in an item line, details depending on org-support-shift-select.

C-c ^

> Sort the plain list. You will be prompted for the sorting method: numerically, alphabetically, by time, or by custom function.

---

[18] See bullet rule in org-list-automatic-rules for more information.

2.8 Drawers

Sometimes you want to keep information associated with an entry, but you normally don't want to see it. For this, Org-mode has *drawers*. Drawers need to be configured with the variable org-drawers.[19] Drawers look like this:

```
** This is a headline
   Still outside the drawer
   :DRAWERNAME:
      This is inside the drawer.
   :END:
   After the drawer.
```

Visibility cycling (see Section 2.3 [Visibility cycling], page 10) on the headline will hide and show the entry, but keep the drawer collapsed to a single line. In order to look inside the drawer, you need to move the cursor to the drawer line and press (TAB) there. Org-mode uses the PROPERTIES drawer for storing properties (see Chapter 7 [Properties and Columns], page 59), and you can also arrange for state change notes (see Section 5.3.2 [Tracking TODO state changes], page 47) and clock times (see Section 8.4 [Clocking work time], page 76) to be stored in a drawer LOGBOOK. If you want to store a quick note in the LOGBOOK drawer, in a similar way to state changes, use

C-c C-z
Add a time-stamped note to the LOGBOOK drawer.

2.9 Blocks

Org-mode uses begin...end blocks for various purposes from including source code examples (see Section 11.3 [Literal examples], page 126) to capturing time logging information (see Section 8.4 [Clocking work time], page 76). These blocks can be folded and unfolded by pressing TAB in the begin line. You can also get all blocks folded at startup by configuring the variable org-hide-block-startup or on a per-file basis by using

```
#+STARTUP: hideblocks
#+STARTUP: nohideblocks
```

---

[19] You can define drawers on a per-file basis with a line like #+DRAWERS: HIDDEN PROPERTIES STATE

2.10 Footnotes

Org-mode supports the creation of footnotes. In contrast to the 'footnote.el' package, Org-mode's footnotes are designed for work on a larger document, not only for one-off documents like emails. The basic syntax is similar to the one used by 'footnote.el', i.e., a footnote is defined in a paragraph that is started by a footnote marker in square brackets in column 0, no indentation allowed. If you need a paragraph break inside a footnote, use the LaTeX idiom '\par'. The footnote reference is simply the marker in square brackets, inside text. For example:

```
The Org homepage[fn:1] now looks a lot better than it used to.
...
[fn:1] The link is: http://orgmode.org
```

Org-mode extends the number-based syntax to *named* footnotes and optional inline definition. Using plain numbers as markers (as 'footnote.el' does) is supported for backward compatibility, but not encouraged because of possible conflicts with LaTeX snippets (see Section 11.7 [Embedded LaTeX], page 129). Here are the valid references:

[1]
> A plain numeric footnote marker. Compatible with 'footnote.el', but not recommended because something like '[1]' could easily be part of a code snippet.

[fn:name]
> A named footnote reference, where name is a unique label word, or, for simplicity of automatic creation, a number.

[fn:: This is the inline definition of this footnote]
> A LaTeX-like anonymous footnote where the definition is given directly at the reference point.

[fn:name: a definition]
> An inline definition of a footnote, which also specifies a name for the note. Since Org allows multiple references to the same note, you can then use [fn:name] to create additional references.

Footnote labels can be created automatically, or you can create names yourself. This is handled by the variable org-footnote-auto-label and its corresponding #+STARTUP keywords. See the docstring[20] of that variable for details. The following command handles footnotes:

C-c C-x f
> The footnote action command.
>
> When the cursor is on a footnote reference, jump to the definition. When it is at a definition, jump to the (first) reference.
>
> Otherwise, create a new footnote. Depending on the variable org-footnote-define-inline,[21] the definition will be placed right into the

---

[20] Docstrings for variables can be displayed with M-x describe-variable or C-h v.

[21] The corresponding in-buffer setting is: #+STARTUP: fninline or #+STARTUP: nofninline

text as part of the reference, or separately into the location determined by the variable `org-footnote-section`.

When this command is called with a prefix argument, a menu of additional options is offered:

s   Sort the footnote definitions by reference sequence. During editing, Org makes no effort to sort footnote definitions into a particular sequence. If you want them sorted, use this command, which will also move entries according to `org-footnote-section`. Automatic sorting after each insertion/deletion can be configured using the variable `org-footnote-auto-adjust`.

r   Renumber the simple `fn:N` footnotes. Automatic renumbering after each insertion/deletion can be configured using the variable `org-footnote-auto-adjust`.

S   Short for first r, then s action.

n   Normalize the footnotes by collecting all definitions (including inline definitions) into a special section, and then numbering them in sequence. The references will then also be numbers. This is meant to be the final step before finishing a document (e.g., sending off an email). The exporters do this automatically, and so could something like `message-send-hook`.

d   Delete the footnote at point, and all definitions of and references to it.

Depending on the variable `org-footnote-auto-adjust`,[22] renumbering and sorting footnotes can be automatic after each insertion or deletion.

C-c C-c
If the cursor is on a footnote reference, jump to the definition. If it is a the definition, jump back to the reference. When called at a footnote location with a prefix argument, offer the same menu as C-c C-x f.

C-c C-o or mouse-1/2
Footnote labels are also links to the corresponding definition/reference, and you can use the usual commands to follow these links.

---

[22] the corresponding in-buffer options are fnadjust and nofnadjust.

2.11 The Orgstruct minor mode

If you like the intuitive way the Org-mode structure editing and list formatting works, you might want to use these commands in other modes like Text mode or Mail mode as well. The minor mode `orgstruct-mode` makes this possible. Toggle the mode with `M-x orgstruct-mode`, or turn it on by default, for example in Mail mode, with one of:

```
(add-hook 'mail-mode-hook 'turn-on-orgstruct)
(add-hook 'mail-mode-hook 'turn-on-orgstruct++)
```

When this mode is active and the cursor is on a line that looks to Org like a headline or the first line of a list item, most structure editing commands will work, even if the same keys normally have different functionality in the major mode you are using. If the cursor is not in one of those special lines, Orgstruct mode lurks silently in the shadows. When you use `orgstruct++-mode`, Org will also export indentation and autofill settings into that mode, and detect item context after the first line of an item.

3 Tables

Org comes with a fast and intuitive table editor. Spreadsheet-like calculations are supported using the Emacs 'calc' package (see the Emacs Calculator manual for more information about the Emacs calculator).

3.1 The built-in table editor

Org makes it easy to format tables in plain ASCII. Any line with '|' as the first non-whitespace character is considered part of a table. '|' is also the column separator. A table might look like this:

```
| Name  | Phone  | Age |
|-------+-------+-----|
| Peter |  1234  |  17 |
| Anna  |  4321  |  25 |
```

A table is re-aligned automatically each time you press (TAB) or (RET) or C-c C-c inside the table. (TAB) also moves to the next field ((RET) to the next row) and creates new table rows at the end of the table or before horizontal lines. The indentation of the table is set by the first line. Any line starting with '|-' is considered as a horizontal separator line and will be expanded on the next re-align to span the whole table width. So, to create the above table, you would only type

```
|Name|Phone|Age|
|-
```

and then press (TAB) to align the table and start filling in fields. Even faster would be to type |Name|Phone|Age followed by C-c (RET).

When typing text into a field, Org treats (DEL), (Backspace), and all character keys in a special way, so that inserting and deleting avoids shifting other fields. Also, when typing *immediately after the cursor was moved into a new field with* (TAB), S-(TAB) *or* (RET), the field is automatically made blank. If this behavior is too unpredictable for you, configure the variables org-enable-table-editor and org-table-auto-blank-field.

Creation and conversion

C-c | org-table-create-or-convert-from-region
    Convert the active region to table. If every line contains at least one TAB character, the function assumes that the material is tab separated. If every line contains a comma, comma-separated values (CSV) are assumed. If not, lines are split at whitespace into fields. You can use a prefix argument to force a specific separator: C-u forces CSV, C-u C-u forces TAB, and a numeric argument N indicates that at least N consecutive spaces, or alternatively a TAB will be the separator.
    If there is no active region, this command creates an empty Org table. But it's easier just to start typing, like |Name|Phone|Age (RET) |- (TAB).

Re-aligning and field motion

C-c C-c   org-ctrl-c-ctrl-c
> Re-align the table without moving the cursor.

<TAB>   org-cycle
> Re-align the table, move to the next field. Creates a new row if necessary.

S-(TAB)   org-shifttab
> Re-align, move to previous field.

(RET)   org-return
> Re-align the table and move down to next row. Creates a new row if
> necessary. At the beginning or end of a line, (RET) still does NEWLINE,
> so it can be used to split a table.

M-a
> Move to beginning of the current table field, or on to the previous field.

M-e
> Move to end of the current table field, or on to the next field.

Column and row editing

M-(left)
M-(right)
> Move the current column left/right.

M-S-(left)
> Kill the current column.

M-S-(right)
> Insert a new column to the left of the cursor position.

M-(up)
M-(down)
> Move the current row up/down.

M-S-(up)
> Kill the current row or horizontal line.

M-S-(down)
> Insert a new row above the current row. With a prefix argument, the line
> is created below the current one.

C-c -
> Insert a horizontal line below current row. With a prefix argument, the
> line is created above the current line.

C-c (RET)
> Insert a horizontal line below current row, and move the cursor into the
> row below that line.

C-c ^

> Sort the table lines in the region. The position of point indicates the
> column to be used for sorting, and the range of lines is the range between
> the nearest horizontal separator lines, or the entire table. If point is before
> the first column, you will be prompted for the sorting column. If there is
> an active region, the mark specifies the first line and the sorting column,
> while point should be in the last line to be included into the sorting. The
> command prompts for the sorting type (alphabetically, numerically, or by
> time). When called with a prefix argument, alphabetic sorting will be
> case-sensitive.

Regions

C-c C-x M-w

> Copy a rectangular region from a table to a special clipboard. Point and
> mark determine edge fields of the rectangle. If there is no active region,
> copy just the current field. The process ignores horizontal separator lines.

C-c C-x C-w

> Copy a rectangular region from a table to a special clipboard, and blank
> all fields in the rectangle. So this is the "cut" operation.

C-c C-x C-y

> Paste a rectangular region into a table. The upper left corner ends up in
> the current field. All involved fields will be overwritten. If the rectangle
> does not fit into the present table, the table is enlarged as needed. The
> process ignores horizontal separator lines.

M-RET

> Wrap several fields in a column like a paragraph. If there is an active
> region, and both point and mark are in the same column, the text in the
> column is wrapped to minimum width for the given number of lines. A
> numeric prefix argument may be used to change the number of desired
> lines. If there is no region, the current field is split at the cursor position
> and the text fragment to the right of the cursor is prepended to the field
> one line down. If there is no region, but you specify a prefix argument, the
> current field is made blank, and the content is appended to the field above.

Calculations

C-c +

> Sum the numbers in the current column, or in the rectangle defined by the
> active region. The result is shown in the echo area and can be inserted
> with C-y.

S-(RET)

> When current field is empty, copy from first non-empty field above. When
> not empty, copy current field down to next row and move cursor along
> with it. Depending on the variable org-table-copy-increment, integer
> field values will be incremented during copy. Integers that are too large
> will not be incremented. Also, a 0 prefix argument temporarily disables

the increment. This key is also used by shift-selection and related modes (see Section 16.10.2 [Conflicts], page 208).

Miscellaneous

C-c '

Edit the current field in a separate window. This is useful for fields that are not fully visible (see Section 3.2 [Column width and alignment], page 27). When called with a C-u prefix, just make the full field visible, so that it can be edited in place.

M-x org-table-import

Import a file as a table. The table should be TAB or whitespace separated. Use, for example, to import a spreadsheet table or data from a database, because these programs generally can write TAB-separated text files. This command works by inserting the file into the buffer and then converting the region to a table. Any prefix argument is passed on to the converter, which uses it to determine the separator.

C-c |

Tables can also be imported by pasting tabular text into the Org buffer, selecting the pasted text with C-x C-x and then using the C-c | command (see above under *Creation and conversion*).

M-x org-table-export

Export the table, by default as a TAB-separated file. Use for data exchange with, for example, spreadsheet or database programs. The format used to export the file can be configured in the variable org-table-export-default-format. You may also use properties TABLE_EXPORT_FILE and TABLE_EXPORT_FORMAT to specify the file name and the format for table export in a subtree. Org supports quite general formats for exported tables. The exporter format is the same as the format used by Orgtbl radio tables, see Section A.5.3 [Translator functions], page 217, for a detailed description.

If you don't like the automatic table editor because it gets in your way on lines which you would like to start with '|', you can turn it off with

    (setq org-enable-table-editor nil)

Then the only table command that still works is C-c C-c to do a manual re-align.

3.2 Column width and alignment

The width of columns is automatically determined by the table editor. And also the alignment of a column is determined automatically from the fraction of number-like versus non-number fields in the column.

Sometimes a single field or a few fields need to carry more text, leading to inconveniently wide columns. Or maybe you want to make a table with several columns having a fixed width, regardless of content. To set[1] the width of a column, one field anywhere in the column may contain just the string '<N>' where 'N' is an integer specifying the width of the column in characters. The next re-align will then set the width of this column to this value.

```
|---+----------------------------|          |---+--------|
|   |                            |          |   | <6>    |
| 1 | one                        |          | 1 | one    |
| 2 | two                        |   ---\   | 2 | two    |
| 3 | This is a long chunk of text |   ---/   | 3 | This=> |
| 4 | four                       |          | 4 | four   |
|---+----------------------------|          |---+--------|
```

Fields that are wider become clipped and end in the string '=>'. Note that the full text is still in the buffer but is hidden. To see the full text, hold the mouse over the field—a tool-tip window will show the full content. To edit such a field, use the command C-c ' (that is C-c followed by the backquote). This will open a new window with the full field. Edit it and finish with C-c C-c.

When visiting a file containing a table with narrowed columns, the necessary character hiding has not yet happened, and the table needs to be aligned before it looks nice. Setting the option org-startup-align-all-tables will realign all tables in a file upon visiting, but also slow down startup. You can also set this option on a per-file basis with:

```
#+STARTUP: align
#+STARTUP: noalign
```

If you would like to overrule the automatic alignment of number-rich columns to the right and of string-rich column to the left, you can use '<r>', 'c'[2] or '<l>' in a similar fashion. You may also combine alignment and field width like this: '<l10>'.

Lines which only contain these formatting cookies will be removed automatically when exporting the document.

---

[1] This feature does not work on XEmacs.

[2] Centering does not work inside Emacs, but it does have an effect when exporting to HTML.

3.3 Column groups

When Org exports tables, it does so by default without vertical lines because
that is visually more satisfying in general. Occasionally however, vertical lines
can be useful to structure a table into groups of columns, much like horizontal
lines can do for groups of rows. In order to specify column groups, you can use
a special row where the first field contains only '/'. The further fields can either
contain '<' to indicate that this column should start a group, '>' to indicate
the end of a column, or '<>' to make a column a group of its own. Boundaries
between column groups will upon export be marked with vertical lines. Here is
an example:

```
| N | N^2 | N^3 | N^4 | sqrt(n) | sqrt[4](N) |
|---+-----+-----+-----+---------+------------|
| / |  <  |     |  >  |    <    |         >  |
| 1 |  1  |  1  |  1  |    1    |         1  |
| 2 |  4  |  8  | 16  | 1.4142  |    1.1892  |
| 3 |  9  | 27  | 81  | 1.7321  |    1.3161  |
|---+-----+-----+-----+---------+------------|
```
#+TBLFM: $2=$1^2::$3=$1^3::$4=$1^4::$5=sqrt($1)::$6=sqrt(sqrt(($1)))

It is also sufficient to just insert the column group starters after every vertical
line you would like to have:

```
|  N | N^2 | N^3 | N^4 | sqrt(n) | sqrt[4](N) |
|----+-----+-----+-----+---------+------------|
| /  | <   |     | <   |    <    |            |
```

3.4 The Orgtbl minor mode

If you like the intuitive way the Org table editor works, you might also
want to use it in other modes like Text mode or Mail mode. The minor mode
Orgtbl mode makes this possible. You can always toggle the mode with M-x
orgtbl-mode. To turn it on by default, for example in mail mode, use

    (add-hook 'mail-mode-hook 'turn-on-orgtbl)

Furthermore, with some special setup, it is possible to maintain tables in arbitrary syntax with Orgtbl mode. For example, it is possible to construct LaTeX
tables with the underlying ease and power of Orgtbl mode, including spreadsheet capabilities. For details, see Section A.5 [Tables in arbitrary syntax],
page 213.

3.5 The spreadsheet

The table editor makes use of the Emacs 'calc' package to implement spreadsheet-like capabilities. It can also evaluate Emacs Lisp forms to derive fields from other fields. While fully featured, Org's implementation is not identical to other spreadsheets. For example, Org knows the concept of a *column formula* that will be applied to all non-header fields in a column without having to copy the formula to each relevant field. There is also a formula debugger, and a formula editor with features for highlighting fields in the table corresponding to the references at the point in the formula, and moving these references by arrow keys.

See Chapter 15 [The spreadsheet], page 185 for full details of the spreadsheet and Org-Plot graph plotting functionality.

4 Hyperlinks

Like HTML, Org provides links inside a file, external links to other files, Usenet articles, emails, and much more.

4.1 Link format

Org will recognize plain URL-like links and activate them as clickable links. The general link format, however, looks like this:

    [[link][description]]   or alternatively   [[link]]

Once a link in the buffer is complete (all brackets present), Org will change the display so that 'description' is displayed instead of '[[link][description]]' and 'link' is displayed instead of '[[link]]'. Links will be highlighted in the face org-link, which by default is an underlined face. You can directly edit the visible part of a link. Note that this can be either the 'link' part (if there is no description) or the 'description' part. To edit also the invisible 'link' part, use C-c C-l with the cursor on the link.

If you place the cursor at the beginning or just behind the end of the displayed text and press (BACKSPACE), you will remove the (invisible) bracket at that location. This makes the link incomplete and the internals are again displayed as plain text. Inserting the missing bracket hides the link internals again. To show the internal structure of all links, use the menu entry Org->Hyperlinks->Literal links.

4.2 Internal links

If the link does not look like a URL, it is considered to be internal in the current file. The most important case is a link like '[[#my-custom-id]]' which will link to the entry with the CUSTOM_ID property 'my-custom-id'. Such custom IDs are very good for HTML export (see Section 12.5 [HTML export], page 136) where they produce pretty section links. You are responsible yourself to make sure these custom IDs are unique in a file.

Links such as '[[My Target]]' or '[[My Target][Find my target]]' lead to a text search in the current file.

The link can be followed with C-c C-o when the cursor is on the link, or with a mouse click (see Section 4.4 [Handling links], page 34). Links to custom IDs will point to the corresponding headline. The preferred match for a text link is a *dedicated target*: the same string in double angular brackets. Targets may be located anywhere; sometimes it is convenient to put them into a comment line. For example

    # <<My Target>>

In HTML export (see Section 12.5 [HTML export], page 136), such targets will become named anchors for direct access through 'http' links.[1]

---

[1] Note that text before the first headline is usually not exported, so the first such target should be after the first headline, or in the line directly before the first headline.

If no dedicated target exists, Org will search for a headline that is exactly the link text but may also include a TODO keyword and tags.[2] In non-Org files, the search will look for the words in the link text. In the above example the search would be for 'my target'.

Following a link pushes a mark onto Org's own mark ring. You can return to the previous position with C-c &. Using this command several times in direct succession goes back to positions recorded earlier.

4.2.1 Radio targets

Org can automatically turn any occurrences of certain target names in normal text into a link. So without explicitly creating a link, the text connects to the target radioing its position. Radio targets are enclosed by triple angular brackets. For example, a target '<<<My Target>>>' causes each occurrence of 'my target' in normal text to become activated as a link. The Org file is scanned automatically for radio targets only when the file is first loaded into Emacs. To update the target list during editing, press C-c C-c with the cursor on or at a target.

4.3 External links

Org supports links to files, websites, Usenet and email messages, BBDB database entries and links to both IRC conversations and their logs. External links are URL-like locators. They start with a short identifying string followed by a colon. There can be no space after the colon. The following list shows examples for each link type.

http://www.astro.uva.nl/~dominik
  on the web

doi:10.1000/182
  DOI for an electronic resource

file:/home/dominik/images/jupiter.jpg
  file, absolute path

/home/dominik/images/jupiter.jpg
  same as above

file:papers/last.pdf
  file, relative path

./papers/last.pdf
  same as above

file:/myself@some.where:papers/last.pdf
  file, path on remote machine

---

[2] To insert a link targeting a headline, in-buffer completion can be used. Just type a star followed by a few optional letters into the buffer and press M-(TAB). All headlines in the current buffer will be offered as completions.

`/myself@some.where:papers/last.pdf`
> same as above

`file:sometextfile::NNN`
> file with line number to jump to

`file:projects.org`
> another Org file

`file:projects.org::some words`
> text search in Org file

`file:projects.org::*task title`
> heading search in Org file

`docview:papers/last.pdf::NNN`
> open file in doc-view mode at page NNN

`id:B7423F4D-2E8A-471B-8810-C40F074717E9`
> Link to heading by ID

`news:comp.emacs`
> Usenet link

`mailto:adent@galaxy.net`
> Mail link

`vm:folder`
> VM folder link

`vm:folder#id`
> VM message link

`vm://myself@some.where.org/folder#id`
> VM on remote machine

`wl:folder`
> WANDERLUST folder link

`wl:folder#id`
> WANDERLUST message link

`mhe:folder`
> MH-E folder link

`mhe:folder#id`
> MH-E message link

`rmail:folder`
> RMAIL folder link

`rmail:folder#id`
> RMAIL message link

`gnus:group`
> Gnus group link

gnus:group#id
>   Gnus article link

bbdb:R.*Stallman
>   BBDB link (with regexp)

irc:/irc.com/#emacs/bob
>   IRC link

info:org:External%20links
>   Info node link (with encoded space)

shell:ls *.org
>   A shell command

elisp:org-agenda
>   Interactive Elisp command

elisp:(find-file-other-frame "Elisp.org")
>   Elisp form to evaluate

A link should be enclosed in double brackets and may contain a descriptive text to be displayed instead of the URL (see Section 4.1 [Link format], page 31), for example:

>   [[http://www.gnu.org/software/emacs/][GNU Emacs]]

If the description is a file name or URL that points to an image, HTML export (see Section 12.5 [HTML export], page 136) will inline the image as a clickable button. If there is no description at all and the link points to an image, that image will be inlined into the exported HTML file.

Org also finds external links in the normal text and activates them as links. If spaces must be part of the link (for example in 'bbdb:Richard Stallman'), or if you need to remove ambiguities about the end of the link, enclose them in square brackets.

4.4 Handling links

Org provides methods to create a link in the correct syntax, to insert it into an Org file, and to follow the link.

C-c l
>   Store a link to the current location. This is a *global* command (you must create the key binding yourself) which can be used in any buffer to create a link. The link will be stored for later insertion into an Org buffer (see below). What kind of link will be created depends on the current buffer:

>   **Org-mode buffers**
>   >   For Org files, if there is a '<<target>>' at the cursor, the link points to the target. Otherwise it points to the current headline, which will also be the description.

>   >   If the headline has a CUSTOM_ID property, a link to this custom ID will be stored. In addition or alternatively (depending on the value of org-link-to-org-use-id), a globally unique ID property will be

created and/or used to construct a link. So using this command in Org buffers will potentially create two links: a human-readable from the custom ID, and one that is globally unique and works even if the entry is moved from file to file. Later, when inserting the link, you need to decide which one to use.

Email/News clients: VM, Rmail, Wanderlust, MH-E, Gnus
Pretty much all Emacs mail clients are supported. The link will point to the current article, or, in some GNUS buffers, to the group. The description is constructed from the author and the subject.

Web browsers: W3 and W3M
Here the link will be the current URL, with the page title as description.

Contacts: BBDB
Links created in a BBDB buffer will point to the current entry.

Chat: IRC
For IRC links, if you set the variable `org-irc-link-to-logs` to t, a 'file:/' style link to the relevant point in the logs for the current conversation is created. Otherwise an 'irc:/' style link to the user/channel/server under the point will be stored.

Other files
For any other files, the link will point to the file, with a search string (see Section 4.7 [Search options], page 38) pointing to the contents of the current line. If there is an active region, the selected words will form the basis of the search string. If the automatically created link is not working correctly or accurately enough, you can write custom functions to select the search string and to do the search for particular file types—see Section 4.8 [Custom searches], page 39. The key binding C-c l is only a suggestion—see Section 1.2 [Installation], page 4.

Agenda view
When the cursor is in an agenda view, the created link points to the entry referenced by the current line.

C-c C-l
Insert a link.[3] This prompts for a link to be inserted into the buffer. You can just type a link, using text for an internal link, or one of the link type prefixes mentioned in the examples above. The link will be inserted into the buffer,[4] along with a descriptive text. If some text was selected when this command is called, the selected text becomes the default description.

---

[3] Note that you don't have to use this command to insert a link. Links in Org are plain text, and you can type or paste them straight into the buffer. By using this command, the links are automatically enclosed in double brackets, and you will be asked for the optional descriptive text.

[4] After insertion of a stored link, the link will be removed from the list of stored links. To keep it in the list later use, use a triple C-u prefix argument to C-c C-l, or configure the option `org-keep-stored-link-after-insertion`.

Inserting stored links

All links stored during the current session are part of the history for this prompt, so you can access them with (up) and (down) (or M-p/n).

Completion support

Completion with (TAB) will help you to insert valid link prefixes like 'http:' or 'ftp:', including the prefixes defined through link abbreviations (see Section 4.6 [Link abbreviations], page 38). If you press (RET) after inserting only the *prefix*, Org will offer specific completion support for some link types[5] For example, if you type file (RET), file name completion (alternative access: C-u C-c C-l, see below) will be offered, and after bbdb (RET) you can complete contact names.

C-u C-c C-l

When C-c C-l is called with a C-u prefix argument, a link to a file will be inserted and you may use file name completion to select the name of the file. The path to the file is inserted relative to the directory of the current Org file, if the linked file is in the current directory or in a sub-directory of it, or if the path is written relative to the current directory using '../'. Otherwise an absolute path is used, if possible with '~/' for your home directory. You can force an absolute path with two C-u prefixes.

C-c C-l   (with cursor on existing link)

When the cursor is on an existing link, C-c C-l allows you to edit the link and description parts of the link.

C-c C-o   (or, if org-return-follows-link is set, also (RET))

Open link at point. This will launch a web browser for URLs (using browse-url-at-point), run VM/MH-E/Wanderlust/Rmail/Gnus/BBDB for the corresponding links, and execute the command in a shell link. When the cursor is on an internal link, this command runs the corresponding search. When the cursor is on a TAG list in a headline, it creates the corresponding TAGS view. If the cursor is on a timestamp, it compiles the agenda for that date. Furthermore, it will visit text and remote files in 'file:' links with Emacs and select a suitable application for local non-text files. Classification of files is based on file extension only. See option org-file-apps. If you want to override the default application and visit the file with Emacs, use a C-u prefix. If you want to avoid opening in Emacs, use a C-u C-u prefix.

If the cursor is on a headline, but not on a link, offer all links in the headline and entry text.

mouse-2
mouse-1

On links, mouse-2 will open the link just as C-c C-o would. Under Emacs 22, mouse-1 will also follow a link.

---

[5] This works by calling a special function org-PREFIX-complete-link.

mouse-3
> Like mouse-2, but force file links to be opened with Emacs, and internal
> links to be displayed in another window.[6]

C-c C-x C-v
> Toggle the inline display of linked images. Normally this will only inline
> images that have no description part in the link, i.e., images that will also
> be inlined during export. When called with a prefix argument, also display
> images that do have a link description. You can ask for inline images to
> be displayed at startup by configuring the variable org-startup-with-
> inline-images.[7]

C-c %
> Push the current position onto the mark ring, to be able to return easily.
> Commands following an internal link do this automatically.

C-c &
> Jump back to a recorded position. A position is recorded by the commands
> following internal links, and by C-c %. Using this command several times
> in direct succession moves through a ring of previously recorded positions.

C-c C-x C-n
C-c C-x C-p
> Move forward/backward to the next link in the buffer. At the limit of the
> buffer, the search fails once, and then wraps around. The key bindings for
> this are really too long; you might want to bind this also to C-n and C-p

```
(add-hook 'org-load-hook
  (lambda ()
    (define-key 'org-mode-map "\C-n" 'org-next-link)
    (define-key 'org-mode-map "\C-p" 'org-previous-link)))
```

4.5 Using links outside Org

You can insert and follow links that have Org syntax not only in Org, but in
any Emacs buffer. For this, you should create two global commands, like this
(please select suitable global keys yourself):

```
(global-set-key "\C-c L" 'org-insert-link-global)
(global-set-key "\C-c o" 'org-open-at-point-global)
```

---

[6] See the variable org-display-internal-link-with-indirect-buffer

[7] with corresponding #+STARTUP keywords inlineimages and inlineimages

4.6 Link abbreviations

Long URLs can be cumbersome to type, and often many similar links are needed in a document. For this you can use link abbreviations. An abbreviated link looks like this

```
[[linkword:tag][description]]
```

where the tag is optional. The *linkword* must be a word, starting with a letter, followed by letters, numbers, '-', and '_'. Abbreviations are resolved according to the information in the variable `org-link-abbrev-alist` that relates the linkwords to replacement text. Here is an example:

```
(setq org-link-abbrev-alist
 '(("bugzilla" . "http://10.1.2.9/bugzilla/show_bug.cgi?id=")
   ("google"   . "http://www.google.com/search?q=")
   ("gmap"     . "http://maps.google.com/maps?q=%s")
   ("omap"     . "http://nominatim.openstreetmap.org/search?q=%s&polygon=1")
   ("ads"      . "http://adsabs.harvard.edu/cgi-bin/nph-abs_connect?author=%s")))
```

If the replacement text contains the string '%s', it will be replaced with the tag. Otherwise the tag will be appended to the string in order to create the link. You may also specify a function that will be called with the tag as the only argument to create the link.

With the above setting, you could link to a specific bug with `[[bugzilla:129]]`, search the web for 'OrgMode' with `[[google:OrgMode]]`, show the map location of the Free Software Foundation `[[gmap:51 Franklin Street, Boston]]` or of Carsten office `[[omap:Science Park 904, Amsterdam, The Netherlands]]` and find out what the Org author is doing besides Emacs hacking with `[[ads:Dominik,C]]`.

If you need special abbreviations just for a single Org buffer, you can define them in the file with

```
#+LINK: bugzilla  http://10.1.2.9/bugzilla/show_bug.cgi?id=
#+LINK: google    http://www.google.com/search?q=%s
```

In-buffer completion (see Section 16.1 [Completion], page 197) can be used after '[' to complete link abbreviations. You may also define a function `org-PREFIX-complete-link` that implements special (e.g., completion) support for inserting such a link with `C-c C-l`. Such a function should not accept any arguments, and return the full link with prefix.

4.7 Search options in file links

File links can contain additional information to make Emacs jump to a particular location in the file when following a link. This can be a line number or a search option after a double[8] colon. For example, when the command `C-c l` creates a link (see Section 4.4 [Handling links], page 34) to a file, it encodes the words in the current line as a search string that can be used to find this line back later when following the link with `C-c C-o`.

Here is the syntax of the different ways to attach a search to a file link, together with an explanation:

---

[8] For backward compatibility, line numbers can also follow a single colon.

```
[[file:~/code/main.c::255]]
[[file:~/xx.org::My Target]]
[[file:~/xx.org::*My Target]]
[[file:~/xx.org::#my-custom-id]]
[[file:~/xx.org::/regexp/]]
```

`255`

Jump to line 255.

`My Target`

Search for a link target '<<My Target>>', or do a text search for 'my target', similar to the search in internal links, see Section 4.2 [Internal links], page 31. In HTML export (see Section 12.5 [HTML export], page 136), such a file link will become an HTML reference to the corresponding named anchor in the linked file.

`*My Target`

In an Org file, restrict search to headlines.

`#my-custom-id`

Link to a heading with a CUSTOM_ID property

`/regexp/`

Do a regular expression search for regexp. This uses the Emacs command occur to list all matches in a separate window. If the target file is in Org-mode, org-occur is used to create a sparse tree with the matches.

As a degenerate case, a file link with an empty file name can be used to search the current file. For example, [[file:::find me]] does a search for 'find me' in the current file, just as '[[find me]]' would.

4.8 Custom Searches

The default mechanism for creating search strings and for doing the actual search related to a file link may not work correctly in all cases. For example, BibTEX database files have many entries like 'year="1993"' which would not result in good search strings, because the only unique identification for a BibTEX entry is the citation key.

If you come across such a problem, you can write custom functions to set the right search string for a particular file type, and to do the search for the string in the file. Using add-hook, these functions need to be added to the hook variables org-create-file-search-functions and org-execute-file-search-functions. See the docstring for these variables for more information. Org actually uses this mechanism for BibTEX database files, and you can use the corresponding code as an implementation example. See the file 'org-bibtex.el'.

5 TODO items

Org-mode does not maintain TODO lists as separate documents.[1] Instead, TODO items are an integral part of the notes file, because TODO items usually come up while taking notes! With Org mode, simply mark any entry in a tree as being a TODO item. In this way, information is not duplicated, and the entire context from which the TODO item emerged is always present.

Of course, this technique for managing TODO items scatters them throughout your notes file. Org-mode compensates for this by providing methods to give you an overview of all the things that you have to do.

5.1 Basic TODO functionality

Any headline becomes a TODO item when it starts with the word 'TODO', for example:

    *** TODO Write letter to Sam Fortune

The most important commands to work with TODO entries are:

C-c C-t
>   Rotate the TODO state of the current item among

>   The same rotation can also be done "remotely" from the timeline and agenda buffers with the t command key (see Section 10.5 [Agenda commands], page 108).

C-u C-c C-t
>   Select a specific keyword using completion or (if it has been set up) the fast selection interface. For the latter, you need to assign keys to TODO states, see Section 5.2.5 [Per-file keywords], page 44, and Section 6.2 [Setting tags], page 56, for more information.

S-⟨right⟩
S-⟨left⟩
>   Select the following/preceding TODO state, similar to cycling. Useful mostly if more than two TODO states are possible (see Section 5.2 [TODO extensions], page 42). See also Section 16.10.2 [Conflicts], page 208, for a discussion of the interaction with shift-selection-mode. See also the variable org-treat-S-cursor-todo-selection-as-state-change.

C-c / t
>   View TODO items in a *sparse tree* (see Section 2.6 [Sparse trees], page 14). Folds the entire buffer, but shows all TODO items (with not-DONE state)

---

[1] Of course, you can make a document that contains only long lists of TODO items, but this is not required.

and the headings hierarchy above them. With a prefix argument (or by
using C-c / T), search for a specific TODO. You will be prompted for the
keyword, and you can also give a list of keywords like KWD1|KWD2|... to
list entries that match any one of these keywords. With numeric prefix
argument N, show the tree for the Nth keyword in the variable org-todo-
keywords. With two prefix arguments, find all TODO states, both un-done
and done.

C-c a t
> Show the global TODO list. Collects the TODO items (with not-DONE
> states) from all agenda files (see Chapter 10 [Agenda Views], page 97) into
> a single buffer. The new buffer will be in agenda-mode, which provides
> commands to examine and manipulate the TODO entries from the new
> buffer (see Section 10.5 [Agenda commands], page 108). See Section 10.3.2
> [Global TODO list], page 102, for more information.

S-M-(RET)
> Insert a new TODO entry below the current one.

Changing a TODO state can also trigger tag changes. See the docstring of the
option org-todo-state-tags-triggers for details.

5.2 Extended use of TODO keywords

By default, marked TODO entries have one of only two states: TODO and
DONE. Org-mode allows you to classify TODO items in more complex ways
with *TODO keywords* (stored in org-todo-keywords). With special setup, the
TODO keyword system can work differently in different files.

Note that *tags* are another way to classify headlines in general and TODO
items in particular (see Chapter 6 [Tags], page 55).

5.2.1 TODO keywords as workflow states

You can use TODO keywords to indicate different *sequential* states in the
process of working on an item, for example:[2]

```
(setq org-todo-keywords
  '((sequence "TODO" "FEEDBACK" "VERIFY" "|" "DONE" "DELEGATED")))
```

The vertical bar separates the TODO keywords (states that *need action*)
from the DONE states (which need *no further action*). If you don't provide
the separator bar, the last state is used as the DONE state. With this setup,
the command C-c C-t will cycle an entry from TODO to FEEDBACK, then
to VERIFY, and finally to DONE and DELEGATED. You may also use a
numeric prefix argument to quickly select a specific state. For example C-3 C-c
C-t will change the state immediately to VERIFY. Or you can use S-(left)
to go backward through the sequence. If you define many keywords, you can
use in-buffer completion (see Section 16.1 [Completion], page 197) or even a
special one-key selection scheme (see Section 5.2.4 [Fast access to TODO states],
page 44) to insert these words into the buffer. Changing a TODO state can be

---

[2] Changing this variable only becomes effective after restarting Org-mode in a buffer.

logged with a timestamp, see Section 5.3.2 [Tracking TODO state changes], page 47, for more information.

5.2.2 TODO keywords as types

The second possibility is to use TODO keywords to indicate different *types* of action items. For example, you might want to indicate that items are for "work" or "home". Or, when you work with several people on a single project, you might want to assign action items directly to persons, by using their names as TODO keywords. This would be set up like this:

```
(setq org-todo-keywords
      '((type "Fred" "Sara" "Lucy" "|" "DONE")))
```

In this case, different keywords do not indicate a sequence, but rather different types. So the normal work flow would be to assign a task to a person, and later to mark it DONE. Org-mode supports this style by adapting the workings of the command C-c C-t.[3] When used several times in succession, it will still cycle through all names, in order to first select the right type for a task. But when you return to the item after some time and execute C-c C-t again, it will switch from any name directly to DONE. Use prefix arguments or completion to quickly select a specific name. You can also review the items of a specific TODO type in a sparse tree by using a numeric prefix to C-c / t. For example, to see all things Lucy has to do, you would use C-3 C-c / t. To collect Lucy's items from all agenda files into a single buffer, you would use the numeric prefix argument as well when creating the global TODO list: C-3 C-c a t.

5.2.3 Multiple keyword sets in one file

Sometimes you may want to use different sets of TODO keywords in parallel. For example, you may want to have the basic TODO/DONE, but also a workflow for bug fixing, and a separate state indicating that an item has been canceled (so it is not DONE, but also does not require action). Your setup would then look like this:

```
(setq org-todo-keywords
      '((sequence "TODO" "|" "DONE")
        (sequence "REPORT" "BUG" "KNOWNCAUSE" "|" "FIXED")
        (sequence "|" "CANCELED")))
```

The keywords should all be different, this helps Org-mode to keep track of which subsequence should be used for a given entry. In this setup, C-c C-t only operates within a subsequence, so it switches from DONE to (nothing) to TODO, and from FIXED to (nothing) to REPORT. Therefore you need a mechanism to initially select the correct sequence. Besides the obvious ways like typing a keyword or using completion, you may also apply the following commands:

---

[3] This is also true for the t command in the timeline and agenda buffers.

C-u C-u C-c C-t
C-S-(right)
C-S-(left)

> These keys jump from one TODO subset to the next. In the above ex-
> ample, C-u C-u C-c C-t or C-S-(right) would jump from TODO or DONE to
> REPORT, and any of the words in the second row to CANCELED. Note that the
> C-S- key binding conflict with shift-selection-mode (see Section 16.10.2
> [Conflicts], page 208).

S-(right)
S-(left)

> S-(<left>) and S-(<right>) and walk through *all* keywords from all sets,
> so for example S-(<right>) would switch from DONE to REPORT in the ex-
> ample above. See also Section 16.10.2 [Conflicts], page 208, for a discussion
> of the interaction with shift-selection-mode.

5.2.4 Fast access to TODO states

If you would like to quickly change an entry to an arbitrary TODO state
instead of cycling through the states, you can set up keys for single-letter access
to the states. This is done by adding the section key after each keyword, in
parentheses. For example:

```
(setq org-todo-keywords
      '((sequence "TODO(t)" "|" "DONE(d)")
        (sequence "REPORT(r)" "BUG(b)" "KNOWNCAUSE(k)" "|"
                  "FIXED(f)")
        (sequence "|" "CANCELED(c)")))
```

If you then press C-c C-t followed by the selection key, the entry will be
switched to this state. (SPC) can be used to remove any TODO keyword from
an entry.[4]

5.2.5 Setting up keywords for individual files

It can be very useful to use different aspects of the TODO mechanism in
different files. For file-local settings, you need to add special lines to the file
which set the keywords and interpretation for that file only. For example, to set
one of the two examples discussed above, you need one of the following lines,
starting in column zero anywhere in the file:

```
#+TODO: TODO FEEDBACK VERIFY | DONE CANCELED
```

(you may also write #+SEQ_TODO to be explicit about the interpretation, but it
means the same as #+TODO), or

```
#+TYP_TODO: Fred Sara Lucy Mike | DONE
```

A setup for using several sets in parallel would be:

---

[4] Check also the variable org-fast-tag-selection-include-todo, it allows you to
change the TODO state through the tags interface (see Section 6.2 [Setting tags],
page 56), in case you like to mingle the two concepts. Note that this means you
need to come up with unique keys across both sets of keywords.

```
#+TODO: TODO | DONE
#+TODO: REPORT BUG KNOWNCAUSE | FIXED
#+TODO: | CANCELED
```

To make sure you are using the correct keyword, type '#+' into the buffer and then use M-(TAB) completion.

Remember that the keywords after the vertical bar (or the last keyword if no bar is there) must always mean that the item is DONE (although you may use a different word). After changing one of these lines, use C-c C-c with the cursor still in the line to make the changes known to Org-mode.[5]

5.2.6 Faces for TODO keywords

Org-mode highlights TODO keywords with special faces: org-todo for keywords indicating that an item still has to be acted upon, and org-done for keywords indicating that an item is finished. If you are using more than 2 different states, you might want to use special faces for some of them. This can be done using the variable org-todo-keyword-faces. For example:

```
(setq org-todo-keyword-faces
      '(("TODO" . org-warning) ("STARTED" . "yellow")
        ("CANCELED" . (:foreground "blue" :weight bold))))
```

While using a list with face properties as shown for CANCELED *should* work, this does not always seem to be the case. If necessary, define a special face and use that. A string is interpreted as a color. The variable org-faces-easy-properties determines if that color is interpreted as a foreground or a background color.

5.2.7 TODO dependencies

The structure of Org files (hierarchy and lists) makes it easy to define TODO dependencies. Usually, a parent TODO task should not be marked DONE until all subtasks (defined as children tasks) are marked as DONE. And sometimes there is a logical sequence to a number of (sub)tasks, so that one task cannot be acted upon before all siblings above it are done. If you customize the variable org-enforce-todo-dependencies, Org will block entries from changing state to DONE while they have children that are not DONE. Furthermore, if an entry has a property ORDERED, each of its children will be blocked until all earlier siblings are marked DONE. Here is an example:

```
* TODO Blocked until (two) is done
** DONE one
** TODO two

* Parent
  :PROPERTIES:
    :ORDERED: t
```

---

[5] Org-mode parses these lines only when Org-mode is activated after visiting a file. C-c C-c with the cursor in a line starting with '#+' is simply restarting Org-mode for the current buffer.

```
    :END:
 ** TODO a
 ** TODO b, needs to wait for (a)
 ** TODO c, needs to wait for (a) and (b)
```

C-c C-x o

Toggle the ORDERED property of the current entry. A property is used for this behavior because this should be local to the current entry, not inherited like a tag. However, if you would like to *track* the value of this property with a tag for better visibility, customize the variable org-track-ordered-property-with-tag.

C-u C-u C-u C-c C-t

Change TODO state, circumventing any state blocking.

If you set the variable org-agenda-dim-blocked-tasks, TODO entries that cannot be closed because of such dependencies will be shown in a dimmed font or even made invisible in agenda views (see Chapter 10 [Agenda Views], page 97).

You can also block changes of TODO states by looking at checkboxes (see Section 5.6 [Checkboxes], page 53). If you set the variable org-enforce-todo-checkbox-dependencies, an entry that has unchecked checkboxes will be blocked from switching to DONE.

If you need more complex dependency structures, for example dependencies between entries in different trees or files, check out the contributed module 'org-depend.el'.

5.3 Progress logging

Org-mode can automatically record a timestamp and possibly a note when you mark a TODO item as DONE, or even each time you change the state of a TODO item. This system is highly configurable, settings can be on a per-keyword basis and can be localized to a file or even a subtree. For information on how to clock working time for a task, see Section 8.4 [Clocking work time], page 76.

5.3.1 Closing items

The most basic logging is to keep track of *when* a certain TODO item was finished. This is achieved with[1]

    (setq org-log-done 'time)

Then each time you turn an entry from a TODO (not-done) state into any of the DONE states, a line 'CLOSED: [timestamp]' will be inserted just after the headline. If you turn the entry back into a TODO item through further state cycling, that line will be removed again. If you want to record a note along with the timestamp, use[2]

    (setq org-log-done 'note)

You will then be prompted for a note, and that note will be stored below the entry with a 'Closing Note' heading.

In the timeline (see Section 10.3.4 [Timeline], page 105) and in the agenda (see Section 10.3.1 [Weekly/daily agenda], page 100), you can then use the l key to display the TODO items with a 'CLOSED' timestamp on each day, giving you an overview of what has been done.

5.3.2 Tracking TODO state changes

When TODO keywords are used as workflow states (see Section 5.2.1 [Work-flow states], page 42), you might want to keep track of when a state change occurred and maybe take a note about this change. You can either record just a timestamp, or a time-stamped note for a change. These records will be inserted after the headline as an itemized list, newest first.[3] When taking a lot of notes, you might want to get the notes out of the way into a drawer (see Section 2.8 [Drawers], page 19). Customize the variable org-log-into-drawer to get this behavior—the recommended drawer for this is called LOGBOOK. You can also overrule the setting of this variable for a subtree by setting a LOG_INTO_DRAWER property.

Since it is normally too much to record a note for every state, Org-mode expects configuration on a per-keyword basis for this. This is achieved by adding special markers '!' (for a timestamp) and '@' (for a note) in parentheses after each keyword. For example, with the setting

---

[1] The corresponding in-buffer setting is: #+STARTUP: logdone

[2] The corresponding in-buffer setting is: #+STARTUP: lognotedone

[3] See the variable org-log-states-order-reversed

```
(setq org-todo-keywords
  '((sequence "TODO(t)" "WAIT(w@/!)" "|" "DONE(d!)"
              "CANCELED(c@)")))
```

you not only define global TODO keywords and fast access keys, but also request
that a time is recorded when the entry is set to DONE,[4] and that a note is
recorded when switching to WAIT or CANCELED. The setting for WAIT is
even more special: the '!' after the slash means that in addition to the note
taken when entering the state, a timestamp should be recorded when *leaving*
the WAIT state, if and only if the *target* state does not configure logging for
entering it. So it has no effect when switching from WAIT to DONE, because
DONE is configured to record a timestamp only. But when switching from
WAIT back to TODO, the '/!' in the WAIT setting now triggers a timestamp
even though TODO has no logging configured.

   You can use the exact same syntax for setting logging preferences local to a
buffer:

```
#+TODO: TODO(t) WAIT(w@/!) | DONE(d!) CANCELED(c@)
```

In order to define logging settings that are local to a subtree or a single
item, define a LOGGING property in this entry. Any non-empty LOGGING
property resets all logging settings to nil. You may then turn on logging for this
specific tree using STARTUP keywords like lognotedone or logrepeat, as well
as adding state specific settings like TODO(!). For example

```
* TODO Log each state with only a time
  :PROPERTIES:
  :LOGGING: TODO(!) WAIT(!) DONE(!) CANCELED(!)
  :END:
* TODO Only log when switching to WAIT, and when repeating
  :PROPERTIES:
  :LOGGING: WAIT(@) logrepeat
  :END:
* TODO No logging at all
  :PROPERTIES:
  :LOGGING: nil
  :END:
```

---

[4] It is possible that Org-mode will record two timestamps when you are using both
org-log-done and state change logging. However, it will never prompt for two
notes—if you have configured both, the state change recording note will take precedence and cancel the 'Closing Note'.

5.3.3 Tracking your habits

Org has the ability to track the consistency of a special category of TODOs, called "habits". A habit has the following properties:

1. You have enabled the habits module by customizing the variable org-modules.

2. The habit is a TODO, with a TODO keyword representing an open state.

3. The property STYLE is set to the value habit.

4. The TODO has a scheduled date, usually with a .+ style repeat interval. A ++ style may be appropriate for habits with time constraints, e.g., must be done on weekends, or a + style for an unusual habit that can have a backlog, e.g., weekly reports.

5. The TODO may also have minimum and maximum ranges specified by using the syntax '.+2d/3d', which says that you want to do the task at least every three days, but at most every two days.

6. You must also have state logging for the DONE state enabled, in order for historical data to be represented in the consistency graph. If it's not enabled it's not an error, but the consistency graphs will be largely meaningless.

To give you an idea of what the above rules look like in action, here's an actual habit with some history:

```
** TODO Shave
   SCHEDULED: <2009-10-17 Sat .+2d/4d>
   - State "DONE"        from "TODO"        [2009-10-15 Thu]
   - State "DONE"        from "TODO"        [2009-10-12 Mon]
   - State "DONE"        from "TODO"        [2009-10-10 Sat]
   - State "DONE"        from "TODO"        [2009-10-04 Sun]
   - State "DONE"        from "TODO"        [2009-10-02 Fri]
   - State "DONE"        from "TODO"        [2009-09-29 Tue]
   - State "DONE"        from "TODO"        [2009-09-25 Fri]
   - State "DONE"        from "TODO"        [2009-09-19 Sat]
   - State "DONE"        from "TODO"        [2009-09-16 Wed]
   - State "DONE"        from "TODO"        [2009-09-12 Sat]
   :PROPERTIES:
   :STYLE:      habit
   :LAST_REPEAT: [2009-10-19 Mon 00:36]
   :END:
```

What this habit says is: I want to shave at most every 2 days (given by the SCHEDULED date and repeat interval) and at least every 4 days. If today is the 15th, then the habit first appears in the agenda on Oct 17, after the minimum of 2 days has elapsed, and will appear overdue on Oct 19, after four days have elapsed.

What's really useful about habits is that they are displayed along with a consistency graph, to show how consistent you've been at getting that task done in the past. This graph shows every day that the task was done over the past three weeks, with colors for each day. The colors used are:

Blue
> If the task wasn't to be done yet on that day.

Green
> If the task could have been done on that day.

Yellow
> If the task was going to be overdue the next day.

Red
> If the task was overdue on that day.

In addition to coloring each day, the day is also marked with an asterisk if the task was actually done that day, and an exclamation mark to show where the current day falls in the graph.

There are several configuration variables that can be used to change the way habits are displayed in the agenda.

org-habit-graph-column
> The buffer column at which the consistency graph should be drawn. This will overwrite any text in that column, so it's a good idea to keep your habits' titles brief and to the point.

org-habit-preceding-days
> The amount of history, in days before today, to appear in consistency graphs.

org-habit-following-days
> The number of days after today that will appear in consistency graphs.

org-habit-show-habits-only-for-today
> If non-nil, only show habits in today's agenda view. This is set to true by default.

Lastly, pressing K in the agenda buffer will cause habits to temporarily be disabled and they won't appear at all. Press K again to bring them back. They are also subject to tag filtering, if you have habits which should only be done in certain contexts, for example.

5.4 Priorities

If you use Org-mode extensively, you may end up with enough TODO items that it starts to make sense to prioritize them. Prioritizing can be done by placing a *priority cookie* into the headline of a TODO item, like this

```
*** TODO [#A] Write letter to Sam Fortune
```

By default, Org-mode supports three priorities: 'A', 'B', and 'C'. 'A' is the highest priority. An entry without a cookie is treated just like priority 'B'. Priorities make a difference only for sorting in the agenda (see Section 10.3.1 [Weekly/daily agenda], page 100); outside the agenda, they have no inherent meaning to Org-mode. The cookies can be highlighted with special faces by customizing the variable `org-priority-faces`.

Priorities can be attached to any outline node; they do not need to be TODO items.

C-c ,

> Set the priority of the current headline. The command prompts for a priority character 'A', 'B' or 'C'. When you press (SPC) instead, the priority cookie is removed from the headline. The priorities can also be changed "remotely" from the timeline and agenda buffer with the , command (see Section 10.5 [Agenda commands], page 108).

S-(up)
S-(down)

> Increase/decrease priority of current headline.[5] Note that these keys are also used to modify timestamps (see Section 8.2 [Creating timestamps], page 70). See also Section 16.10.2 [Conflicts], page 208, for a discussion of the interaction with `shift-selection-mode`.

You can change the range of allowed priorities by setting the variables `org-highest-priority`, `org-lowest-priority`, and `org-default-priority`. For an individual buffer, you may set these values (highest, lowest, default) like this (please make sure that the highest priority is earlier in the alphabet than the lowest priority):

```
#+PRIORITIES: A C B
```

---

[5] See also the option `org-priority-start-cycle-with-default`.

5.5 Breaking tasks down into subtasks

It is often advisable to break down large tasks into smaller, manageable subtasks. You can do this by creating an outline tree below a TODO item, with detailed subtasks on the tree.[6] To keep the overview over the fraction of subtasks that are already completed, insert either '[/]' or '[%]' anywhere in the headline. These cookies will be updated each time the TODO status of a child changes, or when pressing C-c C-c on the cookie. For example:

```
* Organize Party [33%]
** TODO Call people [1/2]
*** TODO Peter
*** DONE Sarah
** TODO Buy food
** DONE Talk to neighbor
```

If a heading has both checkboxes and TODO children below it, the meaning of the statistics cookie become ambiguous. Set the property COOKIE_DATA to either 'checkbox' or 'todo' to resolve this issue.

If you would like to have the statistics cookie count any TODO entries in the subtree (not just direct children), configure the variable org-hierarchical-todo-statistics. To do this for a single subtree, include the word 'recursive' into the value of the COOKIE_DATA property.

```
* Parent capturing statistics [2/20]
  :PROPERTIES:
  :COOKIE_DATA: todo recursive
  :END:
```

If you would like a TODO entry to automatically change to DONE when all children are done, you can use the following setup:

```
(defun org-summary-todo (n-done n-not-done)
    "Switch entry to DONE when all subentries are done, to
TODO otherwise."
    (let (org-log-done org-log-states)   ; turn off logging
      (org-todo (if (= n-not-done 0) "DONE" "TODO"))))

(add-hook 'org-after-todo-statistics-hook 'org-summary-todo)
```

Another possibility is the use of checkboxes to identify (a hierarchy of) a large number of subtasks (see Section 5.6 [Checkboxes], page 53).

---

[6] To keep subtasks out of the global TODO list, see the org-agenda-todo-list-sublevels.

5.6 Checkboxes

Every item in a plain list[7] (see Section 2.7 [Plain lists], page 15) can be made into a checkbox by starting it with the string '[ ]'. This feature is similar to TODO items (see Chapter 5 [TODO Items], page 41), but is more lightweight. Checkboxes are not included into the global TODO list, so they are often great to split a task into a number of simple steps. Or you can use them in a shopping list. To toggle a checkbox, use C-c C-c, or use the mouse (thanks to Piotr Zielinski's 'org-mouse.el').

Here is an example of a checkbox list.

```
* TODO Organize party [2/4]
  - [-] call people [1/3]
    - [ ] Peter
    - [X] Sarah
    - [ ] Sam
  - [X] order food
  - [ ] think about what music to play
  - [X] talk to the neighbors
```

Checkboxes work hierarchically, so if a checkbox item has children that are checkboxes, toggling one of the children checkboxes will make the parent checkbox reflect if none, some, or all of the children are checked.

The '[2/4]' and '[1/3]' in the first and second line are cookies indicating how many checkboxes present in this entry have been checked off, and the total number of checkboxes present. This can give you an idea on how many checkboxes remain, even without opening a folded entry. The cookies can be placed into a headline or into (the first line of) a plain list item. Each cookie covers checkboxes of direct children structurally below the headline/item on which the cookie appears.[8] You have to insert the cookie yourself by typing either '[/]' or '[%]'. With '[/]' you get an 'n out of m' result, as in the examples above. With '[%]' you get information about the percentage of checkboxes checked (in the above example, this would be '[50%]' and '[33%]', respectively). In a headline, a cookie can count either checkboxes below the heading or TODO states of children, and it will display whatever was changed last. Set the property COOKIE_DATA to either 'checkbox' or 'todo' to resolve this issue.

If the current outline node has an ORDERED property, checkboxes must be checked off in sequence, and an error will be thrown if you try to check off a box while there are unchecked boxes above it.

The following commands work with checkboxes:

C-c C-c

> Toggle checkbox status or (with prefix arg) checkbox presence at point. With double prefix argument, set it to '[-]', which is considered to be an intermediate state.

---

[7] With the exception of description lists. But you can allow it by modifying org-list-automatic-rules accordingly.

[8] Set the variable org-hierarchical-checkbox-statistics if you want such cookies to represent the all checkboxes below the cookie, not just the direct children.

C-c C-x C-b

> Toggle checkbox status or (with prefix arg) checkbox presence at point. With double prefix argument, set it to '[-]', which is considered to be an intermediate state.
>
> — If there is an active region, toggle the first checkbox in the region and set all remaining boxes to the same status as the first. With a prefix arg, add or remove the checkbox for all items in the region.
>
> — If the cursor is in a headline, toggle checkboxes in the region between this headline and the next (so *not* the entire subtree).
>
> — If there is no active region, just toggle the checkbox at point.

M-S-(RET)

> Insert a new item with a checkbox. This works only if the cursor is already in a plain list item (see Section 2.7 [Plain lists], page 15).

C-c C-x o

> Toggle the ORDERED property of the entry, to toggle if checkboxes must be checked off in sequence. A property is used for this behavior because this should be local to the current entry, not inherited like a tag. However, if you would like to *track* the value of this property with a tag for better visibility, customize the variable org-track-ordered-property-with-tag.

C-c #

> Update the statistics cookie in the current outline entry. When called with a C-u prefix, update the entire file. Checkbox statistic cookies are updated automatically if you toggle checkboxes with C-c C-c and make new ones with M-S-(RET). TODO statistics cookies update when changing TODO states. If you delete boxes/entries or add/change them by hand, use this command to get things back into sync. Or simply toggle any entry twice (checkboxes with C-c C-c).

6 Tags

An excellent way to implement labels and contexts for cross-correlating information is to assign *tags* to headlines. Org-mode has extensive support for tags.

Every headline can contain a list of tags; they occur at the end of the headline. Tags are normal words containing letters, numbers, '_', and '@'. Tags must be preceded and followed by a single colon, e.g., ':work:'. Several tags can be specified, as in ':work:urgent:'. Tags will by default be in bold face with the same color as the headline. You may specify special faces for specific tags using the variable org-tag-faces, in much the same way as you can for TODO keywords (see Section 5.2.6 [Faces for TODO keywords], page 45).

6.1 Tag inheritance

Tags make use of the hierarchical structure of outline trees. If a heading has a certain tag, all subheadings will inherit the tag as well. For example, in the list

```
* Meeting with the French group        :work:
** Summary by Frank                     :boss:notes:
*** TODO Prepare slides for him         :action:
```

the final heading will have the tags ':work:', ':boss:', ':notes:', and ':action:' even though the final heading is not explicitly marked with those tags. You can also set tags that all entries in a file should inherit just as if these tags were defined in a hypothetical level zero that surrounds the entire file. Use a line like this:[1]

```
#+FILETAGS:  :Peter:Boss:Secret:
```

To limit tag inheritance to specific tags, or to turn it off entirely, use the variables org-use-tag-inheritance and org-tags-exclude-from-inheritance.

When a headline matches during a tags search while tag inheritance is turned on, all the sublevels in the same tree will (for a simple match form) match as well.[2] The list of matches may then become very long. If you only want to see the first tags match in a subtree, configure the variable org-tags-match-list-sublevels (not recommended).

---

[1] As with all these in-buffer settings, pressing C-c C-c activates any changes in the line.

[2] This is only true if the search does not involve more complex tests including properties (see Section 7.3 [Property searches], page 61).

6.2 Setting tags

Tags can simply be typed into the buffer at the end of a headline. After a colon, M-(TAB) offers completion on tags. There is also a special command for inserting tags:

C-c C-q

Enter new tags for the current headline. Org-mode will either offer completion or a special single-key interface for setting tags, see below. After pressing (RET), the tags will be inserted and aligned to org-tags-column. When called with a C-u prefix, all tags in the current buffer will be aligned to that column, just to make things look nice. TAGS are automatically realigned after promotion, demotion, and TODO state changes (see Section 5.1 [TODO basics], page 41).

C-c C-c

When the cursor is in a headline, this does the same as C-c C-q.

Org will support tag insertion based on a *list of tags*. By default this list is constructed dynamically, containing all tags currently used in the buffer. You may also globally specify a hard list of tags with the variable org-tag-alist. Finally you can set the default tags for a given file with lines like

```
#+TAGS: @work @home @tennisclub
#+TAGS: laptop car pc sailboat
```

If you have globally defined your preferred set of tags using the variable org-tag-alist, but would like to use a dynamic tag list in a specific file, add an empty TAGS option line to that file:

```
#+TAGS:
```

If you have a preferred set of tags that you would like to use in every file, in addition to those defined on a per-file basis by TAGS option lines, then you may specify a list of tags with the variable org-tag-persistent-alist. You may turn this off on a per-file basis by adding a STARTUP option line to that file:

```
#+STARTUP: noptag
```

By default Org-mode uses the standard minibuffer completion facilities for entering tags. However, it also implements another, quicker, tag selection method called *fast tag selection*. This allows you to select and deselect tags with just a single key press. For this to work well you should assign unique letters to most of your commonly used tags. You can do this globally by configuring the variable org-tag-alist in your '.emacs' file. For example, you may find the need to tag many items in different files with ':@home:'. In this case you can set something like:

```
(setq org-tag-alist '(("@work" . ?w) ("@home" . ?h)
                       ("laptop" . ?l)))
```

If the tag is only relevant to the file you are working on, then you can instead set the TAGS option line as:

```
#+TAGS: @work(w) @home(h) @tennisclub(t)  laptop(l)  pc(p)
```
The tags interface will show the available tags in a splash window. If you want to start a new line after a specific tag, insert '\n' into the tag list

```
#+TAGS: @work(w) @home(h) @tennisclub(t) \n laptop(l) pc(p)
```
or write them in two lines:

```
#+TAGS: @work(w) @home(h) @tennisclub(t)
#+TAGS: laptop(l) pc(p)
```
You can also group together tags that are mutually exclusive by using braces, as in:

```
#+TAGS: { @work(w) @home(h) @tennisclub(t) } laptop(l) pc(p)
```
you indicate that at most one of '@work', '@home', and '@tennisclub' should be selected. Multiple such groups are allowed.

Don't forget to press C-c C-c with the cursor in one of these lines to activate any changes.

To set these mutually exclusive groups in the variable org-tags-alist, you must use the dummy tags :startgroup and :endgroup instead of the braces. Similarly, you can use :newline to indicate a line break. The previous example would be set globally by the following configuration:

```
(setq org-tag-alist '((:startgroup . nil)
                      ("@work" . ?w) ("@home" . ?h)
                      ("@tennisclub" . ?t)
                      (:endgroup . nil)
                      ("laptop" . ?l) ("pc" . ?p)))
```

If at least one tag has a selection key then pressing C-c C-c will automatically present you with a special interface, listing inherited tags, the tags of the current headline, and a list of all valid tags with corresponding keys.[3] In this interface, you can use the following keys:

a-z...

> Pressing keys assigned to tags will add or remove them from the list of tags in the current line. Selecting a tag in a group of mutually exclusive tags will turn off any other tags from that group.

(TAB)

> Enter a tag in the minibuffer, even if the tag is not in the predefined list. You will be able to complete on all tags present in the buffer.

(SPC)

> Clear all tags for this line.

(RET)

> Accept the modified set.

C-g

> Abort without installing changes.

q   If q is not assigned to a tag, it aborts like C-g.

---

[3] Keys will automatically be assigned to tags which have no configured keys.

!   Turn off groups of mutually exclusive tags. Use this to (as an exception)
     assign several tags from such a group.

C-c

     Toggle auto-exit after the next change (see below). If you are using expert
     mode, the first C-c will display the selection window.

This method lets you assign tags to a headline with very few keys. With the
above setup, you could clear the current tags and set '@home', 'laptop' and 'pc'
tags with just the following keys: C-c C-c (SPC) h l p (RET). Switching from
'@home' to '@work' would be done with C-c C-c w (RET) or alternatively with
C-c C-c C-c w. Adding the non-predefined tag 'Sarah' could be done with C-c
C-c (TAB) S a r a h (RET) (RET).

    If you find that most of the time you need only a single key press to modify
your list of tags, set the variable org-fast-tag-selection-single-key. Then
you no longer have to press (RET) to exit fast tag selection—it will immediately
exit after the first change. If you then occasionally need more keys, press C-c to
turn off auto-exit for the current tag selection process (in effect: start selection
with C-c C-c C-c instead of C-c C-c). If you set the variable to the value expert,
the special window is not even shown for single-key tag selection, it comes up
only when you press an extra C-c.

6.3 Tag searches

    Once a system of tags has been set up, it can be used to collect related
information into special lists.

C-c \
C-c / m

     Create a sparse tree with all headlines matching a tags search. With a C-u
     prefix argument, ignore headlines that are not a TODO line.

C-c a m

     Create a global list of tag matches from all agenda files. See Section 10.3.3
     [Matching tags and properties], page 103.

C-c a M

     Create a global list of tag matches from all agenda files, but check only
     TODO items and force checking subitems (see variable org-tags-match-
     list-sublevels).

    These commands all prompt for a match string which allows basic Boolean
logic like '+boss+urgent-project1', to find entries with tags 'boss' and
'urgent', but not 'project1', or 'Kathy|Sally' to find entries which are
tagged, like 'Kathy' or 'Sally'. The full syntax of the search string is rich and
allows also matching against TODO keywords, entry levels and properties. For
a complete description with many examples, see Section 10.3.3 [Matching tags
and properties], page 103.

7 Properties and columns

Properties are a set of key-value pairs associated with an entry. There are two main applications for properties in Org-mode. First, properties are like tags, but with a value. Second, you can use properties to implement (very basic) database capabilities in an Org buffer. For an example of the first application, imagine maintaining a file where you document bugs and plan releases for a piece of software. Instead of using tags like :release_1:, :release_2:, one can use a property, say :Release:, that in different subtrees has different values, such as 1.0 or 2.0. For an example of the second application of properties, imagine keeping track of your music CDs, where properties could be things such as the album, artist, date of release, number of tracks, and so on.

Properties can be conveniently edited and viewed in column view (see Section 7.5 [Column view], page 63).

7.1 Property syntax

Properties are key-value pairs. They need to be inserted into a special drawer (see Section 2.8 [Drawers], page 19) with the name PROPERTIES. Each property is specified on a single line, with the key (surrounded by colons) first, and the value after it. Here is an example:

```
* CD collection
** Classic
*** Goldberg Variations
    :PROPERTIES:
    :Title:     Goldberg Variations
    :Composer:  J.S. Bach
    :Artist:    Glen Gould
    :Publisher: Deutsche Grammophon
    :NDisks:    1
    :END:
```

You may define the allowed values for a particular property ':Xyz:' by setting a property ':Xyz_ALL:'. This special property is *inherited*, so if you set it in a level 1 entry, it will apply to the entire tree. When allowed values are defined, setting the corresponding property becomes easier and is less prone to typing errors. For the example with the CD collection, we can predefine publishers and the number of disks in a box like this:

```
* CD collection
  :PROPERTIES:
  :NDisks_ALL:  1 2 3 4
  :Publisher_ALL: "Deutsche Grammophon" Philips EMI
  :END:
```

If you want to set properties that can be inherited by any entry in a file, use a line like

```
#+PROPERTY: NDisks_ALL 1 2 3 4
```

Property values set with the global variable `org-global-properties` can be inherited by all entries in all Org files.

The following commands help to work with properties:

M-⌷TAB⌷
> After an initial colon in a line, complete property keys. All keys used in the current file will be offered as possible completions.

C-c C-x p
> Set a property. This prompts for a property name and a value. If necessary, the property drawer is created as well.

M-x org-insert-property-drawer
> Insert a property drawer into the current entry. The drawer will be inserted early in the entry, but after the lines with planning information like deadlines.

C-c C-c
> With the cursor in a property drawer, this executes property commands.

C-c C-c s
> Set a property in the current entry. Both the property and the value can be inserted using completion.

S-⌷left⌷/⌷right⌷
> Switch property at point to the next/previous allowed value.

C-c C-c d
> Remove a property from the current entry.

C-c C-c D
> Globally remove a property, from all entries in the current file.

C-c C-c c
> Compute the property at point, using the operator and scope from the nearest column format definition.

7.2 Special properties

Special properties provide an alternative access method to Org-mode features, like the TODO state or the priority of an entry, discussed in the previous chapters. This interface exists so that you can include these states in a column view (see Section 7.5 [Column view], page 63), or to use them in queries. The following property names are special and should not be used as keys in the properties drawer:

TODO	The TODO keyword of the entry.
TAGS	The tags defined directly in the headline.
ALLTAGS	All tags, including inherited ones.
CATEGORY	The category of an entry.
PRIORITY	The priority of the entry, a string with a single letter.
DEADLINE	The deadline time string, without the angular brackets.
SCHEDULED	The scheduling timestamp, without the angular brackets.
CLOSED	When was this entry closed?
TIMESTAMP	The first keyword-less timestamp in the entry.
TIMESTAMP_IA	The first inactive timestamp in the entry.
CLOCKSUM	The sum of CLOCK intervals in the subtree. org-clock-sum must be run first to compute the values.
BLOCKED	"t" if task is currently blocked by children or siblings
ITEM	The content of the entry.

7.3 Property searches

To create sparse trees and special lists with selection based on properties, the same commands are used as for tag searches (see Section 6.3 [Tag searches], page 58).

C-c \
C-c / m

> Create a sparse tree with all matching entries. With a C-u prefix argument, ignore headlines that are not a TODO line.

C-c a m

> Create a global list of tag/property matches from all agenda files. See Section 10.3.3 [Matching tags and properties], page 103.

C-c a M

> Create a global list of tag matches from all agenda files, but check only TODO items and force checking of subitems (see variable org-tags-match-list-sublevels).

The syntax for the search string is described in Section 10.3.3 [Matching tags and properties], page 103.

There is also a special command for creating sparse trees based on a single property:

C-c / p

> Create a sparse tree based on the value of a property. This first prompts for the name of a property, and then for a value. A sparse tree is created with all entries that define this property with the given value. If you enclose the value in curly braces, it is interpreted as a regular expression and matched against the property values.

7.4 Property Inheritance

The outline structure of Org-mode documents lends itself to an inheritance model of properties: if the parent in a tree has a certain property, the children can inherit this property. Org-mode does not turn this on by default, because it can slow down property searches significantly and is often not needed. However, if you find inheritance useful, you can turn it on by setting the variable org-use-property-inheritance. It may be set to t to make all properties inherited from the parent, to a list of properties that should be inherited, or to a regular expression that matches inherited properties. If a property has the value 'nil', this is interpreted as an explicit undefine of the property, so that inheritance search will stop at this value and return nil.

Org-mode has a few properties for which inheritance is hard-coded, at least for the special applications for which they are used:

COLUMNS

> The :COLUMNS: property defines the format of column view (see Section 7.5 [Column view], page 63). It is inherited in the sense that the level where a :COLUMNS: property is defined is used as the starting point for a column view table, independently of the location in the subtree from where columns view is turned on.

CATEGORY

> For agenda view, a category set through a :CATEGORY: property applies to the entire subtree.

ARCHIVE

> For archiving, the :ARCHIVE: property may define the archive location for the entire subtree (see Section 9.6.1 [Moving subtrees], page 94).

LOGGING

> The LOGGING property may define logging settings for an entry or a subtree (see Section 5.3.2 [Tracking TODO state changes], page 47).

7.5 Column view

A great way to view and edit properties in an outline tree is *column view*. In column view, each outline node is turned into a table row. Columns in this table provide access to properties of the entries. Org-mode implements columns by overlaying a tabular structure over the headline of each item. While the headlines have been turned into a table row, you can still change the visibility of the outline tree. For example, you get a compact table by switching to CONTENTS view (S-(TAB) S-(TAB), or simply c while column view is active), but you can still open, read, and edit the entry below each headline. Or, you can switch to column view after executing a sparse tree command and in this way get a table only for the selected items. Column view also works in agenda buffers (see Chapter 10 [Agenda Views], page 97) where queries have collected selected items, possibly from a number of files.

7.5.1 Defining columns

Setting up a column view first requires defining the columns. This is done by defining a column format line.

7.5.1.1 Scope of column definitions

To define a column format for an entire file, use a line like

```
#+COLUMNS: %25ITEM %TAGS %PRIORITY %TODO
```

To specify a format that only applies to a specific tree, add a :COLUMNS: property to the top node of that tree, for example:

```
** Top node for columns view
   :PROPERTIES:
   :COLUMNS: %25ITEM %TAGS %PRIORITY %TODO
   :END:
```

If a :COLUMNS: property is present in an entry, it defines columns for the entry itself, and for the entire subtree below it. Since the column definition is part of the hierarchical structure of the document, you can define columns on level 1 that are general enough for all sublevels, and more specific columns further down, when you edit a deeper part of the tree.

7.5.1.2 Column attributes

A column definition sets the attributes of a column. The general definition looks like this:

```
%[width]property[(title)][{summary-type}]
```

Except for the percent sign and the property name, all items are optional. The individual parts have the following meaning:

width

    An integer specifying the width of the column in characters. If omitted, the width will be determined automatically.

property

> The property that should be edited in this column. Special properties representing meta data are allowed here as well (see Section 7.2 [Special properties], page 61)

title

> The header text for the column. If omitted, the property name is used.

{summary-type}

> The summary type. If specified, the column values for parent nodes are computed from the children. Supported summary types are:

{+}	Sum numbers in this column.
{+;%.1f}	Like '+', but format result with '%.1f'.
{$}	Currency, short for '+;%.2f'.
{:}	Sum times, HH:MM, plain numbers are hours.
{X}	Checkbox status, '[X]' if all children are '[X]'.
{X/}	Checkbox status, '[n/m]'.
{X%}	Checkbox status, '[n%]'.
{min}	Smallest number in column.
{max}	Largest number.
{mean}	Arithmetic mean of numbers.
{:min}	Smallest time value in column.
{:max}	Largest time value.
{:mean}	Arithmetic mean of time values.
{@min}	Minimum age (in days/hours/mins/seconds).
{@max}	Maximum age (in days/hours/mins/seconds).
{@mean}	Arithmetic mean of ages (in days/hours/mins/seconds).
{est+}	Add low-high estimates.

Be aware that you can only have one summary type for any property you include. Subsequent columns referencing the same property will all display the same summary information.

The est+ summary type requires further explanation. It is used for combining estimates, expressed as low-high ranges. For example, instead of estimating a particular task will take 5 days, you might estimate it as 5-6 days if you're fairly confident you know how much work is required, or 1-10 days if you don't really know what needs to be done. Both ranges average at 5.5 days, but the first represents a more predictable delivery.

When combining a set of such estimates, simply adding the lows and highs produces an unrealistically wide result. Instead, est+ adds the statistical mean and variance of the sub-tasks, generating a final estimate from the sum. For example, suppose you had ten tasks, each of which was estimated at 0.5 to 2 days of work. Straight addition produces an estimate of 5 to 20 days, representing what to expect if everything goes either extremely well or extremely poorly. In contrast, est+ estimates the full job more realistically, at 10-15 days.

Here is an example for a complete columns definition, along with allowed values.

```
:COLUMNS: %25ITEM %9Approved(Approved?){X} %Owner %11Status \(1)
          %10Time_Estimate{:} %CLOCKSUM
:Owner_ALL:      Tammy Mark Karl Lisa Don
:Status_ALL:     "In progress" "Not started yet" "Finished" ""
:Approved_ALL:   "[ ]" "[X]"
```

The first column, '%25ITEM', means the first 25 characters of the item itself, i.e.,
of the headline. You probably always should start the column definition with
the 'ITEM' specifier. The other specifiers create columns 'Owner' with a list of
names as allowed values, for 'Status' with four different possible values, and
for a checkbox field 'Approved'. When no width is given after the '%' character,
the column will be exactly as wide as it needs to be in order to fully display all
values. The 'Approved' column does have a modified title ('Approved?', with a
question mark). Summaries will be created for the 'Time_Estimate' column by
adding time duration expressions like HH:MM, and for the 'Approved' column,
by providing an '[X]' status if all children have been checked. The 'CLOCKSUM'
column is special, it lists the sum of CLOCK intervals in the subtree.

7.5.2 Using column view

Turning column view on and off

C-c C-x C-c
: Turn on column view. If the cursor is before the first headline in the
file, column view is turned on for the entire file, using the #+COLUMNS
definition. If the cursor is somewhere inside the outline, this command
searches the hierarchy, up from point, for a :COLUMNS: property that defines
a format. When one is found, the column view table is established for the
tree starting at the entry that contains the :COLUMNS: property. If no such
property is found, the format is taken from the #+COLUMNS line or from the
variable org-columns-default-format, and column view is established for
the current entry and its subtree.

r
: Recreate the column view, to include recent changes made in the buffer.

g
: Same as r.

q
: Exit column view.

Editing values

(left) (right) (up) (down)
: Move through the column view from field to field.

S-(left)/(right)
: Switch to the next/previous allowed value of the field. For this, you have
to have specified allowed values for a property.

----

(1) Please note that the COLUMNS definition must be on a single line—it is wrapped
here only because of formatting constraints.

1..9,0

> Directly select the Nth allowed value, 0 selects the 10th value.

n / p

> Same as S-(left)/(right)

e   Edit the property at point. For the special properties, this will invoke the
     same interface that you normally use to change that property. For exam-
     ple, when editing a TAGS property, the tag completion or fast selection
     interface will pop up.

C-c C-c

> When there is a checkbox at point, toggle it.

v   View the full value of this property. This is useful if the width of the
     column is smaller than that of the value.

a   Edit the list of allowed values for this property. If the list is found in the
     hierarchy, the modified values is stored there. If no list is found, the new
     value is stored in the first entry that is part of the current column view.

Modifying the table structure

< / >

> Make the column narrower/wider by one character.

S-M-(right)

> Insert a new column, to the left of the current column.

S-M-(left)

> Delete the current column.

7.5.3 Capturing column view

Since column view is just an overlay over a buffer, it cannot be exported
or printed directly. If you want to capture a column view, use a columnview
dynamic block (see Section A.6 [Dynamic blocks], page 218). The frame of this
block looks like this:

```
* The column view
#+BEGIN: columnview :hlines 1 :id "label"

#+END:
```

This dynamic block has the following parameters:

:id

> This is the most important parameter. Column view is a feature that is
> often localized to a certain (sub)tree, and the capture block might be at a
> different location in the file. To identify the tree whose view to capture,
> you can use 4 values:
>
> local
>
> > use the tree in which the capture block is located
>
> global
>
> > make a global view, including all headings in the file

"file:*path-to-file*"
> run column view at the top of this file

"*ID*"
> call column view in the tree that has an :ID: property with the value *label*. You can use M-x org-id-copy to create a globally unique ID for the current entry and copy it to the kill-ring.

:hlines
> When t, insert an hline after every line. When a number *N*, insert an hline before each headline with level <= *N*.

:vlines
> When set to t, force column groups to get vertical lines.

:maxlevel
> When set to a number, don't capture entries below this level.

:skip-empty-rows
> When set to t, skip rows where the only non-empty specifier of the column view is ITEM.

The following commands insert or update the dynamic block:

C-c C-x i
> Insert a dynamic block capturing a column view. You will be prompted for the scope or ID of the view.

C-c C-c
C-c C-x C-u
> Update dynamic block at point. The cursor needs to be in the #+BEGIN line of the dynamic block.

C-u C-c C-x C-u
> Update all dynamic blocks (see Section A.6 [Dynamic blocks], page 218). This is useful if you have several clock table blocks in a buffer.

You can add formulas to the column view table and you may add plotting instructions in front of the table—these will survive an update of the block. If there is a #+TBLFM: after the table, the table will actually be recalculated automatically after an update.

An alternative way to capture and process property values into a table is provided by Eric Schulte's 'org-collector.el' which is a contributed package.[2] It provides a general API to collect properties from entries in a certain scope, and arbitrary Lisp expressions to process these values before inserting them into a table or a dynamic block.

---

[2] Contributed packages are not part of Emacs, but are distributed with the main distribution of Org (visit http://orgmode.org).

7.6 The Property API

There is a full API for accessing and changing properties. This API can be used by Emacs Lisp programs to work with properties and to implement features based on them. For more information see Section A.9 [Using the property API], page 223.

8 Dates and times

To assist project planning, TODO items can be labeled with a date and/or a time. The specially formatted string carrying the date and time information is called a *timestamp* in Org-mode. This may be a little confusing because time-stamp is often used as indicating when something was created or last changed. However, in Org-mode this term is used in a much wider sense.

8.1 Timestamps, deadlines, and scheduling

A timestamp is a specification of a date (possibly with a time or a range of times) in a special format, either '<2003-09-16 Tue>' or '<2003-09-16 Tue 09:39>' or '<2003-09-16 Tue 12:00-12:30>'.[1] A timestamp can appear any-where in the headline or body of an Org tree entry. Its presence causes entries to be shown on specific dates in the agenda (see Section 10.3.1 [Weekly/daily agenda], page 100). We distinguish:

Plain timestamp; Event; Appointment
> A simple timestamp just assigns a date/time to an item. This is just like writing down an appointment or event in a paper agenda. In the timeline and agenda displays, the headline of an entry associated with a plain timestamp will be shown exactly on that date.
>
> > * Meet Peter at the movies <2006-11-01 Wed 19:15>
> > * Discussion on climate change <2006-11-02 Thu 20:00-22:00>

Timestamp with repeater interval
> A timestamp may contain a *repeater interval*, indicating that it applies not only on the given date, but again and again after a certain interval of N days (d), weeks (w), months (m), or years (y). The following will show up in the agenda every Wednesday:
>
> > * Pick up Sam at school <2007-05-16 Wed 12:30 +1w>

Diary-style sexp entries
> For more complex date specifications, Org-mode supports using the special sexp diary entries implemented in the Emacs calendar/diary package. For example
>
> > * The nerd meeting on every 2nd Thursday of the month
> > <%%(diary-float t 4 2)>

Time/Date range
> Two timestamps connected by '--' denote a range. The headline will be shown on the first and last day of the range, and on any dates that are displayed and fall in the range. Here is an example:
>
> > ** Meeting in Amsterdam
> > <2004-08-23 Mon>--<2004-08-26 Thu>

---

[1] This is inspired by the standard ISO 8601 date/time format. To use an alternative format, see Section 8.2.2 [Custom time format], page 72.

Inactive timestamp
> Just like a plain timestamp, but with square brackets instead of angular ones. These timestamps are inactive in the sense that they do *not* trigger an entry to show up in the agenda.
>
> > * Gillian comes late for the fifth time [2006-11-01 Wed]

8.2 Creating timestamps

For Org-mode to recognize timestamps, they need to be in the specific format. All commands listed below produce timestamps in the correct format.

C-c .   org-time-stamp
> Prompt for a date and insert a corresponding timestamp. When the cursor is at an existing timestamp in the buffer, the command is used to modify this timestamp instead of inserting a new one. When this command is used twice in succession, a time range is inserted.

C-c !   org-time-stamp-inactive
> Like C-c ., but insert an inactive timestamp that will not cause an agenda entry.

C-u C-c .
C-u C-c !
> Like C-c . and C-c !, but use the alternative format which contains date and time. The default time can be rounded to multiples of 5 minutes, see the option org-time-stamp-rounding-minutes.

C-c <   org-date-from-calendar
> Insert a timestamp corresponding to the cursor date in the Calendar.

C-c >   org-goto-calendar
> Access the Emacs calendar for the current date. If there is a timestamp in the current line, go to the corresponding date instead.

C-c C-o   org-open-at-point
> Access the agenda for the date given by the timestamp or -range at point (see Section 10.3.1 [Weekly/daily agenda], page 100).

S-(left)
S-(right)
> Change date at cursor by one day. These key bindings conflict with shift-selection and related modes (see Section 16.10.2 [Conflicts], page 208).

S-(up)
S-(down)
> Change the item under the cursor in a timestamp. The cursor can be on a year, month, day, hour or minute. When the timestamp contains a time range like '15:30-16:30', modifying the first time will also shift the second, shifting the time block with constant length. To change the length, modify the second time. Note that if the cursor is in a headline and not at a timestamp, these same keys modify the priority of an item. (see Section 5.4 [Priorities], page 51). The key bindings also conflict with

shift-selection and related modes (see Section 16.10.2 [Conflicts], page 208).

C-c C-y

> Evaluate a time range by computing the difference between start and end. With a prefix argument, insert result after the time range (in a table: into the following column).

8.2.1 The date/time prompt

When Org-mode prompts for a date/time, the default is shown in default date/time format, and the prompt therefore seems to ask for a specific format. But it will in fact accept any string containing some date and/or time information, and it is really smart about interpreting your input. You can, for example, use C-y to paste a (possibly multi-line) string copied from an email message. Org-mode will find whatever information is in there and derive anything you have not specified from the *default date and time*. The default is usually the current date and time, but when modifying an existing timestamp, or when entering the second stamp of a range, it is taken from the stamp in the buffer. When filling in information, Org-mode assumes that most of the time you will want to enter a date in the future: if you omit the month/year and the given day/month is *before* today, it will assume that you mean a future date.[2] If the date has been automatically shifted into the future, the time prompt will show this with '(=>F).'

For example, let's assume that today is **June 13, 2006**. Here is how various inputs will be interpreted, the items filled in by Org-mode are in **bold**.

3-2-5	⇒ 2003-02-05
2/5/3	⇒ 2003-02-05
14	⇒ **2006-06**-14
12	⇒ **2006-07**-12
2/5	⇒ **2007**-02-05
Fri	⇒ **nearest Friday (default date or later)**
sep 15	⇒ **2006**-09-15
feb 15	⇒ **2007**-02-15
sep 12 9	⇒ 2009-09-12
12:45	⇒ **2006-06-13** 12:45
22 sept 0:34	⇒ **2006**-09-22 0:34
w4	⇒ **ISO week for of the current year 2006**
2012 w4 fri	⇒ **Friday of ISO week 4 in 2012**
2012-w04-5	⇒ **Same as above**

Furthermore you can specify a relative date by giving, as the *first* thing in the input: a plus/minus sign, a number and a letter ([dwmy]) to indicate change in days, weeks, months, or years. With a single plus or minus, the date is always relative to today. With a double plus or minus, it is relative to the default date. If instead of a single letter, you use the abbreviation of day name, the date will be the Nth such day. E.g.,

---

[2] See the variable org-read-date-prefer-future. You may set that variable to the symbol time to even make a time before now shift the date to tomorrow.

```
+0                ⇒ today
.                 ⇒ today
+4d               ⇒ four days from today
+4                ⇒ same as above
+2w               ⇒ two weeks from today
++5               ⇒ five days from default date
+2tue             ⇒ second Tuesday from now.
```

The function understands English month and weekday abbreviations. If you want to use unabbreviated names and/or other languages, configure the variables parse-time-months and parse-time-weekdays.

You can specify a time range by giving start and end times or by giving a start time and a duration (in HH:MM format). Use '-' or '--' as the separator in the former case and use '+' as the separator in the latter case. E.g.,

```
11am-1:15pm       ⇒ 11:00-13:15
11am--1:15pm      ⇒ same as above
11am+2:15         ⇒ same as above
```

Parallel to the minibuffer prompt, a calendar is popped up.[3] When you exit the date prompt, either by clicking on a date in the calendar, or by pressing (RET), the date selected in the calendar will be combined with the information entered at the prompt. You can control the calendar fully from the minibuffer:

(RET)	Choose date at cursor in calendar.
mouse-1	Select date by clicking on it.
S-(right)/(left)	One day forward/backward.
S-(down)/(up)	One week forward/backward.
M-S-(right)/(left)	One month forward/backward.
> / <	Scroll calendar forward/backward by one month.
M-v / C-v	Scroll calendar forward/backward by 3 months.

The actions of the date/time prompt may seem complex, but I assure you they will grow on you, and you will start getting annoyed by pretty much any other way of entering a date/time out there. To help you understand what is going on, the current interpretation of your input will be displayed live in the minibuffer.[4]

8.2.2 Custom time format

Org-mode uses the standard ISO notation for dates and times as it is defined in ISO 8601. If you cannot get used to this and require another representation of date and time to keep you happy, you can get it by customizing the variables org-display-custom-times and org-time-stamp-custom-formats.

C-c C-x C-t
    Toggle the display of custom formats for dates and times.

---

[3] If you don't need/want the calendar, configure the variable org-popup-calendar-for-date-prompt.

[4] If you find this distracting, turn the display of with org-read-date-display-live.

Org-mode needs the default format for scanning, so the custom date/time format does not *replace* the default format—instead it is put *over* the default format using text properties. This has the following consequences:

- You cannot place the cursor onto a timestamp anymore, only before or after.

- The S-(up)/(down) keys can no longer be used to adjust each component of a timestamp. If the cursor is at the beginning of the stamp, S-(up)/(down) will change the stamp by one day, just like S-(left)/(right). At the end of the stamp, the time will be changed by one minute.

- If the timestamp contains a range of clock times or a repeater, these will not be overlaid, but remain in the buffer as they were.

- When you delete a timestamp character-by-character, it will only disappear from the buffer after *all* (invisible) characters belonging to the ISO timestamp have been removed.

- If the custom timestamp format is longer than the default and you are using dates in tables, table alignment will be messed up. If the custom format is shorter, things do work as expected.

8.3 Deadlines and scheduling

A timestamp may be preceded by special keywords to facilitate planning:

DEADLINE

Meaning: the task (most likely a TODO item, though not necessarily) is supposed to be finished on that date.

On the deadline date, the task will be listed in the agenda. In addition, the agenda for *today* will carry a warning about the approaching or missed deadline, starting `org-deadline-warning-days` before the due date, and continuing until the entry is marked DONE. An example:

```
*** TODO write article about the Earth for the Guide
    The editor in charge is [[bbdb:Ford Prefect]]
    DEADLINE: <2004-02-29 Sun>
```

You can specify a different lead time for warnings for a specific deadlines using the following syntax. Here is an example with a warning period of 5 days `DEADLINE: <2004-02-29 Sun -5d>`.

SCHEDULED

Meaning: you are planning to start working on that task on the given date.

The headline will be listed under the given date.[5] In addition, a reminder that the scheduled date has passed will be present in the compilation for *today*, until the entry is marked DONE, i.e., the task will automatically be forwarded until completed.

---

[5] It will still be listed on that date after it has been marked DONE. If you don't like this, set the variable `org-agenda-skip-scheduled-if-done`.

```
*** TODO Call Trillian for a date on New Years Eve.
    SCHEDULED: <2004-12-25 Sat>
```

Important: Scheduling an item in Org-mode should *not* be understood in the same way that we understand *scheduling a meeting*. Setting a date for a meeting is just a simple appointment, you should mark this entry with a simple plain timestamp, to get this item shown on the date where it applies. This is a frequent misunderstanding by Org users. In Org-mode, *scheduling* means setting a date when you want to start working on an action item.

You may use timestamps with repeaters in scheduling and deadline entries. Org-mode will issue early and late warnings based on the assumption that the timestamp represents the *nearest instance* of the repeater. However, the use of diary sexp entries like `<%%(diary-float t 42)>` in scheduling and deadline timestamps is limited. Org-mode does not know enough about the internals of each sexp function to issue early and late warnings. However, it will show the item on each day where the sexp entry matches.

8.3.1 Inserting deadlines or schedules

The following commands allow you to quickly insert a deadline or to schedule an item:

C-c C-d

Insert 'DEADLINE' keyword along with a stamp. The insertion will happen in the line directly following the headline. When called with a prefix arg, an existing deadline will be removed from the entry. Depending on the variable `org-log-redeadline`,[6] a note will be taken when changing an existing deadline.

C-c C-s

Insert 'SCHEDULED' keyword along with a stamp. The insertion will happen in the line directly following the headline. Any CLOSED timestamp will be removed. When called with a prefix argument, remove the scheduling date from the entry. Depending on the variable `org-log-reschedule`,[7] a note will be taken when changing an existing scheduling time.

C-c C-x C-k

Mark the current entry for agenda action. After you have marked the entry like this, you can open the agenda or the calendar to find an appropriate date. With the cursor on the selected date, press k s or k d to schedule the marked item.

---

[6] with corresponding #+STARTUP keywords logredeadline, lognoteredeadline, and nologredeadline

[7] with corresponding #+STARTUP keywords logredeadline, lognoteredeadline, and nologredeadline

C-c / d

> Create a sparse tree with all deadlines that are either past-due, or which will become due within `org-deadline-warning-days`. With C-u prefix, show all deadlines in the file. With a numeric prefix, check that many days. For example, C-1 C-c / d shows all deadlines due tomorrow.

C-c / b

> Sparse tree for deadlines and scheduled items before a given date.

C-c / a

> Sparse tree for deadlines and scheduled items after a given date.

8.3.2 Repeated tasks

Some tasks need to be repeated again and again. Org-mode helps to organize such tasks using a so-called repeater in a DEADLINE, SCHEDULED, or plain timestamp. In the following example

```
** TODO Pay the rent
   DEADLINE: <2005-10-01 Sat +1m>
```

the +1m is a repeater; the intended interpretation is that the task has a deadline on <2005-10-01> and repeats itself every (one) month starting from that time. If you need both a repeater and a special warning period in a deadline entry, the repeater should come first and the warning period last: DEADLINE: <2005-10-01 Sat +1m -3d>.

Deadlines and scheduled items produce entries in the agenda when they are over-due, so it is important to be able to mark such an entry as completed once you have done so. When you mark a DEADLINE or a SCHEDULE with the TODO keyword DONE, it will no longer produce entries in the agenda. The problem with this is, however, that then also the *next* instance of the repeated entry will not be active. Org-mode deals with this in the following way: When you try to mark such an entry DONE (using C-c C-t), it will shift the base date of the repeating timestamp by the repeater interval, and immediately set the entry state back to TODO.[8] In the example above, setting the state to DONE would actually switch the date like this:

```
** TODO Pay the rent
   DEADLINE: <2005-11-01 Tue +1m>
```

A timestamp[9] will be added under the deadline, to keep a record that you actually acted on the previous instance of this deadline.

As a consequence of shifting the base date, this entry will no longer be visible in the agenda when checking past dates, but all future instances will be visible.

---

[8] In fact, the target state is taken from, in this sequence, the `REPEAT_TO_STATE` property or the variable `org-todo-repeat-to-state`. If neither of these is specified, the target state defaults to the first state of the TODO state sequence.

[9] You can change this using the option `org-log-repeat`, or the `#+STARTUP` options logrepeat, lognoterepeat, and nologrepeat. With lognoterepeat, you will also be prompted for a note.

With the '+1m' cookie, the date shift will always be exactly one month. So
if you have not paid the rent for three months, marking this entry DONE will
still keep it as an overdue deadline. Depending on the task, this may not be
the best way to handle it. For example, if you forgot to call your father for 3
weeks, it does not make sense to call him 3 times in a single day to make up for
it. Finally, there are tasks like changing batteries which should always repeat
a certain time *after* the last time you did it. For these tasks, Org-mode has
special repeaters '++' and '.+'. For example:

```
  ** TODO Call Father
     DEADLINE: <2008-02-10 Sun ++1w>
     Marking this DONE will shift the date by at least one week,
     but also by as many weeks as it takes to get this date into
     the future. However, it stays on a Sunday, even if you
     called and marked it done on Saturday.
  ** TODO Check the batteries in the smoke detectors
     DEADLINE: <2005-11-01 Tue .+1m>
     Marking this DONE will shift the date to one month after
     today.
```

You may have both scheduling and deadline information for a specific task—
just make sure that the repeater intervals on both are the same.

An alternative to using a repeater is to create a number of copies of a task
subtree, with dates shifted in each copy. The command C-c C-x c was created
for this purpose, it is described in Section 2.5 [Structure editing], page 12.

8.4 Clocking work time

Org-mode allows you to clock the time you spend on specific tasks in a project.
When you start working on an item, you can start the clock. When you stop
working on that task, or when you mark the task done, the clock is stopped
and the corresponding time interval is recorded. It also computes the total time
spent on each subtree of a project. And it remembers a history or tasks recently
clocked, to that you can jump quickly between a number of tasks absorbing your
time.

To save the clock history across Emacs sessions, use

```
  (setq org-clock-persist 'history)
  (org-clock-persistence-insinuate)
```

When you clock into a new task after resuming Emacs, the incomplete
clock[10] will be found (see Section 8.5 [Resolving idle time], page 80) and
you will be prompted about what to do with it.

C-c C-x C-i
        Start the clock on the current item (clock-in). This inserts the CLOCK
        keyword together with a timestamp. If this is not the first clocking of this
        item, the multiple CLOCK lines will be wrapped into a :LOGBOOK: drawer
        (see also the variable org-clock-into-drawer). When called with a C-u

---

[10] To resume the clock under the assumption that you have worked on this task while
      outside Emacs, use (setq org-clock-persist t).

prefix argument, select the task from a list of recently clocked tasks. With two C-u C-u prefixes, clock into the task at point and mark it as the default task. The default task will always be available when selecting a clocking task, with letter d.

While the clock is running, the current clocking time is shown in the mode line, along with the title of the task. The clock time shown will be all time ever clocked for this task and its children. If the task has an effort estimate (see Section 8.6 [Effort estimates], page 81), the mode line displays the current clocking time against it[11] If the task is a repeating one (see Section 8.3.2 [Repeated tasks], page 75), only the time since the last reset of the task[12] will be shown. More control over what time is shown can be exercised with the CLOCK_MODELINE_TOTAL property. It may have the values current to show only the current clocking instance, today to show all time clocked on this tasks today (see also the variable org-extend-today-until), all to include all time, or auto which is the default.[13]

Clicking with mouse-1 onto the mode line entry will pop up a menu with clocking options.

C-c C-x C-o

Stop the clock (clock-out). This inserts another timestamp at the same location where the clock was last started. It also directly computes the resulting time in inserts it after the time range as '=> HH:MM'. See the variable org-log-note-clock-out for the possibility to record an additional note together with the clock-out timestamp.[14]

C-c C-x C-e

Update the effort estimate for the current clock task.

C-c C-y   or   C-c C-c

Recompute the time interval after changing one of the timestamps. This is only necessary if you edit the timestamps directly. If you change them with S-cursor keys, the update is automatic.

C-c C-t

Changing the TODO state of an item to DONE automatically stops the clock if it is running in this same item.

C-c C-x C-x

Cancel the current clock. This is useful if a clock was started by mistake, or if you ended up working on something else.

C-c C-x C-j

Jump to the headline of the currently clocked in task. With a C-u prefix arg, select the target task from a list of recently clocked tasks.

---

[11] To add an effort estimate "on the fly", hook a function doing this to org-clock-in-prepare-hook.

[12] as recorded by the LAST_REPEAT property

[13] See also the variable org-clock-modeline-total.

[14] The corresponding in-buffer setting is: #+STARTUP: lognoteclock-out

C-c C-x C-d

Display time summaries for each subtree in the current buffer. This puts
overlays at the end of each headline, showing the total time recorded under
that heading, including the time of any subheadings. You can use visibility
cycling to study the tree, but the overlays disappear when you change the
buffer (see variable `org-remove-highlights-with-change`) or press C-c
C-c.

C-c C-x C-r

Insert a dynamic block (see Section A.6 [Dynamic blocks], page 218) containing a clock report as an Org-mode table into the current file. When
the cursor is at an existing clock table, just update it. When called with
a prefix argument, jump to the first clock report in the current document
and update it.

```
#+BEGIN: clocktable :maxlevel 2 :emphasize nil :scope file
#+END: clocktable
```

If such a block already exists at point, its content is replaced by the new
table. The 'BEGIN' line can specify options:

:maxlevel

Maximum level depth to which times are listed in the table.

:emphasize

When t, emphasize level one and level two items.

:scope

The scope to consider. This can be any of the following:

nil	the current buffer or narrowed region
file	the full current buffer
subtree	the subtree where the clocktable is located
tree$N$	the surrounding level N tree, for example tree3
tree	the surrounding level 1 tree
agenda	all agenda files
("file"..)	scan these files
file-with-archives	current file and its archives
agenda-with-archives	all agenda files, including archives

:block

The time block to consider. This block is specified either absolute, or
relative to the current time and may be any of these formats:

2007-12-31	New year eve 2007
2007-12	December 2007
2007-W50	ISO-week 50 in 2007
2007	the year 2007
today, yesterday, today-N	a relative day
thisweek, lastweek, thisweek-N	a relative week
thismonth, lastmonth, thismonth-N	a relative month

> thisyear, lastyear, thisyear-*N*   a relative year
> Use S-⟨left⟩/⟨right⟩ keys to shift the time interval.

:tstart
> A time string specifying when to start considering times.

:tend
> A time string specifying when to stop considering times.

:step
> week or day, to split the table into chunks. To use this, :block or
> :tstart, :tend are needed.

:stepskip0
> Don't show steps that have zero time

:tags
> A tags match to select entries that should contribute

:link
> Link the item headlines in the table to their origins.

:formula
> Content of a #+TBLFM line to be added and evaluated. As a special
> case, ':formula %' adds a column with % time. If you do not specify
> a formula here, any existing formula below the clock table will survive
> updates and be evaluated.

:timestamp
> A timestamp for the entry, when available. Look for SCHEDULED,
> DEADLINE, TIMESTAMP and TIMESTAMP_IA, in this order.

To get a clock summary of the current level 1 tree, for the current day, you
could write[15]

```
#+BEGIN: clocktable :maxlevel 2 :block today :scope tree1
                    :link t
#+END: clocktable
```

and to use a specific time range you could write

```
#+BEGIN: clocktable :tstart "<2006-08-10 Thu 10:00>"
                    :tend "<2006-08-10 Thu 12:00>"
#+END: clocktable
```

A summary of the current subtree with % times would be

```
#+BEGIN: clocktable :scope subtree :link t :formula %
#+END: clocktable
```

C-c C-c
C-c C-x C-u
> Update dynamic block at point. The cursor needs to be in the #+BEGIN
> line of the dynamic block.

---

[15] Note that all parameters must be specified in a single line—the lines are broken here
only to fit them into the manual.

C-u C-c C-x C-u
> Update all dynamic blocks (see Section A.6 [Dynamic blocks], page 218). This is useful if you have several clock table blocks in a buffer.

S-`left`
S-`right`
> Shift the current :block interval and update the table. The cursor needs to be in the #+BEGIN: clocktable line for this command. If :block is today, it will be shifted to today-1 etc.

The l key may be used in the timeline (see Section 10.3.4 [Timeline], page 105) and in the agenda (see Section 10.3.1 [Weekly/daily agenda], page 100) to show which tasks have been worked on or closed during a day.

8.5 Resolving idle time

If you clock in on a work item, and then walk away from your computer—perhaps to take a phone call—you often need to "resolve" the time you were away by either subtracting it from the current clock, or applying it to another one.

By customizing the variable org-clock-idle-time to some integer, such as 10 or 15, Emacs can alert you when you get back to your computer after being idle for that many minutes,[16] and ask what you want to do with the idle time. There will be a question waiting for you when you get back, indicating how much idle time has passed (constantly updated with the current amount), as well as a set of choices to correct the discrepancy:

k   To keep some or all of the minutes and stay clocked in, press k. Org will ask how many of the minutes to keep. Press `RET` to keep them all, effectively changing nothing, or enter a number to keep that many minutes.

K   If you use the shift key and press K, it will keep however many minutes you request and then immediately clock out of that task. If you keep all of the minutes, this is the same as just clocking out of the current task.

s   To keep none of the minutes, use s to subtract all the away time from the clock, and then check back in from the moment you returned.

S   To keep none of the minutes and just clock out at the start of the away time, use the shift key and press S. Remember that using shift will always leave you clocked out, no matter which option you choose.

C   To cancel the clock altogether, use C. Note that if instead of canceling you subtract the away time, and the resulting clock amount is less than a minute, the clock will still be canceled rather than clutter up the log with an empty entry.

---

[16] On computers using Mac OS X, idleness is based on actual user idleness, not just Emacs' idle time. For X11, you can install a utility program 'x11idle.c', available in the UTILITIES directory of the Org git distribution, to get the same general treatment of idleness. On other systems, idle time refers to Emacs idle time only.

What if you subtracted those away minutes from the current clock, and now want to apply them to a new clock? Simply clock in to any task immediately after the subtraction. Org will notice that you have subtracted time "on the books", so to speak, and will ask if you want to apply those minutes to the next task you clock in on.

There is one other instance when this clock resolution magic occurs. Say you were clocked in and hacking away, and suddenly your cat chased a mouse who scared a hamster that crashed into your UPS's power button! You suddenly lose all your buffers, but thanks to auto-save you still have your recent Org mode changes, including your last clock in.

If you restart Emacs and clock into any task, Org will notice that you have a dangling clock which was never clocked out from your last session. Using that clock's starting time as the beginning of the unaccounted-for period, Org will ask how you want to resolve that time. The logic and behavior is identical to dealing with away time due to idleness; it's just happening due to a recovery event rather than a set amount of idle time.

You can also check all the files visited by your Org agenda for dangling clocks at any time using M-x org-resolve-clocks.

8.6 Effort estimates

If you want to plan your work in a very detailed way, or if you need to produce offers with quotations of the estimated work effort, you may want to assign effort estimates to entries. If you are also clocking your work, you may later want to compare the planned effort with the actual working time, a great way to improve planning estimates. Effort estimates are stored in a special property 'Effort'.[17] You can set the effort for an entry with the following commands:

C-c C-x e

> Set the effort estimate for the current entry. With a numeric prefix argument, set it to the Nth allowed value (see below). This command is also accessible from the agenda with the e key.

C-c C-x C-e

> Modify the effort estimate of the item currently being clocked.

Clearly the best way to work with effort estimates is through column view (see Section 7.5 [Column view], page 63). You should start by setting up discrete values for effort estimates, and a COLUMNS format that displays these values together with clock sums (if you want to clock your time). For a specific buffer you can use

    #+PROPERTY: Effort_ALL 0 0:10 0:30 1:00 2:00 3:00 4:00 5:00 \(18)
               6:00 7:00 8:00

---

[17] You may change the property being used with the variable org-effort-property.

[18] Please note that the PROPERTY definition must be on a single line—it is wrapped here only because of formatting constraints.

```
#+COLUMNS: %40ITEM(Task) %17Effort(Estimated Effort){:} \(19)
            %CLOCKSUM
```

or, even better, you can set up these values globally by customizing the variables `org-global-properties` and `org-columns-default-format`. In particular if you want to use this setup also in the agenda, a global setup may be advised.

The way to assign estimates to individual items is then to switch to column mode, and to use S-[right] and S-[left] to change the value. The values you enter will immediately be summed up in the hierarchy. In the column next to it, any clocked time will be displayed.

If you switch to column view in the daily/weekly agenda, the effort column will summarize the estimated work effort for each day,[20] and you can use this to find space in your schedule. To get an overview of the entire part of the day that is committed, you can set the option `org-agenda-columns-add-appointments-to-effort-sum`. The appointments on a day that take place over a specified time interval will then also be added to the load estimate of the day.

Effort estimates can be used in secondary agenda filtering that is triggered with the / key in the agenda (see Section 10.5 [Agenda commands], page 108). If you have these estimates defined consistently, two or three key presses will narrow down the list to stuff that fits into an available time slot.

8.7 Taking notes with a relative timer

When taking notes during, for example, a meeting or a video viewing, it can be useful to have access to times relative to a starting time. Org provides such a relative timer and make it easy to create timed notes.

C-c C-x .

    Insert a relative time into the buffer. The first time you use this, the timer will be started. When called with a prefix argument, the timer is restarted.

C-c C-x -

    Insert a description list item with the current relative time. With a prefix argument, first reset the timer to 0.

M-[RET]

    Once the timer list is started, you can also use M-[RET] to insert new timer items.

C-c C-x ,

    Pause the timer, or continue it if it is already paused.

C-u C-c C-x ,

    Stop the timer. After this, you can only start a new timer, not continue the old one. This command also removes the timer from the mode line.

---

[19] Please note that the COLUMNS definition must be on a single line—it is wrapped here only because of formatting constraints.

[20] Please note the pitfalls of summing hierarchical data in a flat list (see Section 10.8 [Agenda column view], page 121).

C-c C-x 0

    Reset the timer without inserting anything into the buffer. By default, the timer is reset to 0. When called with a C-u prefix, reset the timer to specific starting offset. The user is prompted for the offset, with a default taken from a timer string at point, if any, So this can be used to restart taking notes after a break in the process. When called with a double prefix argument C-u C-u, change all timer strings in the active region by a certain amount. This can be used to fix timer strings if the timer was not started at exactly the right moment.

8.8 Countdown timer

    Calling `org-timer-set-timer` from an Org-mode buffer runs a countdown timer. Use `;` from agenda buffers, `C-c C-x ;` everwhere else.

    `org-timer-set-timer` prompts the user for a duration and displays a countdown timer in the modeline. `org-timer-default-timer` sets the default countdown value. Giving a prefix numeric argument overrides this default value.

9 Capture - Refile - Archive

An important part of any organization system is the ability to quickly capture new ideas and tasks, and to associate reference material with them. Org does this using a process called *capture*. It also can store files related to a task (*attachments*) in a special directory. Once in the system, tasks and projects need to be moved around. Moving completed project trees to an archive file keeps the system compact and fast.

9.1 Capture

Org's method for capturing new items is heavily inspired by John Wiegley excellent remember package. Up to version 6.36 Org used a special setup for 'remember.el'. 'org-remember.el' is still part of Org-mode for backward compatibility with existing setups. You can find the documentation for org-remember at http://orgmode.org/org-remember.pdf.

The new capturing setup described here is preferred and should be used by new users. To convert your org-remember-templates, run the command

    M-x org-capture-import-remember-templates (RET)

and then customize the new variable with M-x customize-variable org-capture-templates, check the result, and save the customization. You can then use both remember and capture until you are familiar with the new mechanism.

Capture lets you quickly store notes with little interruption of your work flow. The basic process of capturing is very similar to remember, but Org does enhance it with templates and more.

9.1.1 Setting up capture

The following customization sets a default target file for notes, and defines a global key[1] for capturing new material.

    (setq org-default-notes-file (concat org-directory "/notes.org"))
    (define-key global-map "\C-cc" 'org-capture)

9.1.2 Using capture

C-c c

Call the command org-capture. If you have templates defined see Section 9.1.3 [Capture templates], page 86, it will offer these templates for selection or use a new Org outline node as the default template. It will insert the template into the target file and switch to an indirect buffer narrowed to this new node. You may then insert the information you want.

---

[1] Please select your own key, C-c c is only a suggestion.

C-c C-c

> Once you have finished entering information into the capture buffer, C-c
> C-c will return you to the window configuration before the capture process,
> so that you can resume your work without further distraction.

C-c C-w

> Finalize the capture process by refiling (see Section 9.5 [Refiling notes],
> page 93) the note to a different place. Please realize that this is a normal
> refiling command that will be executed—so the cursor position at the mo-
> ment you run this command is important. If you have inserted a tree with
> a parent and children, first move the cursor back to the parent.

C-c C-k

> Abort the capture process and return to the previous state.

You can also call org-capture in a special way from the agenda, using the k
c key combination. With this access, any timestamps inserted by the selected
capture template will default to the cursor date in the agenda, rather than to
the current date.

9.1.3 Capture templates

You can use templates for different types of capture items, and for different target locations. The easiest way to create such templates is through the
customize interface.

C-c c C

> Customize the variable org-capture-templates.

Before we give the formal description of template definitions, let's look at
an example. Say you would like to use one template to create general TODO
entries, and you want to put these entries under the heading 'Tasks' in your
file '~/org/gtd.org'. Also, a date tree in the file 'journal.org' should capture
journal entries. A possible configuration would look like:

```
(setq org-capture-templates
 '(("t" "Todo" entry (file+headline "~/org/gtd.org" "Tasks")
        "* TODO %?\n  %i\n  %a")
   ("j" "Journal" entry (file+datetree "~/org/journal.org")
        "* %?\nEntered on %U\n  %i\n  %a")))
```

If you then press C-c c t, Org will prepare the template for you like this:

```
* TODO
  [[file:link to where you initiated capture]]
```

During expansion of the template, %a has been replaced by a link to the location
from where you called the capture command. This can be extremely useful for
deriving tasks from emails, for example. You fill in the task definition, press
C-c C-c and Org returns you to the same place where you started the capture
process.

9.1.3.1 Template elements

Now lets look at the elements of a template definition. Each entry in org-capture-templates is a list with the following items:

keys

> The keys that will select the template, as a string, characters only, for example "a" for a template to be selected with a single key, or "bt" for selection with two keys. When using several keys, keys using the same prefix key must be sequential in the list and preceded by a 2-element entry explaining the prefix key, for example
>
> > ("b" "Templates for marking stuff to buy")
>
> If you do not define a template for the C key, this key will be used to open the customize buffer for this complex variable.

description

> A short string describing the template, which will be shown during selection.

type

> The type of entry, a symbol. Valid values are:
>
> entry
>
> > An Org-mode node, with a headline. Will be filed as the child of the target entry or as a top-level entry. The target file should be an Org-mode file.
>
> item
>
> > A plain list item, placed in the first plain list at the target location. Again the target file should be an Org file.
>
> checkitem
>
> > A checkbox item. This only differs from the plain list item by the default template.
>
> table-line
>
> > a new line in the first table at the target location. Where exactly the line will be inserted depends on the properties :prepend and :table-line-pos (see below).
>
> plain
>
> > Text to be inserted as it is.

target

> Specification of where the captured item should be placed. In Org-mode files, targets usually define a node. Entries will become children of this node. Other types will be added to the table or list in the body of this node. Most target specifications contain a file name. If that file name is the empty string, it defaults to org-default-notes-file.
>
> Valid values are:
>
> (file "path/to/file")
>
> > Text will be placed at the beginning or end of that file.

(id "id of existing org entry")
>   Filing as child of this entry, or in the body of the entry.

(file+headline "path/to/file" "node headline")
>   Fast configuration if the target heading is unique in the file.

(file+olp "path/to/file" "Level 1 heading" "Level 2" ...)
>   For non-unique headings, the full path is safer.

(file+regexp "path/to/file" "regexp to find location")
>   Use a regular expression to position the cursor.

(file+datetree "path/to/file")
>   Will create a heading in a date tree.

(file+function "path/to/file" function-finding-location)
>   A function to find the right location in the file.

(clock)
>   File to the entry that is currently being clocked.

(function function-finding-location)
>   Most general way, write your own function to find both file and location.

template
>   The template for creating the capture item. If you leave this empty, an appropriate default template will be used. Otherwise this is a string with escape codes, which will be replaced depending on time and context of the capture call. The string with escapes may be loaded from a template file, using the special syntax (file "path/to/template"). See below for more details.

properties
>   The rest of the entry is a property list of additional options. Recognized properties are:

:prepend
>   Normally new captured information will be appended at the target location (last child, last table line, last list item...). Setting this property will change that.

:immediate-finish
>   When set, do not offer to edit the information, just file it away immediately. This makes sense if the template only needs information that can be added automatically.

:empty-lines
>   Set this to the number of lines to insert before and after the new item. Default 0, only common other value is 1.

:clock-in
>   Start the clock in this item.

`:clock-resume`
> If starting the capture interrupted a clock, restart that clock when finished with the capture.

`:unnarrowed`
> Do not narrow the target buffer, simply show the full buffer. Default is to narrow it so that you only see the new material.

`:kill-buffer`
> If the target file was not yet visited when capture was invoked, kill the buffer again after capture is completed.

9.1.3.2 Template expansion

In the template itself, special %-escapes[2] allow dynamic insertion of content:

`%^{prompt}`	prompt the user for a string and replace this sequence with it. You may specify a default value and a completion table with `%^{prompt|default|completion2|completion3...}` The arrow keys access a prompt-specific history.
`%a`	annotation, normally the link created with `org-store-link`
`%A`	like `%a`, but prompt for the description part
`%i`	initial content, the region when capture is called while the region is active. The entire text will be indented like `%i` itself.
`%t`	timestamp, date only
`%T`	timestamp with date and time
`%u`, `%U`	like the above, but inactive timestamps
`%^t`	like `%t`, but prompt for date. Similarly `%^T`, `%^u`, `%^U` You may define a prompt like `%^{Birthday}t`
`%n`	user name (taken from `user-full-name`)
`%c`	Current kill ring head.
`%x`	Content of the X clipboard.
`%^C`	Interactive selection of which kill or clip to use.
`%^L`	Like `%^C`, but insert as link.
`%k`	title of the currently clocked task
`%K`	link to the currently clocked task
`%^g`	prompt for tags, with completion on tags in target file.
`%^G`	prompt for tags, with completion all tags in all agenda files.
`%^{prop}p`	Prompt the user for a value for property *prop*
`%:keyword`	specific information for certain link types, see below
`%[file]`	insert the contents of the file given by *file*
`%(sexp)`	evaluate Elisp *sexp* and replace with the result

For specific link types, the following keywords will be defined:[3]

---

[2] If you need one of these sequences literally, escape the % with a backslash.

[3] If you define your own link types (see Section A.3 [Adding hyperlink types], page 211), any property you store with `org-store-link-props` can be accessed in capture templates in a similar way.

Link type	Available keywords
bbdb	%:name %:company
irc	%:server %:port %:nick
vm, wl, mh, mew, rmail	%:type %:subject %:message-id
	%:from %:fromname %:fromaddress
	%:to %:toname %:toaddress
	%:date
	(message date header field)
	%:date-timestamp
	(date as active timestamp)
	%:date-timestamp-inactive
	(date as inactive timestamp)
	%:fromto
	(either "to NAME" or "from NAME")[4]
gnus	%:group,
	for messages also all email fields
w3, w3m	%:url
info	%:file %:node
calendar	%:date

To place the cursor after template expansion use:

%?   After completing the template, position cursor here.

9.2 Attachments

It is often useful to associate reference material with an outline node/task. Small chunks of plain text can simply be stored in the subtree of a project. Hyperlinks (see Chapter 4 [Hyperlinks], page 31) can establish associations with files that live elsewhere on your computer or in the cloud, like emails or source code files belonging to a project. Another method is *attachments*, which are files located in a directory belonging to an outline node. Org uses directories named by the unique ID of each entry. These directories are located in the 'data' directory which lives in the same directory where your Org file lives.[5] If you initialize this directory with git init, Org will automatically commit changes when it sees them. The attachment system has been contributed to Org by John Wiegley.

In cases where it seems better to do so, you can also attach a directory of your choice to an entry. You can also make children inherit the attachment directory from a parent, so that an entire subtree uses the same attached directory.

The following commands deal with attachments:

---

[4] This will always be the other, not the user. See the variable org-from-is-user-regexp.

[5] If you move entries or Org files from one directory to another, you may want to configure org-attach-directory to contain an absolute path.

C-c C-a

The dispatcher for commands related to the attachment system. After these keys, a list of commands is displayed and you must press an additional key to select a command:

a   Select a file and move it into the task's attachment directory. The file will be copied, moved, or linked, depending on org-attach-method. Note that hard links are not supported on all systems.

c/m/l

Attach a file using the copy/move/link method. Note that hard links are not supported on all systems.

n   Create a new attachment as an Emacs buffer.

z   Synchronize the current task with its attachment directory, in case you added attachments yourself.

o   Open current task's attachment. If there is more than one, prompt for a file name first. Opening will follow the rules set by org-file-apps. For more details, see the information on following hyperlinks (see Section 4.4 [Handling links], page 34).

O   Also open the attachment, but force opening the file in Emacs.

f   Open the current task's attachment directory.

F   Also open the directory, but force using dired in Emacs.

d   Select and delete a single attachment.

D   Delete all of a task's attachments. A safer way is to open the directory in dired and delete from there.

C-c C-a s

Set a specific directory as the entry's attachment directory. This works by putting the directory path into the ATTACH_DIR property.

C-c C-a i

Set the ATTACH_DIR_INHERIT property, so that children will use the same directory for attachments as the parent does.

9.3 RSS feeds

Org can add and change entries based on information found in RSS feeds and Atom feeds. You could use this to make a task out of each new podcast in a podcast feed. Or you could use a phone-based note-creating service on the web to import tasks into Org. To access feeds, configure the variable `org-feed-alist`. The docstring of this variable has detailed information. Here is just an example:

```
(setq org-feed-alist
      '(("Slashdot"
         "http://rss.slashdot.org/Slashdot/slashdot"
         "~/txt/org/feeds.org" "Slashdot Entries")))
```

will configure that new items from the feed provided by `rss.slashdot.org` will result in new entries in the file '`~/org/feeds.org`' under the heading 'Slashdot Entries', whenever the following command is used:

`C-c C-x g`

Collect items from the feeds configured in `org-feed-alist` and act upon them.

`C-c C-x G`

Prompt for a feed name and go to the inbox configured for this feed.

Under the same headline, Org will create a drawer 'FEEDSTATUS' in which it will store information about the status of items in the feed, to avoid adding the same item several times. You should add 'FEEDSTATUS' to the list of drawers in that file:

```
#+DRAWERS: LOGBOOK PROPERTIES FEEDSTATUS
```

For more information, including how to read atom feeds, see '`org-feed.el`' and the docstring of `org-feed-alist`.

9.4 Protocols for external access

You can set up Org for handling protocol calls from outside applications that are passed to Emacs through the 'emacsserver'. For example, you can configure bookmarks in your web browser to send a link to the current page to Org and create a note from it using capture (see Section 9.1 [Capture], page 85). Or you could create a bookmark that will tell Emacs to open the local source file of a remote website you are looking at with the browser. See `http://orgmode.org/worg/org-contrib/org-protocol.php` for detailed documentation and setup instructions.

9.5 Refiling notes

When reviewing the captured data, you may want to refile some of the entries into a different list, for example into a project. Cutting, finding the right location, and then pasting the note is cumbersome. To simplify this process, you can use the following special command:

C-c C-w

> Refile the entry or region at point. This command offers possible locations for refiling the entry and lets you select one with completion. The item (or all items in the region) is filed below the target heading as a subitem. Depending on org-reverse-note-order, it will be either the first or last subitem.
>
> By default, all level 1 headlines in the current buffer are considered to be targets, but you can have more complex definitions across a number of files. See the variable org-refile-targets for details. If you would like to select a location via a file-path-like completion along the outline path, see the variables org-refile-use-outline-path and org-outline-path-complete-in-steps. If you would like to be able to create new nodes as new parents for refiling on the fly, check the variable org-refile-allow-creating-parent-nodes. When the variable org-log-refile[6] is set, a timestamp or a note will be recorded when an entry has been refiled.

C-u C-c C-w

> Use the refile interface to jump to a heading.

C-u C-u C-c C-w

> Jump to the location where org-refile last moved a tree to.

C-2 C-c C-w

> Refile as the child of the item currently being clocked.

C-0 C-c C-w   or   C-u C-u C-u C-c C-w

> Clear the target cache. Caching of refile targets can be turned on by setting org-refile-use-cache. To make the command see new possible targets, you have to clear the cache with this command.

9.6 Archiving

When a project represented by a (sub)tree is finished, you may want to move the tree out of the way and to stop it from contributing to the agenda. Archiving is important to keep your working files compact and global searches like the construction of agenda views fast.

C-c C-x C-a

> Archive the current entry using the command specified in the variable org-archive-default-command.

---

[6] with corresponding #+STARTUP keywords logrefile, lognoterefile, and nologrefile

9.6.1 Moving a tree to the archive file

The most common archiving action is to move a project tree to another file, the archive file.

C-c C-x C-s or short C-c $
> Archive the subtree starting at the cursor position to the location given by org-archive-location.

C-u C-c C-x C-s
> Check if any direct children of the current headline could be moved to the archive. To do this, each subtree is checked for open TODO entries. If none are found, the command offers to move it to the archive location. If the cursor is *not* on a headline when this command is invoked, the level 1 trees will be checked.

The default archive location is a file in the same directory as the current file, with the name derived by appending '_archive' to the current file name. For information and examples on how to change this, see the documentation string of the variable org-archive-location. There is also an in-buffer option for setting this variable, for example:[7]

> #+ARCHIVE: %s_done::

If you would like to have a special ARCHIVE location for a single entry or a (sub)tree, give the entry an :ARCHIVE: property with the location as the value (see Chapter 7 [Properties and Columns], page 59).

When a subtree is moved, it receives a number of special properties that record context information like the file from where the entry came, its outline path the archiving time etc. Configure the variable org-archive-save-context-info to adjust the amount of information added.

9.6.2 Internal archiving

If you want to just switch off (for agenda views) certain subtrees without moving them to a different file, you can use the ARCHIVE tag.

A headline that is marked with the ARCHIVE tag (see Chapter 6 [Tags], page 55) stays at its location in the outline tree, but behaves in the following way:

- It does not open when you attempt to do so with a visibility cycling command (see Section 2.3 [Visibility cycling], page 10). You can force cycling archived subtrees with C-(TAB), or by setting the option org-cycle-open-archived-trees. Also normal outline commands like show-all will open archived subtrees.

---

[7] For backward compatibility, the following also works: If there are several such lines in a file, each specifies the archive location for the text below it. The first such line also applies to any text before its definition. However, using this method is *strongly* deprecated as it is incompatible with the outline structure of the document. The correct method for setting multiple archive locations in a buffer is using properties.

- During sparse tree construction (see Section 2.6 [Sparse trees], page 14), matches in archived subtrees are not exposed, unless you configure the option `org-sparse-tree-open-archived-trees`.

- During agenda view construction (see Chapter 10 [Agenda Views], page 97), the content of archived trees is ignored unless you configure the option `org-agenda-skip-archived-trees`, in which case these trees will always be included. In the agenda you can press v a to get archives temporarily included.

- Archived trees are not exported (see Chapter 12 [Exporting], page 133), only the headline is. Configure the details using the variable `org-export-with-archived-trees`.

- Archived trees are excluded from column view unless the variable `org-columns-skip-archived-trees` is configured to nil.

The following commands help manage the ARCHIVE tag:

C-c C-x a

> Toggle the ARCHIVE tag for the current headline. When the tag is set, the headline changes to a shadowed face, and the subtree below it is hidden.

C-u C-c C-x a

> Check if any direct children of the current headline should be archived. To do this, each subtree is checked for open TODO entries. If none are found, the command offers to set the ARCHIVE tag for the child. If the cursor is *not* on a headline when this command is invoked, the level 1 trees will be checked.

C-TAB

> Cycle a tree even if it is tagged with ARCHIVE.

C-c C-x A

> Move the current entry to the *Archive Sibling*. This is a sibling of the entry with the heading 'Archive' and the tag 'ARCHIVE'. The entry becomes a child of that sibling and in this way retains a lot of its original context, including inherited tags and approximate position in the outline.

10 Agenda views

Due to the way Org works, TODO items, time-stamped items, and tagged headlines can be scattered throughout a file or even a number of files. To get an overview of open action items, or of events that are important for a particular date, this information must be collected, sorted and displayed in an organized way.

Org can select items based on various criteria and display them in a separate buffer. Seven different view types are provided:

- an *agenda* that is like a calendar and shows information for specific dates,
- a *TODO list* that covers all unfinished action items,
- a *match view*, showings headlines based on the tags, properties, and TODO state associated with them,
- a *timeline view* that shows all events in a single Org file, in time-sorted view,
- a *text search view* that shows all entries from multiple files that contain specified keywords,
- a *stuck projects view* showing projects that currently don't move along, and
- *custom views* that are special searches and combinations of different views.

The extracted information is displayed in a special *agenda buffer*. This buffer is read-only, but provides commands to visit the corresponding locations in the original Org files, and even to edit these files remotely.

Two variables control how the agenda buffer is displayed and whether the window configuration is restored when the agenda exits: `org-agenda-window-setup` and `org-agenda-restore-windows-after-quit`.

10.1 Agenda files

The information to be shown is normally collected from all *agenda files*, the files listed in the variable `org-agenda-files`.[1] If a directory is part of this list, all files with the extension '`.org`' in this directory will be part of the list.

Thus, even if you only work with a single Org file, that file should be put into the list.[2] You can customize `org-agenda-files`, but the easiest way to maintain it is through the following commands

---

[1] If the value of that variable is not a list, but a single file name, then the list of agenda files will be maintained in that external file.

[2] When using the dispatcher, pressing < before selecting a command will actually limit the command to the current file, and ignore `org-agenda-files` until the next dispatcher command.

C-c [

Add current file to the list of agenda files. The file is added to the front
of the list. If it was already in the list, it is moved to the front. With a
prefix argument, file is added/moved to the end.

C-c]

Remove current file from the list of agenda files.

C-,
C-'

Cycle through agenda file list, visiting one file after the other.

M-x org-iswitchb

Command to use an iswitchb-like interface to switch to and between Org
buffers.

The Org menu contains the current list of files and can be used to visit any of
them.

If you would like to focus the agenda temporarily on a file not in this list,
or on just one file in the list, or even on only a subtree in a file, then this
can be done in different ways. For a single agenda command, you may press <
once or several times in the dispatcher (see Section 10.2 [Agenda dispatcher],
page 99). To restrict the agenda scope for an extended period, use the following
commands:

C-c C-x <

Permanently restrict the agenda to the current subtree. When with a
prefix argument, or with the cursor before the first headline in a file, the
agenda scope is set to the entire file. This restriction remains in effect until
removed with C-c C-x >, or by typing either < or > in the agenda dispatcher.
If there is a window displaying an agenda view, the new restriction takes
effect immediately.

C-c C-x >

Remove the permanent restriction created by C-c C-x <.

When working with 'speedbar.el', you can use the following commands in the
Speedbar frame:

< in the speedbar frame

Permanently restrict the agenda to the item—either an Org file or a subtree
in such a file—at the cursor in the Speedbar frame. If there is a window
displaying an agenda view, the new restriction takes effect immediately.

> in the speedbar frame

Lift the restriction.

10.2 The agenda dispatcher

The views are created through a dispatcher, which should be bound to a global key—for example C-c a (see Section 1.2 [Installation], page 4). In the following we will assume that C-c a is indeed how the dispatcher is accessed and list keyboard access to commands accordingly. After pressing C-c a, an additional letter is required to execute a command. The dispatcher offers the following default commands:

a   Create the calendar-like agenda (see Section 10.3.1 [Weekly/daily agenda], page 100).

t / T
        Create a list of all TODO items (see Section 10.3.2 [Global TODO list], page 102).

m / M
        Create a list of headlines matching a TAGS expression (see Section 10.3.3 [Matching tags and properties], page 103).

L   Create the timeline view for the current buffer (see Section 10.3.4 [Timeline], page 105).

s   Create a list of entries selected by a boolean expression of keywords and/or regular expressions that must or must not occur in the entry.

/   Search for a regular expression in all agenda files and additionally in the files listed in org-agenda-text-search-extra-files. This uses the Emacs command multi-occur. A prefix argument can be used to specify the number of context lines for each match, default is 1.

/ !
        Create a list of stuck projects (see Section 10.3.6 [Stuck projects], page 106).

<   Restrict an agenda command to the current buffer.[3] After pressing <, you still need to press the character selecting the command.

< <   If there is an active region, restrict the following agenda command to the region. Otherwise, restrict it to the current subtree.[4] After pressing < <, you still need to press the character selecting the command.

You can also define custom commands that will be accessible through the dispatcher, just like the default commands. This includes the possibility to create extended agenda buffers that contain several blocks together, for example the weekly agenda, the global TODO list and a number of special tags matches. See Section 10.6 [Custom agenda views], page 116.

---

[3] For backward compatibility, you can also press 1 to restrict to the current buffer.

[4] For backward compatibility, you can also press 0 to restrict to the current region/subtree.

10.3 The built-in agenda views

In this section we describe the built-in views.

10.3.1 The weekly/daily agenda

The purpose of the weekly/daily *agenda* is to act like a page of a paper agenda, showing all the tasks for the current week or day.

C-c a a

> Compile an agenda for the current week from a list of Org files. The agenda shows the entries for each day. With a numeric prefix[5] (like C-u 2 1 C-c a a) you may set the number of days to be displayed (see also the variable org-agenda-ndays)

Remote editing from the agenda buffer means, for example, that you can change the dates of deadlines and appointments from the agenda buffer. The commands available in the Agenda buffer are listed in Section 10.5 [Agenda commands], page 108.

Calendar/Diary integration

Emacs contains the calendar and diary by Edward M. Reingold. The calendar displays a three-month calendar with holidays from different countries and cultures. The diary allows you to keep track of anniversaries, lunar phases, sunrise/set, recurrent appointments (weekly, monthly) and more. In this way, it is quite complementary to Org. It can be very useful to combine output from Org with the diary.

In order to include entries from the Emacs diary into Org-mode's agenda, you only need to customize the variable

> (setq org-agenda-include-diary t)

After that, everything will happen automatically. All diary entries including holidays, anniversaries, etc., will be included in the agenda buffer created by Org-mode. (SPC), (TAB), and (RET) can be used from the agenda buffer to jump to the diary file in order to edit existing diary entries. The i command to insert new entries for the current date works in the agenda buffer, as well as the commands S, M, and C to display Sunrise/Sunset times, show lunar phases and to convert to other calendars, respectively. c can be used to switch back and forth between calendar and agenda.

If you are using the diary only for sexp entries and holidays, it is faster to not use the above setting, but instead to copy or even move the entries into an Org file. Org-mode evaluates diary-style sexp entries, and does it faster because there is no overhead for first creating the diary display. Note that the sexp entries must start at the left margin, no whitespace is allowed before them. For example, the following segment of an Org file will be processed and entries will be made in the agenda:

---

[5] For backward compatibility, the universal prefix C-u causes all TODO entries to be listed before the agenda. This feature is deprecated, use the dedicated TODO list, or a block agenda instead (see Section 10.6.2 [Block agenda], page 118).

```
* Birthdays and similar stuff
#+CATEGORY: Holiday
%%(org-calendar-holiday)    ; special function for holiday names
#+CATEGORY: Ann
%%(diary-anniversary  5 14 1956)⁽⁶⁾ Arthur Dent is %d years old
%%(diary-anniversary 10  2 1869) Mahatma Gandhi would be %d
```

Anniversaries from BBDB

If you are using the Big Brothers Database to store your contacts, you will very likely prefer to store anniversaries in BBDB rather than in a separate Org or diary file. Org supports this and will show BBDB anniversaries as part of the agenda. All you need to do is to add the following to one your your agenda files:

```
* Anniversaries
  :PROPERTIES:
  :CATEGORY: Anniv
  :END:
%%(org-bbdb-anniversaries)
```

You can then go ahead and define anniversaries for a BBDB record. Basically, you need to press C-o anniversary (RET) with the cursor in a BBDB record and then add the date in the format YYYY-MM-DD, followed by a space and the class of the anniversary ('birthday' or 'wedding', or a format string). If you omit the class, it will default to 'birthday'. Here are a few examples, the header for the file 'org-bbdb.el' contains more detailed information.

```
1973-06-22
1955-08-02 wedding
2008-04-14 %s released version 6.01 of org-mode, %d years ago
```

After a change to BBDB, or for the first agenda display during an Emacs session, the agenda display will suffer a short delay as Org updates its hash with anniversaries. However, from then on things will be very fast—much faster in fact than a long list of '%%(diary-anniversary)' entries in an Org or Diary file.

Appointment reminders

Org can interact with Emacs appointments notification facility. To add all the appointments of your agenda files, use the command org-agenda-to-appt. This command also lets you filter through the list of your appointments and add only those belonging to a specific category or matching a regular expression. See the docstring for details.

⁽⁶⁾ Note that the order of the arguments (month, day, year) depends on the setting of calendar-date-style.

10.3.2 The global TODO list

The global TODO list contains all unfinished TODO items formatted and collected into a single place.

C-c a t

> Show the global TODO list. This collects the TODO items from all agenda files (see Chapter 10 [Agenda Views], page 97) into a single buffer. By default, this lists items with a state the is not a DONE state. The buffer is in agenda-mode, so there are commands to examine and manipulate the TODO entries directly from that buffer (see Section 10.5 [Agenda commands], page 108).

C-c a T

> Like the above, but allows selection of a specific TODO keyword. You can also do this by specifying a prefix argument to C-c a t. You are prompted for a keyword, and you may also specify several keywords by separating them with '|' as the boolean OR operator. With a numeric prefix, the Nth keyword in org-todo-keywords is selected. The r key in the agenda buffer regenerates it, and you can give a prefix argument to this command to change the selected TODO keyword, for example 3 r. If you often need a search for a specific keyword, define a custom command for it (see Section 10.2 [Agenda dispatcher], page 99).
>
> Matching specific TODO keywords can also be done as part of a tags search (see Section 6.3 [Tag searches], page 58).

Remote editing of TODO items means that you can change the state of a TODO entry with a single key press. The commands available in the TODO list are described in Section 10.5 [Agenda commands], page 108.

Normally the global TODO list simply shows all headlines with TODO keywords. This list can become very long. There are two ways to keep it more compact:

- Some people view a TODO item that has been *scheduled* for execution or have a *deadline* (see Section 8.1 [Timestamps], page 69) as no longer *open*. Configure the variables org-agenda-todo-ignore-scheduled, org-agenda-todo-ignore-deadlines, and/or org-agenda-todo-ignore-with-date to exclude such items from the global TODO list.

- TODO items may have sublevels to break up the task into subtasks. In such cases it may be enough to list only the highest level TODO headline and omit the sublevels from the global list. Configure the variable org-agenda-todo-list-sublevels to get this behavior.

10.3.3 Matching tags and properties

If headlines in the agenda files are marked with *tags* (see Chapter 6 [Tags], page 55), or have properties (see Chapter 7 [Properties and Columns], page 59), you can select headlines based on this metadata and collect them into an agenda buffer. The match syntax described here also applies when creating sparse trees with C-c / m.

C-c a m

> Produce a list of all headlines that match a given set of tags. The command prompts for a selection criterion, which is a boolean logic expression with tags, like '+work+urgent-withboss' or 'work|home' (see Chapter 6 [Tags], page 55). If you often need a specific search, define a custom command for it (see Section 10.2 [Agenda dispatcher], page 99).

C-c a M

> Like C-c a m, but only select headlines that are also TODO items in a not-DONE state and force checking subitems (see variable org-tags-match-list-sublevels). To exclude scheduled/deadline items, see the variable org-agenda-tags-todo-honor-ignore-options. Matching specific TODO keywords together with a tags match is also possible, see Section 6.3 [Tag searches], page 58.

The commands available in the tags list are described in Section 10.5 [Agenda commands], page 108.

Match syntax

A search string can use Boolean operators '&' for AND and '|' for OR. '&' binds more strongly than '|'. Parentheses are currently not implemented. Each element in the search is either a tag, a regular expression matching tags, or an expression like PROPERTY OPERATOR VALUE with a comparison operator, accessing a property value. Each element may be preceded by '-', to select against it, and '+' is syntactic sugar for positive selection. The AND operator '&' is optional when '+' or '-' is present. Here are some examples, using only tags.

'+work-boss'

> Select headlines tagged ':work:', but discard those also tagged ':boss:'.

'work|laptop'

> Selects lines tagged ':work:' or ':laptop:'.

'work|laptop+night'

> Like before, but require the ':laptop:' lines to be tagged also ':night:'.

Instead of a tag, you may also specify a regular expression enclosed in curly braces. For example, 'work+{^boss.*}' matches headlines that contain the tag ':work:' and any tag *starting* with 'boss'.

You may also test for properties (see Chapter 7 [Properties and Columns], page 59) at the same time as matching tags. The properties may be real properties, or special properties that represent other metadata (see Section 7.2 [Special properties], page 61). For example, the "property" TODO represents the TODO keyword of the entry. Or, the "property" LEVEL represents the level of an entry.

So a search '+LEVEL=3+boss-TODO="DONE"' lists all level three headlines that have the tag 'boss' and are *not* marked with the TODO keyword DONE. In buffers with `org-odd-levels-only` set, 'LEVEL' does not count the number of stars, but 'LEVEL=2' will correspond to 3 stars etc.

Here are more examples:

'work+TODO="WAITING"'
> Select ':work:'-tagged TODO lines with the specific TODO keyword 'WAITING'.

'work+TODO="WAITING"|home+TODO="WAITING"'
> Waiting tasks both at work and at home.

When matching properties, a number of different operators can be used to test the value of a property. Here is a complex example:

```
+work-boss+PRIORITY="A"+Coffee="unlimited"+Effort<2           \
       +With={Sarah\|Denny}+SCHEDULED>="<2008-10-11>"
```

The type of comparison will depend on how the comparison value is written:

- If the comparison value is a plain number, a numerical comparison is done, and the allowed operators are '<', '=', '>', '<=', '>=', and '<>'.

- If the comparison value is enclosed in double-quotes, a string comparison is done, and the same operators are allowed.

- If the comparison value is enclosed in double-quotes *and* angular brackets (like 'DEADLINE<="<2008-12-24 18:30>"'), both values are assumed to be date/time specifications in the standard Org way, and the comparison will be done accordingly. Special values that will be recognized are "<now>" for now (including time), and "<today>", and "<tomorrow>" for these days at 0:00 hours, i.e., without a time specification. Also strings like "<+5d>" or "<-2m>" with units d, w, m, and y for day, week, month, and year, respectively, can be used.

- If the comparison value is enclosed in curly braces, a regexp match is performed, with '=' meaning that the regexp matches the property value, and '<>' meaning that it does not match.

So the search string in the example finds entries tagged ':work:' but not ':boss:', which also have a priority value 'A', a ':Coffee:' property with the value 'unlimited', an 'Effort' property that is numerically smaller than 2, a ':With:' property that is matched by the regular expression 'Sarah\|Denny', and that are scheduled on or after October 11, 2008.

Accessing TODO, LEVEL, and CATEGORY during a search is fast. Accessing any other properties will slow down the search. However, once you have paid the price by accessing one property, testing additional properties is cheap again.

You can configure Org-mode to use property inheritance during a search, but beware that this can slow down searches considerably. See Section 7.4 [Property inheritance], page 62, for details.

For backward compatibility, and also for typing speed, there is also a different way to test TODO states in a search. For this, terminate the tags/property part

of the search string (which may include several terms connected with '|') with a
'/' and then specify a Boolean expression just for TODO keywords. The syntax
is then similar to that for tags, but should be applied with care: for example, a
positive selection on several TODO keywords cannot meaningfully be combined
with boolean AND. However, *negative selection* combined with AND can be
meaningful. To make sure that only lines are checked that actually have any
TODO keyword (resulting in a speed-up), use C-c a M, or equivalently start the
TODO part after the slash with '!'. Using C-c a M or '/!' will not match TODO
keywords in a DONE state. Examples:

'work/WAITING'

> Same as 'work+TODO="WAITING"'

'work/!-WAITING-NEXT'

> Select ':work:'-tagged TODO lines that are neither 'WAITING' nor 'NEXT'

'work/!+WAITING|+NEXT'

> Select ':work:'-tagged TODO lines that are either 'WAITING' or 'NEXT'.

10.3.4 Timeline for a single file

The timeline summarizes all time-stamped items from a single Org-mode file
in a *time-sorted view*. The main purpose of this command is to give an overview
over events in a project.

C-c a L

> Show a time-sorted view of the Org file, with all time-stamped items. When
> called with a C-u prefix, all unfinished TODO entries (scheduled or not)
> are also listed under the current date.

The commands available in the timeline buffer are listed in Section 10.5 [Agenda
commands], page 108.

10.3.5 Search view

This agenda view is a general text search facility for Org-mode entries. It is
particularly useful to find notes.

C-c a s

> This is a special search that lets you select entries by matching a substring
> or specific words using a boolean logic.

For example, the search string 'computer equipment' will find entries that
contain 'computer equipment' as a substring. If the two words are separated
by more space or a line break, the search will still match. Search view can
also search for specific keywords in the entry, using Boolean logic. The search
string '+computer +wifi -ethernet -{8\.11[bg]}' will search for note entries
that contain the keywords computer and wifi, but not the keyword ethernet,
and which are also not matched by the regular expression 8\.11[bg], meaning
to exclude both 8.11b and 8.11g. The first '+' is necessary to turn on word
search, other '+' characters are optional. For more details, see the docstring of
the command org-search-view.

Note that in addition to the agenda files, this command will also search the
files listed in org-agenda-text-search-extra-files.

10.3.6 Stuck projects

If you are following a system like David Allen's GTD to organize your work, one of the "duties" you have is a regular review to make sure that all projects move along. A *stuck* project is a project that has no defined next actions, so it will never show up in the TODO lists Org-mode produces. During the review, you need to identify such projects and define next actions for them.

C-c a #
> List projects that are stuck.

C-c a !
> Customize the variable org-stuck-projects to define what a stuck project is and how to find it.

You almost certainly will have to configure this view before it will work for you. The built-in default assumes that all your projects are level-2 headlines, and that a project is not stuck if it has at least one entry marked with a TODO keyword TODO or NEXT or NEXTACTION.

Let's assume that you, in your own way of using Org-mode, identify projects with a tag PROJECT, and that you use a TODO keyword MAYBE to indicate a project that should not be considered yet. Let's further assume that the TODO keyword DONE marks finished projects, and that NEXT and TODO indicate next actions. The tag @SHOP indicates shopping and is a next action even without the NEXT tag. Finally, if the project contains the special word IGNORE anywhere, it should not be listed either. In this case you would start by identifying eligible projects with a tags/todo match[7] '+PROJECT/-MAYBE-DONE', and then check for TODO, NEXT, @SHOP, and IGNORE in the subtree to identify projects that are not stuck. The correct customization for this is

```
(setq org-stuck-projects
      '("+PROJECT/-MAYBE-DONE" ("NEXT" "TODO") ("@SHOP")
                 "\\<IGNORE\\>"))
```

Note that if a project is identified as non-stuck, the subtree of this entry will still be searched for stuck projects.

10.4 Presentation and sorting

Before displaying items in an agenda view, Org-mode visually prepares the items and sorts them. Each item occupies a single line. The line starts with a *prefix* that contains the *category* (see Section 10.4.1 [Categories], page 107) of the item and other important information. You can customize the prefix using the option org-agenda-prefix-format. The prefix is followed by a cleaned-up version of the outline headline associated with the item.

---

[7] See Section 6.3 [Tag searches], page 58.

10.4.1 Categories

The category is a broad label assigned to each agenda item. By default, the category is simply derived from the file name, but you can also specify it with a special line in the buffer, like this:[8]

```
#+CATEGORY: Thesis
```

If you would like to have a special CATEGORY for a single entry or a (sub)tree, give the entry a :CATEGORY: property with the special category you want to apply as the value.

The display in the agenda buffer looks best if the category is not longer than 10 characters.

10.4.2 Time-of-day specifications

Org-mode checks each agenda item for a time-of-day specification. The time can be part of the timestamp that triggered inclusion into the agenda, for example as in '<2005-05-10 Tue 19:00>'. Time ranges can be specified with two timestamps, like '<2005-05-10 Tue 20:30>--<2005-05-10 Tue 22:15>'.

In the headline of the entry itself, a time(range) may also appear as plain text (like '12:45' or a '8:30-1pm'). If the agenda integrates the Emacs diary (see Section 10.3.1 [Weekly/daily agenda], page 100), time specifications in diary entries are recognized as well.

For agenda display, Org-mode extracts the time and displays it in a standard 24 hour format as part of the prefix. The example times in the previous paragraphs would end up in the agenda like this:

```
8:30-13:00 Arthur Dent lies in front of the bulldozer
12:45...... Ford Prefect arrives and takes Arthur to the pub
19:00...... The Vogon reads his poem
20:30-22:15 Marvin escorts the Hitchhikers to the bridge
```

If the agenda is in single-day mode, or for the display of today, the timed entries are embedded in a time grid, like

```
8:00...... ------------------
8:30-13:00 Arthur Dent lies in front of the bulldozer
10:00...... ------------------
12:00...... ------------------
12:45...... Ford Prefect arrives and takes Arthur to the pub
14:00...... ------------------
16:00...... ------------------
18:00...... ------------------
19:00...... The Vogon reads his poem
20:00...... ------------------
20:30-22:15 Marvin escorts the Hitchhikers to the bridge
```

---

[8] For backward compatibility, the following also works: if there are several such lines in a file, each specifies the category for the text below it. The first category also applies to any text before the first CATEGORY line. However, using this method is *strongly* deprecated as it is incompatible with the outline structure of the document. The correct method for setting multiple categories in a buffer is using a property.

The time grid can be turned on and off with the variable `org-agenda-use-time-grid`, and can be configured with `org-agenda-time-grid`.

10.4.3 Sorting of agenda items

Before being inserted into a view, the items are sorted. How this is done depends on the type of view.

- For the daily/weekly agenda, the items for each day are sorted. The default order is to first collect all items containing an explicit time-of-day specification. These entries will be shown at the beginning of the list, as a *schedule* for the day. After that, items remain grouped in categories, in the sequence given by `org-agenda-files`. Within each category, items are sorted by priority (see Section 5.4 [Priorities], page 51), which is composed of the base priority (2000 for priority 'A', 1000 for 'B', and 0 for 'C'), plus additional increments for overdue scheduled or deadline items.

- For the TODO list, items remain in the order of categories, but within each category, sorting takes place according to priority (see Section 5.4 [Priorities], page 51). The priority used for sorting derives from the priority cookie, with additions depending on how close an item is to its due or scheduled date.

- For tags matches, items are not sorted at all, but just appear in the sequence in which they are found in the agenda files.

Sorting can be customized using the variable `org-agenda-sorting-strategy`, and may also include criteria based on the estimated effort of an entry (see Section 8.6 [Effort estimates], page 81).

10.5 Commands in the agenda buffer

Entries in the agenda buffer are linked back to the Org file or diary file where they originate. You are not allowed to edit the agenda buffer itself, but commands are provided to show and jump to the original entry location, and to edit the Org files "remotely" from the agenda buffer. In this way, all information is stored only once, removing the risk that your agenda and note files may diverge.

Some commands can be executed with mouse clicks on agenda lines. For the other commands, the cursor needs to be in the desired line.

Motion

n   Next line (same as (up) and C-p).

p   Previous line (same as (down) and C-n).

View/Go to Org file

mouse-3
(SPC)

Display the original location of the item in another window. With prefix arg, make sure that the entire entry is made visible in the outline, not only the heading.

L   Display original location and recenter that window.

mouse-2
mouse-1
[TAB]
      Go to the original location of the item in another window. Under Emacs
      22, mouse-1 will also works for this.

[RET]
      Go to the original location of the item and delete other windows.

F   Toggle Follow mode. In Follow mode, as you move the cursor through the
      agenda buffer, the other window always shows the corresponding location
      in the Org file. The initial setting for this mode in new agenda buffers can
      be set with the variable org-agenda-start-with-follow-mode.

C-c C-x b
      Display the entire subtree of the current item in an indirect buffer. With
      a numeric prefix argument N, go up to level N and then take that tree. If
      N is negative, go up that many levels. With a C-u prefix, do not remove
      the previously used indirect buffer.

C-c C-o
      Follow a link in the entry. This will offer a selection of any links in the
      text belonging to the referenced Org node. If there is only one link, it will
      be followed without a selection prompt.

Change display

o   Delete other windows.

v d   or short   d
v w   or short   w
v m
v y   Switch to day/week/month/year view. When switching to day or week
      view, this setting becomes the default for subsequent agenda commands.
      Since month and year views are slow to create, they do not become the
      default. A numeric prefix argument may be used to jump directly to a spe-
      cific day of the year, ISO week, month, or year, respectively. For example,
      32 d jumps to February 1st, 9 w to ISO week number 9. When setting day,
      week, or month view, a year may be encoded in the prefix argument as
      well. For example, 200712 w will jump to week 12 in 2007. If such a year
      specification has only one or two digits, it will be mapped to the interval
      1938-2037.

f   Go forward in time to display the following org-agenda-ndays days. For
      example, if the display covers a week, switch to the following week. With
      prefix arg, go forward that many times org-agenda-ndays days.

b   Go backward in time to display earlier dates.

.   Go to today.

j   Prompt for a date and go there.

J   Go to the currently clocked in task in the agenda buffer.

D   Toggle the inclusion of diary entries. See Section 10.3.1 [Weekly/daily
        agenda], page 100.

v l   or short   l
        Toggle Logbook mode. In Logbook mode, entries that were marked DONE
        while logging was on (variable org-log-done) are shown in the agenda, as
        are entries that have been clocked on that day. You can configure the entry
        types that should be included in log mode using the variable org-agenda-
        log-mode-items. When called with a C-u prefix, show all possible logbook
        entries, including state changes. When called with two prefix args C-u C-u,
        show only logging information, nothing else. v L is equivalent to C-u v l.

v [or short   [
        Include inactive timestamps into the current view. Only for weekly/daily
        agenda and timeline views.

v a
v A   Toggle Archives mode. In Archives mode, trees that are marked ARCHIVED
        are also scanned when producing the agenda. When you use the capital A,
        even all archive files are included. To exit archives mode, press v a again.

v R   or short   R
        Toggle Clockreport mode. In Clockreport mode, the daily/weekly agenda
        will always show a table with the clocked times for the timespan and file
        scope covered by the current agenda view. The initial setting for this
        mode in new agenda buffers can be set with the variable org-agenda-
        start-with-clockreport-mode.

v E   or short   E
        Toggle entry text mode. In entry text mode, a number of lines from the Org
        outline node referenced by an agenda line will be displayed below the line.
        The maximum number of lines is given by the variable org-agenda-entry-
        text-maxlines. Calling this command with a numeric prefix argument will
        temporarily modify that number to the prefix value.

G   Toggle the time grid on and off. See also the variables org-agenda-use-
        time-grid and org-agenda-time-grid.

r   Recreate the agenda buffer, for example to reflect the changes after modifi-
        cation of the timestamps of items with S-(left) and S-(right). When the
        buffer is the global TODO list, a prefix argument is interpreted to create
        a selective list for a specific TODO keyword.

g   Same as r.

s
C-x C-s
        Save all Org buffers in the current Emacs session, and also the locations
        of IDs.

`C-c C-x C-c`
> Invoke column view (see Section 7.5 [Column view], page 63) in the agenda buffer. The column view format is taken from the entry at point, or (if there is no entry at point), from the first entry in the agenda view. So whatever the format for that entry would be in the original buffer (taken from a property, from a #+COLUMNS line, or from the default variable org-columns-default-format), will be used in the agenda.

`C-c C-x >`
> Remove the restriction lock on the agenda, if it is currently restricted to a file or subtree (see Section 10.1 [Agenda files], page 97).

Secondary filtering and query editing

`/`
> Filter the current agenda view with respect to a tag and/or effort estimates. The difference between this and a custom agenda command is that filtering is very fast, so that you can switch quickly between different filters without having to recreate the agenda.[9]
>
> You will be prompted for a tag selection letter; (SPC) will mean any tag at all. Pressing (TAB) at that prompt will offer use completion to select a tag (including any tags that do not have a selection character). The command then hides all entries that do not contain or inherit this tag. When called with prefix arg, remove the entries that *do* have the tag. A second / at the prompt will turn off the filter and unhide any hidden entries. If the first key you press is either + or -, the previous filter will be narrowed by requiring or forbidding the selected additional tag. Instead of pressing + or - after /, you can also immediately use the \ command.
>
> In order to filter for effort estimates, you should set up allowed efforts globally, for example
>
> ```
> (setq org-global-properties
>       '(("Effort_ALL". "0 0:10 0:30 1:00 2:00 3:00 4:00")))
> ```
>
> You can then filter for an effort by first typing an operator, one of <, >, and =, and then the one-digit index of an effort estimate in your array of allowed values, where 0 means the 10th value. The filter will then restrict to entries with effort smaller-or-equal, equal, or larger-or-equal than the selected value. If the digits 0-9 are not used as fast access keys to tags, you can also simply press the index digit directly without an operator. In this case, < will be assumed. For application of the operator, entries without a defined effort will be treated according to the value of org-sort-agenda-noeffort-is-high. To filter for tasks without effort definition, press ? as the operator.
>
> Org also supports automatic, context-aware tag filtering. If the variable org-agenda-auto-exclude-function is set to a user-defined function, that

---

[9] Custom commands can preset a filter by binding the variable org-agenda-filter-preset as an option. This filter will then be applied to the view and persist as a basic filter through refreshes and more secondary filtering. The filter is a global property of the entire agenda view—in a block agenda, you should only set this in the global options section, not in the section of an individual block.

function can decide which tags should be excluded from the agenda automatically. Once this is set, the / command then accepts RET as a sub-option
key and runs the auto exclusion logic. For example, let's say you use a Net
tag to identify tasks which need network access, an Errand tag for errands
in town, and a Call tag for making phone calls. You could auto-exclude
these tags based on the availability of the Internet, and outside of business
hours, with something like this:

```
(defun org-my-auto-exclude-function (tag)
  (and (cond
        ((string= tag "Net")
         (/= 0 (call-process
                "/sbin/ping" nil nil nil
                "-c1" "-q" "-t1" "mail.gnu.org")))
        ((or (string= tag "Errand") (string= tag "Call"))
         (let ((hour (nth 2 (decode-time))))
           (or (< hour 8) (> hour 21)))))
       (concat "-" tag)))

(setq org-agenda-auto-exclude-function
      'org-my-auto-exclude-function)
```

\   Narrow the current agenda filter by an additional condition. When called
        with prefix arg, remove the entries that *do* have the tag, or that do match
        the effort criterion. You can achieve the same effect by pressing + or - as
        the first key after the / command.

[ ] { }

        in *search view*

                add new search words ([and]) or new regular expressions ({ and
                }) to the query string. The opening bracket/brace will add a posi-
                tive search term prefixed by '+', indicating that this search term *must*
                occur/match in the entry. The closing bracket/brace will add a neg-
                ative search term which *must not* occur/match in the entry for it to
                be selected.

Remote editing

0-9
> Digit argument.

C-_
> Undo a change due to a remote editing command. The change is undone both in the agenda buffer and in the remote buffer.

t   Change the TODO state of the item, both in the agenda and in the original org file.

C-S-$\boxed{\texttt{right}}$/$\boxed{\texttt{left}}$
Switch to the next/previous set of TODO keywords.

C-k
> Delete the current agenda item along with the entire subtree belonging to it in the original Org file. If the text to be deleted remotely is longer than one line, the kill needs to be confirmed by the user. See variable org-agenda-confirm-kill.

C-c C-w
> Refile the entry at point.

C-c C-x C-a or short a
> Archive the subtree corresponding to the entry at point using the default archiving command set in org-archive-default-command. When using the a key, confirmation will be required.

C-c C-x a
> Toggle the ARCHIVE tag for the current headline.

C-c C-x A
> Move the subtree corresponding to the current entry to its *archive sibling*.

C-c C-x C-s or short $
> Archive the subtree corresponding to the current headline. This means the entry will be moved to the configured archive location, most likely a different file.

T   Show all tags associated with the current item. This is useful if you have turned off org-agenda-show-inherited-tags, but still want to see all tags of a headline occasionally.

:   Set tags for the current headline. If there is an active region in the agenda, change a tag for all headings in the region.

,   Set the priority for the current item. Org-mode prompts for the priority character. If you reply with $\boxed{\texttt{SPC}}$, the priority cookie is removed from the entry.

P   Display weighted priority of current item.

+

S-⎡up⎤
　　Increase the priority of the current item. The priority is changed in the
　　original buffer, but the agenda is not resorted. Use the r key for this.

-

S-⎡down⎤
　　Decrease the priority of the current item.

z　or also　C-c C-z
　　Add a note to the entry. This note will be recorded, and then filed to the
　　same location where state change notes are put. Depending on org-log-
　　into-drawer, this may be inside a drawer.

C-c C-a
　　Dispatcher for all command related to attachments.

C-c C-s
　　Schedule this item. With prefix arg remove the scheduling timestamp.

C-c C-d
　　Set a deadline for this item. With prefix arg remove the deadline.

k　Agenda actions, to set dates for selected items to the cursor date. This
　　command also works in the calendar! The command prompts for an addi-
　　tional key:

　　m　Mark the entry at point for action. You can also make entries in Org
　　　　files with C-c C-x C-k.

　　d　Set the deadline of the marked entry to the date at point.

　　s　Schedule the marked entry at the date at point.

　　r　Call org-capture with the cursor date as default date.

　　Press r afterward to refresh the agenda and see the effect of the command.

S-⎡right⎤
　　Change the timestamp associated with the current line by one day into
　　the future. With a numeric prefix argument, change it by that many days.
　　For example, 3 6 5 S-⎡right⎤ will change it by a year. With a C-u prefix,
　　change the time by one hour. If you immediately repeat the command, it
　　will continue to change hours even without the prefix arg. With a double
　　C-u C-u prefix, do the same for changing minutes. The stamp is changed in
　　the original Org file, but the change is not directly reflected in the agenda
　　buffer. Use r or g to update the buffer.

S-⎡left⎤
　　Change the timestamp associated with the current line by one day into the
　　past.

>　Change the timestamp associated with the current line. The key > has
　　been chosen, because it is the same as S-. on my keyboard.

I   Start the clock on the current item. If a clock is running already, it is stopped first.

O   Stop the previously started clock.

X   Cancel the currently running clock.

J   Jump to the running clock in another window.

Bulk remote editing selected entries

m   Mark the entry at point for bulk action.

u   Unmark entry for bulk action.

U   Unmark all marked entries for bulk action.

B   Bulk action: act on all marked entries in the agenda. This will prompt for another key to select the action to be applied. The prefix arg to B will be passed through to the s and d commands, to bulk-remove these special timestamps.

  r   Prompt for a single refile target and move all entries. The entries will no longer be in the agenda; refresh (g) to bring them back.

  $ Archive all selected entries.

  A   Archive entries by moving them to their respective archive siblings.

  t   Change TODO state. This prompts for a single TODO keyword and changes the state of all selected entries, bypassing blocking and suppressing logging notes (but not timestamps).

  +   Add a tag to all selected entries.

  -     Remove a tag from all selected entries.

  s   Schedule all items to a new date. To shift existing schedule dates by a fixed number of days, use something starting with double plus at the prompt, for example '++8d' or '++2w'.

  d   Set deadline to a specific date.

Calendar commands

c   Open the Emacs calendar and move to the date at the agenda cursor.

c   When in the calendar, compute and show the Org-mode agenda for the date at the cursor.

i   Insert a new entry into the diary, using the date at the cursor and (for block entries) the date at the mark. This will add to the Emacs diary file,[1] in a way similar to the i command in the calendar. The diary file will pop up in another window, where you can add the entry.

        If you configure org-agenda-diary-file to point to an Org-mode file, Org will create entries (in org-mode syntax) in that file instead. Most

---

[1] This file is parsed for the agenda when org-agenda-include-diary is set.

entries will be stored in a date-based outline tree that will later make it easy to archive appointments from previous months/years. The tree will be built under an entry with a DATE_TREE property, or else with years as top-level entries. Emacs will prompt you for the entry text—if you specify it, the entry will be created in org-agenda-diary-file without further interaction. If you directly press (RET) at the prompt without typing text, the target file will be shown in another window for you to finish the entry there. See also the k r command.

M   Show the phases of the moon for the three months around current date.

S   Show sunrise and sunset times. The geographical location must be set with calendar variables, see the documentation for the Emacs calendar.

C   Convert the date at cursor into many other cultural and historic calendars.

H   Show holidays for three months around the cursor date.

M-x org-export-icalendar-combine-agenda-files
        Export a single iCalendar file containing entries from all agenda files. This is a globally available command, and also available in the agenda menu.

Exporting to a file

C-x C-w
        Write the agenda view to a file. Depending on the extension of the selected file name, the view will be exported as HTML (extension '.html' or '.htm'), Postscript (extension '.ps'), PDF (extension '.pdf'), and plain text (any other extension). When called with a C-u prefix argument, immediately open the newly created file. Use the variable org-agenda-exporter-settings to set options for 'ps-print' and for 'htmlize' to be used during export.

Quit and Exit

q   Quit agenda, remove the agenda buffer.

x   Exit agenda, remove the agenda buffer and all buffers loaded by Emacs for the compilation of the agenda. Buffers created by the user to visit Org files will not be removed.

10.6 Custom agenda views

Custom agenda commands serve two purposes: to store and quickly access frequently used TODO and tags searches, and to create special composite agenda buffers. Custom agenda commands will be accessible through the dispatcher (see Section 10.2 [Agenda dispatcher], page 99), just like the default commands.

10.6.1 Storing searches

The first application of custom searches is the definition of keyboard shortcuts for frequently used searches, either creating an agenda buffer, or a sparse tree (the latter covering of course only the current buffer). Custom commands are configured in the variable org-agenda-custom-commands. You can customize this variable, for example by pressing C-c a C. You can also directly set it with Emacs Lisp in '.emacs'. The following example contains all valid search types:

```
(setq org-agenda-custom-commands
      '(("w" todo "WAITING")
        ("W" todo-tree "WAITING")
        ("u" tags "+boss-urgent")
        ("v" tags-todo "+boss-urgent")
        ("U" tags-tree "+boss-urgent")
        ("f" occur-tree "\\<FIXME\\>")
        ("h" . "HOME+Name tags searches") ; description for "h"
                                            prefix
        ("hl" tags "+home+Lisa")
        ("hp" tags "+home+Peter")
        ("hk" tags "+home+Kim")))
```

The initial string in each entry defines the keys you have to press after the dispatcher command C-c a in order to access the command. Usually this will be just a single character, but if you have many similar commands, you can also define two-letter combinations where the first character is the same in several combinations and serves as a prefix key.[2] The second parameter is the search type, followed by the string or regular expression to be used for the matching. The example above will therefore define:

C-c a w

    as a global search for TODO entries with 'WAITING' as the TODO keyword

C-c a W

    as the same search, but only in the current buffer and displaying the results as a sparse tree

C-c a u

    as a global tags search for headlines marked ':boss:' but not ':urgent:'

C-c a v

    as the same search as C-c a u, but limiting the search to headlines that are also TODO items

C-c a U

    as the same search as C-c a u, but only in the current buffer and displaying the result as a sparse tree

C-c a f

    to create a sparse tree (again: current buffer only) with all entries containing the word 'FIXME'

---

[2] You can provide a description for a prefix key by inserting a cons cell with the prefix and the description.

C-c a h

> as a prefix command for a HOME tags search where you have to press
> an additional key (l, p or k) to select a name (Lisa, Peter, or Kim) as
> additional tag to match.

10.6.2 Block agenda

Another possibility is the construction of agenda views that comprise the
results of *several* commands, each of which creates a block in the agenda buffer.
The available commands include agenda for the daily or weekly agenda (as
created with C-c a a), alltodo for the global TODO list (as constructed with
C-c a t), and the matching commands discussed above: todo, tags, and tags-
todo. Here are two examples:

```
(setq org-agenda-custom-commands
      '(("h" "Agenda and Home-related tasks"
        ((agenda "")
         (tags-todo "home")
         (tags "garden")))
       ("o" "Agenda and Office-related tasks"
        ((agenda "")
         (tags-todo "work")
         (tags "office")))))
```

This will define C-c a h to create a multi-block view for stuff you need to attend
to at home. The resulting agenda buffer will contain your agenda for the current
week, all TODO items that carry the tag 'home', and also all lines tagged with
'garden'. Finally the command C-c a o provides a similar view for office tasks.

10.6.3 Setting options for custom commands

Org-mode contains a number of variables regulating agenda construction and
display. The global variables define the behavior for all agenda commands,
including the custom commands. However, if you want to change some settings
just for a single custom view, you can do so. Setting options requires inserting
a list of variable names and values at the right spot in org-agenda-custom-
commands. For example:

```
(setq org-agenda-custom-commands
      '(("w" todo "WAITING"
        ((org-agenda-sorting-strategy '(priority-down))
         (org-agenda-prefix-format "  Mixed: ")))
       ("U" tags-tree "+boss-urgent"
        ((org-show-following-heading nil)
         (org-show-hierarchy-above nil)))
       ("N" search ""
        ((org-agenda-files '("~org/notes.org"))
         (org-agenda-text-search-extra-files nil)))))
```

Now the C-c a w command will sort the collected entries only by priority, and
the prefix format is modified to just say ' Mixed: ' instead of giving the category
of the entry. The sparse tags tree of C-c a U will now turn out ultra-compact,

because neither the headline hierarchy above the match, nor the headline following the match will be shown. The command C-c a N will do a text search limited to only a single file.

For command sets creating a block agenda, org-agenda-custom-commands has two separate spots for setting options. You can add options that should be valid for just a single command in the set, and options that should be valid for all commands in the set. The former are just added to the command entry; the latter must come after the list of command entries. Going back to the block agenda example (see Section 10.6.2 [Block agenda], page 118), let's change the sorting strategy for the C-c a h commands to priority-down, but let's sort the results for GARDEN tags query in the opposite order, priority-up. This would look like this:

```
(setq org-agenda-custom-commands
      '(("h" "Agenda and Home-related tasks"
        ((agenda)
         (tags-todo "home")
         (tags "garden"
               ((org-agenda-sorting-strategy '(priority-up)))))
        ((org-agenda-sorting-strategy '(priority-down))))
       ("o" "Agenda and Office-related tasks"
        ((agenda)
         (tags-todo "work")
         (tags "office")))))
```

As you see, the values and parentheses setting is a little complex. When in doubt, use the customize interface to set this variable—it fully supports its structure. Just one caveat: when setting options in this interface, the *values* are just Lisp expressions. So if the value is a string, you need to add the double-quotes around the value yourself.

10.7 Exporting Agenda Views

If you are away from your computer, it can be very useful to have a printed version of some agenda views to carry around. Org-mode can export custom agenda views as plain text, HTML,[3] Postscript, PDF,[4] and iCalendar files. If you want to do this only occasionally, use the command

C-x C-w

> Write the agenda view to a file. Depending on the extension of the selected file name, the view will be exported as HTML (extension '.html' or '.htm'), Postscript (extension '.ps'), iCalendar (extension '.ics'), or plain text (any other extension). Use the variable org-agenda-exporter-settings to set options for 'ps-print' and for 'htmlize' to be used during export, for example

---

[3] You need to install Hrvoje Niksic's 'htmlize.el'.

[4] To create PDF output, the ghostscript 'ps2pdf' utility must be installed on the system. Selecting a PDF file with also create the postscript file.

```
(setq org-agenda-exporter-settings
      '((ps-number-of-columns 2)
        (ps-landscape-mode t)
        (org-agenda-add-entry-text-maxlines 5)
        (htmlize-output-type 'css)))
```

If you need to export certain agenda views frequently, you can associate any custom agenda command with a list of output file names .[5] Here is an example that first defines custom commands for the agenda and the global TODO list, together with a number of files to which to export them. Then we define two block agenda commands and specify file names for them as well. File names can be relative to the current working directory, or absolute.

```
(setq org-agenda-custom-commands
      '(("X" agenda "" nil ("agenda.html" "agenda.ps"))
        ("Y" alltodo "" nil ("todo.html" "todo.txt" "todo.ps"))
        ("h" "Agenda and Home-related tasks"
         ((agenda "")
          (tags-todo "home")
          (tags "garden"))
         nil
         ("~/views/home.html"))
        ("o" "Agenda and Office-related tasks"
         ((agenda)
          (tags-todo "work")
          (tags "office"))
         nil
         ("~/views/office.ps" "~/calendars/office.ics"))))
```

The extension of the file name determines the type of export. If it is '.html', Org-mode will use the 'htmlize.el' package to convert the buffer to HTML and save it to this file name. If the extension is '.ps', ps-print-buffer-with-faces is used to produce Postscript output. If the extension is '.ics', iCalendar export is run export over all files that were used to construct the agenda, and limit the export to entries listed in the agenda. Any other extension produces a plain ASCII file.

The export files are *not* created when you use one of those commands interactively because this might use too much overhead. Instead, there is a special command to produce *all* specified files in one step:

C-c a e

   Export all agenda views that have export file names associated with them.

You can use the options section of the custom agenda commands to also set options for the export commands. For example:

---

[5] If you want to store standard views like the weekly agenda or the global TODO list as well, you need to define custom commands for them in order to be able to specify file names.

```
(setq org-agenda-custom-commands
      '(("X" agenda ""
         ((ps-number-of-columns 2)
          (ps-landscape-mode t)
          (org-agenda-prefix-format " [ ] ")
          (org-agenda-with-colors nil)
          (org-agenda-remove-tags t))
         ("theagenda.ps"))))
```

This command sets two options for the Postscript exporter, to make it print
in two columns in landscape format—the resulting page can be cut in two and
then used in a paper agenda. The remaining settings modify the agenda prefix
to omit category and scheduling information, and instead include a checkbox
to check off items. We also remove the tags to make the lines compact, and
we don't want to use colors for the black-and-white printer. Settings specified
in org-agenda-exporter-settings will also apply, but the settings in org-
agenda-custom-commands take precedence.

From the command line you may also use

```
emacs -f org-batch-store-agenda-views -kill
```

or, if you need to modify some parameters[6]

```
emacs -eval '(org-batch-store-agenda-views                     \
              org-agenda-ndays 30                               \
              org-agenda-start-day "2007-11-01"                 \
              org-agenda-include-diary nil                      \
              org-agenda-files (quote ("~/org/project.org")))' \
      -kill
```

which will create the agenda views restricted to the file '~/org/project.org',
without diary entries and with a 30-day extent.

You can also extract agenda information in a way that allows further processing by other programs. See Section A.8 [Extracting agenda information],
page 221, for more information.

10.8 Using column view in the agenda

Column view (see Section 7.5 [Column view], page 63) is normally used to
view and edit properties embedded in the hierarchical structure of an Org file.
It can be quite useful to use column view also from the agenda, where entries
are collected by certain criteria.

C-c C-x C-c
        Turn on column view in the agenda.

To understand how to use this properly, it is important to realize that the
entries in the agenda are no longer in their proper outline environment. This
causes the following issues:

---

[6] Quoting depends on the system you use, please check the FAQ for examples.

1. Org needs to make a decision which COLUMNS format to use. Since the entries in the agenda are collected from different files, and different files may have different COLUMNS formats, this is a non-trivial problem. Org first checks if the variable org-overriding-columns-format is currently set, and if so, takes the format from there. Otherwise it takes the format associated with the first item in the agenda, or, if that item does not have a specific format (defined in a property, or in its file), it uses org-columns-default-format.

2. If any of the columns has a summary type defined (see Section 7.5.1.2 [Column attributes], page 63), turning on column view in the agenda will visit all relevant agenda files and make sure that the computations of this property are up to date. This is also true for the special CLOCKSUM property. Org will then sum the values displayed in the agenda. In the daily/weekly agenda, the sums will cover a single day; in all other views they cover the entire block. It is vital to realize that the agenda may show the same entry *twice* (for example as scheduled and as a deadline), and it may show two entries from the same hierarchy (for example a *parent* and its *child*). In these cases, the summation in the agenda will lead to incorrect results because some values will count double.

3. When the column view in the agenda shows the CLOCKSUM, that is always the entire clocked time for this item. So even in the daily/weekly agenda, the clocksum listed in column view may originate from times outside the current view. This has the advantage that you can compare these values with a column listing the planned total effort for a task—one of the major applications for column view in the agenda. If you want information about clocked time in the displayed period use clock table mode (press R in the agenda).

11 Markup for rich export

When exporting Org-mode documents, the exporter tries to reflect the structure of the document as accurately as possible in the backend. Since export targets like HTML, LaTeX, or DocBook allow much richer formatting, Org-mode has rules on how to prepare text for rich export. This section summarizes the markup rules used in an Org-mode buffer.

11.1 Structural markup elements

Document title

The title of the exported document is taken from the special line

```
#+TITLE: This is the title of the document
```

If this line does not exist, the title is derived from the first non-empty, non-comment line in the buffer. If no such line exists, or if you have turned off exporting of the text before the first headline (see below), the title will be the file name without extension.

If you are exporting only a subtree by marking is as the region, the heading of the subtree will become the title of the document. If the subtree has a property EXPORT_TITLE, that will take precedence.

Headings and sections

The outline structure of the document as described in Chapter 2 [Document Structure], page 9, forms the basis for defining sections of the exported document. However, since the outline structure is also used for (for example) lists of tasks, only the first three outline levels will be used as headings. Deeper levels will become itemized lists. You can change the location of this switch globally by setting the variable org-export-headline-levels, or on a per-file basis with a line

```
#+OPTIONS: H:4
```

Table of contents

The table of contents is normally inserted directly before the first headline of the file. If you would like to get it to a different location, insert the string [TABLE-OF-CONTENTS] on a line by itself at the desired location. The depth of the table of contents is by default the same as the number of headline levels, but you can choose a smaller number, or turn off the table of contents entirely, by configuring the variable org-export-with-toc, or on a per-file basis with a line like

```
#+OPTIONS: toc:2          (only to two levels in TOC)
#+OPTIONS: toc:nil        (no TOC at all)
```

Text before the first headline

Org-mode normally exports the text before the first headline, and even uses the first line as the document title. The text will be fully marked up. If you need to include literal HTML, LaTeX, or DocBook code, use the special constructs described below in the sections for the individual exporters.

Some people like to use the space before the first headline for setup and internal links and therefore would like to control the exported text before the first headline in a different way. You can do so by setting the variable org-export-skip-text-before-1st-heading to t. On a per-file basis, you can get the same effect with '#+OPTIONS: skip:t'.

If you still want to have some text before the first headline, use the #+TEXT construct:

```
#+OPTIONS: skip:t
#+TEXT: This text will go before the *first* headline.
#+TEXT: [TABLE-OF-CONTENTS]
#+TEXT: This goes between table of contents and first headline
```

Lists

Plain lists as described in Section 2.7 [Plain lists], page 15, are translated to the backend's syntax for such lists. Most backends support unordered, ordered, and description lists.

Paragraphs, line breaks, and quoting

Paragraphs are separated by at least one empty line. If you need to enforce a line break within a paragraph, use '\\' at the end of a line.

To keep the line breaks in a region, but otherwise use normal formatting, you can use this construct, which can also be used to format poetry.

```
#+BEGIN_VERSE
 Great clouds overhead
 Tiny black birds rise and fall
 Snow covers Emacs

     -- AlexSchroeder
#+END_VERSE
```

When quoting a passage from another document, it is customary to format this as a paragraph that is indented on both the left and the right margin. You can include quotations in Org-mode documents like this:

```
#+BEGIN_QUOTE
Everything should be made as simple as possible,
but not any simpler -- Albert Einstein
#+END_QUOTE
```

If you would like to center some text, do it like this:

```
#+BEGIN_CENTER
Everything should be made as simple as possible, \\
but not any simpler
#+END_CENTER
```

Footnote markup

Footnotes defined in the way described in Section 2.10 [Footnotes], page 20, will be exported by all backends. Org allows multiple references to the same note, and different backends support this to varying degrees.

Emphasis and monospace

You can make words **bold**, /italic/, _underlined_, =code= and ~verbatim~, and, if you must, '+strike-through+'. Text in the code and verbatim string is not processed for Org-mode specific syntax, it is exported verbatim.

Horizontal rules

A line consisting of only dashes, and at least 5 of them, will be exported as a horizontal line ('<hr/>' in HTML).

Comment lines

Lines starting with '#' in column zero are treated as comments and will never be exported. If you want an indented line to be treated as a comment, start it with '#+ '. Also entire subtrees starting with the word 'COMMENT' will never be exported. Finally, regions surrounded by '#+BEGIN_COMMENT' ... '#+END_COMMENT' will not be exported.

C-c ;
    Toggle the COMMENT keyword at the beginning of an entry.

11.2 Images and Tables

Both the native Org-mode tables (see Chapter 3 [Tables], page 23) and tables formatted with the 'table.el' package will be exported properly. For Org-mode tables, the lines before the first horizontal separator line will become table header lines. You can use the following lines somewhere before the table to assign a caption and a label for cross references, and in the text you can refer to the object with \ref{tab:basic-data}:

```
#+CAPTION: This is the caption for the next table (or link)
#+LABEL:   tbl:basic-data
  | ... | ...|
  |-----|----|
```

Some backends (HTML, LaTeX, and DocBook) allow you to directly include images into the exported document. Org does this, if a link to an image files does not have a description part, for example [[./img/a.jpg]]. If you wish to define a caption for the image and maybe a label for internal cross references, make sure that the link is on a line by itself and precede it with #+CAPTION and #+LABEL as follows:

```
#+CAPTION: The caption for the next figure link (or table)
#+LABEL:   fig:SED-HR4049
[[./img/a.jpg]]
```

You may also define additional attributes for the figure. As this is backend-specific, see the sections about the individual backends for more information.

See Section 4.4 [Handling links], page 34.

11.3 Literal examples

You can include literal examples that should not be subjected to markup. Such examples will be typeset in monospace, so this is well suited for source code and similar examples.

```
#+BEGIN_EXAMPLE
Some example from a text file.
#+END_EXAMPLE
```

Note that such blocks may be *indented* in order to align nicely with indented text and in particular with plain list structure (see Section 2.7 [Plain lists], page 15). For simplicity when using small examples, you can also start the example lines with a colon followed by a space. There may also be additional whitespace before the colon:

```
Here is an example
  : Some example from a text file.
```

If the example is source code from a programming language, or any other text that can be marked up by font-lock in Emacs, you can ask for the example to look like the fontified Emacs buffer.[1] This is done with the 'src' block, where you also need to specify the name of the major mode that should be used to fontify the example:

```
#+BEGIN_SRC emacs-lisp
  (defun org-xor (a b)
    "Exclusive or."
    (if a (not b) b))
#+END_SRC
```

---

[1] This works automatically for the HTML backend (it requires version 1.34 of the 'htmlize.el' package, which is distributed with Org). Fontified code chunks in LATEX can be achieved using either the listings or the minted (http://code.google.com/p/minted) package. To use listings, turn on the variable org-export-latex-listings and ensure that the listings package is included by the LATEX header (e.g., by configuring org-export-latex-packages-alist). See the listings documentation for configuration options, including obtaining colored output. For minted it is necessary to install the program pygments (http://pygments.org), in addition to setting org-export-latex-minted, ensuring that the minted package is included by the LATEX header, and ensuring that the -shell-escape option is passed to 'pdflatex' (see org-latex-to-pdf-process). See the documentation of the variables org-export-latex-listings and org-export-latex-minted for further details.

Both in `example` and in `src` snippets, you can add a -n switch to the end of the BEGIN line, to get the lines of the example numbered. If you use a +n switch, the numbering from the previous numbered snippet will be continued in the current one. In literal examples, Org will interpret strings like '(ref:name)' as labels, and use them as targets for special hyperlinks like [[(name)]] (i.e., the reference name enclosed in single parenthesis). In HTML, hovering the mouse over such a link will remote-highlight the corresponding code line, which is kind of cool.

You can also add a -r switch which *removes* the labels from the source code.[2] With the -n switch, links to these references will be labeled by the line numbers from the code listing, otherwise links will use the labels with no parentheses. Here is an example:

```
#+BEGIN_SRC emacs-lisp -n -r
(save-excursion              (ref:sc)
   (goto-char (point-min))   (ref:jump)
#+END_SRC
In line [[(sc)]] we remember the current position.
[[(jump)][Line (jump)]] jumps to point-min.
```

If the syntax for the label format conflicts with the language syntax, use a -l switch to change the format, for example '#+BEGIN_SRC pascal -n -r -l "((%s))"'. See also the variable `org-coderef-label-format`.

HTML export also allows examples to be published as text areas, See Section 12.5.7 [Text areas in HTML export], page 139.

C-c '

Edit the source code example at point in its native mode. This works by switching to a temporary buffer with the source code. You need to exit by pressing C-c ' again.[3] The edited version will then replace the old version in the Org buffer. Fixed-width regions (where each line starts with a colon followed by a space) will be edited using `artist-mode`[4] to allow creating ASCII drawings easily. Using this command in an empty line will create a new fixed-width region.

C-c l

Calling `org-store-link` while editing a source code example in a temporary buffer created with C-c ' will prompt for a label. Make sure that it is unique in the current buffer, and insert it with the proper formatting like '(ref:label)' at the end of the current line. Then the label is stored as a link '(label)', for retrieval with C-c C-l.

---

[2] Adding -k to -n -r will *keep* the labels in the source code while using line numbers for the links, which might be useful to explain those in an org-mode example code.

[3] Upon exit, lines starting with '*' or '#' will get a comma prepended, to keep them from being interpreted by Org as outline nodes or special comments. These commas will be stripped for editing with C-c ', and also for export.

[4] You may select a different-mode with the variable `org-edit-fixed-width-region-mode`.

11.4 Include files

During export, you can include the content of another file. For example, to include your '.emacs' file, you could use:

```
#+INCLUDE: "~/.emacs" src emacs-lisp
```

The optional second and third parameter are the markup (e.g., 'quote', 'example', or 'src'), and, if the markup is 'src', the language for formatting the contents. The markup is optional: if it is not given, the text will be assumed to be in Org-mode format and will be processed normally. The include line will also allow additional keyword parameters :prefix1 and :prefix to specify pre-fixes for the first line and for each following line, as well as any options accepted by the selected markup. For example, to include a file as an item, use

```
#+INCLUDE: "~/snippets/xx" :prefix1 "   + " :prefix "      "
```

C-c '
Visit the include file at point.

11.5 Index entries

You can specify entries that will be used for generating an index during publishing. This is done by lines starting with #+INDEX. An entry the contains an exclamation mark will create a sub item. See Section 13.1.8 [Generating an index], page 159 for more information.

```
* Curriculum Vitae
#+INDEX: CV
#+INDEX: Application!CV
```

11.6 Macro replacement

You can define text snippets with

```
#+MACRO: name    replacement text $1, $2 are arguments
```

which can be referenced anywhere in the document (even in code examples) with {{{name(arg1,arg2)}}}. In addition to defined macros, {{{title}}}, {{{author}}}, etc., will reference information set by the #+TITLE:, #+AUTHOR:, and similar lines. Also, {{{date(*FORMAT*)}}} and {{{modification-time(*FORMAT*)}}} refer to current date time and to the modification time of the file being exported, respectively. *FORMAT* should be a format string understood by format-time-string.

Macro expansion takes place during export, and some people use it to construct complex HTML code.

11.7 Embedded LaTeX

Plain ASCII is normally sufficient for almost all note taking. Exceptions include scientific notes, which often require mathematical symbols and the occasional formula. LaTeX[5] is widely used to typeset scientific documents. Org-mode supports embedding LaTeX code into its files, because many academics are used to writing and reading LaTeX source code, and because it can be readily processed to produce pretty output for a number of export backends.

11.7.1 Special symbols

You can use LaTeX macros to insert special symbols like '\alpha' to indicate the Greek letter, or '\to' to indicate an arrow. Completion for these macros is available, just type '\' and maybe a few letters, and press M-(TAB) to see possible completions. Unlike LaTeX code, Org-mode allows these macros to be present without surrounding math delimiters, for example:

        Angles are written as Greek letters \alpha, \beta and \gamma.

During export, these symbols will be transformed into the native format of the exporter backend. Strings like \alpha will be exported as α in the HTML output, and as α in the LaTeX output. Similarly, \nbsp will become   in HTML and ~ in LaTeX. If you need such a symbol inside a word, terminate it like this: '\Aacute{}stor'.

A large number of entities is provided, with names taken from both HTML and LaTeX; see the variable org-entities for the complete list. '\-' is treated as a shy hyphen, and '--', '---', and '...' are all converted into special commands creating hyphens of different lengths or a compact set of dots.

If you would like to see entities displayed as UTF8 characters, use the following command:[6]

C-c C-x \
> Toggle display of entities as UTF-8 characters. This does not change the buffer content which remains plain ASCII, but it overlays the UTF-8 character for display purposes only.

---

[5] LaTeX is a macro system based on Donald E. Knuth's TeX system. Many of the features described here as "LaTeX" are really from TeX, but for simplicity I am blurring this distinction.

[6] You can turn this on by default by setting the variable org-pretty-entities, or on a per-file base with the #+STARTUP option entitiespretty.

11.7.2 Subscripts and superscripts

Just like in LaTeX, '`^`' and '`_`' are used to indicate super- and subscripts. Again, these can be used without embedding them in math-mode delimiters. To increase the readability of ASCII text, it is not necessary (but OK) to surround multi-character sub- and superscripts with curly braces. For example

```
The mass of the sun is M_sun = 1.989 x 10^30 kg.  The radius of
the sun is R_{sun} = 6.96 x 10^8 m.
```

To avoid interpretation as raised or lowered text, you can quote '`^`' and '`_`' with a backslash: '`\^`' and '`\_`'. If you write a text where the underscore is often used in a different context, Org's convention to always interpret these as subscripts can get in your way. Configure the variable `org-export-with-sub-superscripts` to globally change this convention, or use, on a per-file basis:

```
#+OPTIONS: ^:{}
```

With this setting, '`a_b`' will not be interpreted as a subscript, but '`a_{b}`' will.

`C-c C-x \`

In addition to showing entities as UTF-8 characters, this command will also format sub- and superscripts in a WYSIWYM way.

11.7.3 LaTeX fragments

Going beyond symbols and sub- and superscripts, a full formula language is needed. Org-mode can contain LaTeX math fragments, and it supports ways to process these for several export backends. When exporting to LaTeX, the code is obviously left as it is. When exporting to HTML, Org invokes the Math-Jax library (http://www.mathjax.org) (see Section 12.5.6 [Math formatting in HTML export], page 139) to process and display the math.[7] Finally, it can also process the mathematical expressions into images[8] that can be displayed in a browser or in DocBook documents.

LaTeX fragments don't need any special marking at all. The following snippets will be identified as LaTeX source code:

- Environments of any kind.[9] The only requirement is that the \begin statement appears on a new line, preceded by only whitespace.

---

[7] If you plan to use this regularly or on pages with significant page views, you should install 'MathJax' on your own server in order to limit the load of our server.

[8] For this to work you need to be on a system with a working LaTeX installation. You also need the 'dvipng' program, available at http://sourceforge.net/projects/dvipng/. The LaTeX header that will be used when processing a fragment can be configured with the variable org-format-latex-header.

[9] When 'MathJax' is used, only the environment recognized by 'MathJax' will be processed. When 'dvipng' is used to create images, any LaTeX environments will be handled.

- Text within the usual LaTeX math delimiters. To avoid conflicts with currency specifications, single '$' characters are only recognized as math delimiters if the enclosed text contains at most two line breaks, is directly attached to the '$' characters with no whitespace in between, and if the closing '$' is followed by whitespace, punctuation or a dash. For the other delimiters, there is no such restriction, so when in doubt, use '\(...\)' as inline math delimiters.

For example:

```
\begin{equation}          % arbitrary environments,
x=\sqrt{b}                % even tables, figures
\end{equation}            % etc
```

```
If $a^2=b$ and \( b=2 \), then the solution must be
either $$ a=+\sqrt{2} $$ or \[ a=-\sqrt{2} \].
```

If you need any of the delimiter ASCII sequences for other purposes, you can configure the option `org-format-latex-options` to deselect the ones you do not wish to have interpreted by the LaTeX converter.

LaTeX processing can be configured with the variable `org-export-with-LaTeX-fragments`. The default setting is t which means 'MathJax' for HTML, and no processing for DocBook, ASCII and LaTeX backends. You can also set this variable on a per-file basis using one of these lines:

`#+OPTIONS: LaTeX:t`	Do the right thing automatically (MathJax)
`#+OPTIONS: LaTeX:dvipng`	Force using dvipng images
`#+OPTIONS: LaTeX:nil`	Do not process LaTeX fragments at all
`#+OPTIONS: LaTeX:verbatim`	Verbatim export, for jsMath or so

11.7.4 Previewing LaTeX fragments

If you have 'dvipng' installed, LaTeX fragments can be processed to produce preview images of the typeset expressions:

`C-c C-x C-l`

Produce a preview image of the LaTeX fragment at point and overlay it over the source code. If there is no fragment at point, process all fragments in the current entry (between two headlines). When called with a prefix argument, process the entire subtree. When called with two prefix arguments, or when the cursor is before the first headline, process the entire buffer.

`C-c C-c`

Remove the overlay preview images.

You can customize the variable `org-format-latex-options` to influence some aspects of the preview. In particular, the `:scale` (and for HTML export, `:html-scale`) property can be used to adjust the size of the preview images.

11.7.5 Using CDLaTeX to enter math

CDLaTeX mode is a minor mode that is normally used in combination with a major LaTeX mode like AUCTeX in order to speed-up insertion of environments and math templates. Inside Org-mode, you can make use of some of the features of CDLaTeX mode. You need to install 'cdlatex.el' and 'texmathp.el' (the latter comes also with AUCTeX) from http://www.astro.uva.nl/~dominik/Tools/cdlatex. Don't use CDLaTeX mode itself under Org-mode, but use the light version org-cdlatex-mode that comes as part of Org-mode. Turn it on for the current buffer with M-x org-cdlatex-mode, or for all Org files with

    (add-hook 'org-mode-hook 'turn-on-org-cdlatex)

When this mode is enabled, the following features are present (for more details see the documentation of CDLaTeX mode):

- Environment templates can be inserted with C-c {.

- The (TAB) key will do template expansion if the cursor is inside a LaTeX fragment.[10] For example, (TAB) will expand fr to \frac{}{} and position the cursor correctly inside the first brace. Another (TAB) will get you into the second brace. Even outside fragments, (TAB) will expand environment abbreviations at the beginning of a line. For example, if you write 'equ' at the beginning of a line and press (TAB), this abbreviation will be expanded to an equation environment. To get a list of all abbreviations, type M-x cdlatex-command-help.

- Pressing _ and ^ inside a LaTeX fragment will insert these characters together with a pair of braces. If you use (TAB) to move out of the braces, and if the braces surround only a single character or macro, they are removed again (depending on the variable cdlatex-simplify-sub-super-scripts).

- Pressing the backquote ` followed by a character inserts math macros, also outside LaTeX fragments. If you wait more than 1.5 seconds after the backquote, a help window will pop up.

- Pressing the single-quote ' followed by another character modifies the symbol before point with an accent or a font. If you wait more than 1.5 seconds after the single-quote, a help window will pop up. Character modification will work only inside LaTeX fragments; outside, the quote is normal.

---

[10] Org-mode has a method to test if the cursor is inside such a fragment, see the documentation of the function org-inside-LaTeX-fragment-p.

12 Exporting

Org-mode documents can be exported into a variety of other formats. For printing and sharing of notes, ASCII export produces a readable and simple version of an Org file. HTML export allows you to publish a notes file on the web, while the XOXO format provides a solid base for exchange with a broad range of other applications. LaTeX export lets you use Org-mode and its structured editing functions to easily create LaTeX files. DocBook export makes it possible to convert Org files to many other formats using DocBook tools. For project management you can create Gantt and resource charts by using TaskJuggler export. To incorporate entries with associated times like deadlines or appointments into a desktop calendar program like iCal, Org-mode can also produce extracts in the iCalendar format. Currently Org-mode only supports export, not import of these different formats.

Org supports export of selected regions when `transient-mark-mode` is enabled (default in Emacs 23).

12.1 Selective export

You may use tags to select the parts of a document that should be exported, or to exclude parts from export. This behavior is governed by two variables: `org-export-select-tags` and `org-export-exclude-tags`.

Org first checks if any of the *select* tags is present in the buffer. If yes, all trees that do not carry one of these tags will be excluded. If a selected tree is a subtree, the heading hierarchy above it will also be selected for export, but not the text below those headings.

If none of the select tags is found, the whole buffer will be selected for export.

Finally, all subtrees that are marked by any of the *exclude* tags will be removed from the export buffer.

12.2 Export options

The exporter recognizes special lines in the buffer which provide additional information. These lines may be put anywhere in the file. The whole set of lines can be inserted into the buffer with C-c C-e t. For individual lines, a good way to make sure the keyword is correct is to type '#+' and then use M-(TAB) completion (see Section 16.1 [Completion], page 197). For a summary of other in-buffer settings not specifically related to export, see Section 16.6 [In-buffer settings], page 200. In particular, note that you can place commonly-used (export) options in a separate file which can be included using #+SETUPFILE.

C-c C-e t

Insert template with export options, see example below.

`#+TITLE:`	the title to be shown (default is the buffer name)
`#+AUTHOR:`	the author (default taken from `user-full-name`)
`#+DATE:`	a date, fixed, or a format string for `format-time-string`
`#+EMAIL:`	his/her email address (default from `user-mail-address`)
`#+DESCRIPTION:`	the page description, e.g., for the XHTML meta tag
`#+KEYWORDS:`	the page keywords, e.g., for the XHTML meta tag
`#+LANGUAGE:`	language for HTML, e.g., 'en' (`org-export-default-language`)
`#+TEXT:`	Some descriptive text to be inserted at the beginning.
`#+TEXT:`	Several lines may be given.
`#+OPTIONS:`	H:2 num:t toc:t \n:nil @:t ::t |:t ^:t f:t TeX:t ...
`#+BIND:`	lisp-var lisp-val, e.g.: org-export-latex-low-levels itemize You need to confirm using these, or configure `org-export-allow-BIND`
`#+LINK_UP:`	the "up" link of an exported page
`#+LINK_HOME:`	the "home" link of an exported page
`#+LATEX_HEADER:`	extra line(s) for the LaTeX header, like \usepackage{xyz}
`#+EXPORT_SELECT_TAGS:`	Tags that select a tree for export
`#+EXPORT_EXCLUDE_TAGS:`	Tags that exclude a tree from export
`#+XSLT:`	the XSLT stylesheet used by DocBook exporter to generate FO file

The OPTIONS line is a compact[1] form to specify export settings. Here you can:

`H:`	set the number of headline levels for export
`num:`	turn on/off section-numbers
`toc:`	turn on/off table of contents, or set level limit (integer)
`\n:`	turn on/off line-break-preservation (DOES NOT WORK)
`@:`	turn on/off quoted HTML tags
`::`	turn on/off fixed-width sections
`|:`	turn on/off tables
`^:`	turn on/off TeX-like syntax for sub- and superscripts. If you write "^:{}", a_{b} will be interpreted, but the simple a_b will be left as it is.
`-:`	turn on/off conversion of special strings.
`f:`	turn on/off footnotes like this[1].
`todo:`	turn on/off inclusion of TODO keywords into exported text
`pri:`	turn on/off priority cookies
`tags:`	turn on/off inclusion of tags, may also be not-in-toc
`<:`	turn on/off inclusion of any time/date stamps like DEADLINES
`*:`	turn on/off emphasized text (bold, italic, underlined)
`TeX:`	turn on/off simple TeX macros in plain text
`LaTeX:`	configure export of LaTeX fragments. Default auto
`skip:`	turn on/off skipping the text before the first heading
`author:`	turn on/off inclusion of author name/email into exported file

---

[1] If you want to configure many options this way, you can use several OPTIONS lines.

email: turn on/off inclusion of author email into exported file
creator: turn on/off inclusion of creator info into exported file
timestamp: turn on/off inclusion creation time into exported file
d: turn on/off inclusion of drawers

These options take effect in both the HTML and LaTeX export, except for TeX and LaTeX, which are respectively t and nil for the LaTeX export.

When exporting only a single subtree by selecting it with C-c @ before calling an export command, the subtree can overrule some of the file's export settings with properties EXPORT_FILE_NAME, EXPORT_TITLE, EXPORT_TEXT, EXPORT_AUTHOR, EXPORT_DATE, and EXPORT_OPTIONS.

12.3 The export dispatcher

All export commands can be reached using the export dispatcher, which is a prefix key that prompts for an additional key specifying the command. Normally the entire file is exported, but if there is an active region that contains one outline tree, the first heading is used as document title and the subtrees are exported.

C-c C-e

Dispatcher for export and publishing commands. Displays a help-window listing the additional key(s) needed to launch an export or publishing command. The prefix arg is passed through to the exporter. A double prefix C-u C-u causes most commands to be executed in the background, in a separate Emacs process.[2]

C-c C-e v

Like C-c C-e, but only export the text that is currently visible (i.e., not hidden by outline visibility).

C-u C-u C-c C-e

Call the exporter, but reverse the setting of org-export-run-in-background, i.e., request background processing if not set, or force processing in the current Emacs process if set.

12.4 ASCII/Latin-1/UTF-8 export

ASCII export produces a simple and very readable version of an Org-mode file, containing only plain ASCII. Latin-1 and UTF-8 export augment the file with special characters and symbols available in these encodings.

C-c C-e a

Export as ASCII file. For an Org file, 'myfile.org', the ASCII file will be 'myfile.txt'. The file will be overwritten without warning. If there is an active region,[3] only the region will be exported. If the selected region is a single tree,[4] the tree head will become the document title. If the tree

---

[2] To make this behavior the default, customize the variable org-export-run-in-background.

[3] This requires transient-mark-mode be turned on.

[4] To select the current subtree, use C-c @.

head entry has or inherits an EXPORT_FILE_NAME property, that name will
be used for the export.

C-c C-e A
    Export to a temporary buffer. Do not create a file.

C-c C-e n   and   C-c C-e N
    Like the above commands, but use Latin-1 encoding.

C-c C-e u   and   C-c C-e U
    Like the above commands, but use UTF-8 encoding.

C-c C-e v a   and   C-c C-e v n   and   C-c C-e v u
    Export only the visible part of the document.

In the exported version, the first 3 outline levels will become headlines, defining a general document structure. Additional levels will be exported as itemized
lists. If you want that transition to occur at a different level, specify it with a
prefix argument. For example,

        C-1 C-c C-e a

creates only top level headlines and does the rest as items. When headlines are
converted to items, the indentation of the text following the headline is changed
to fit nicely under the item. This is done with the assumption that the first body
line indicates the base indentation of the body text. Any indentation larger than
this is adjusted to preserve the layout relative to the first line. Should there be
lines with less indentation than the first, these are left alone.

Links will be exported in a footnote-like style, with the descriptive part in
the text and the link in a note before the next heading. See the variable org-
export-ascii-links-to-notes for details and other options.

12.5 HTML export

Org-mode contains an HTML (XHTML 1.0 strict) exporter with extensive
HTML formatting, in ways similar to John Gruber's *markdown* language, but
with additional support for tables.

12.5.1 HTML export commands

C-c C-e h
    Export as HTML file 'myfile.html'. For an Org file 'myfile.org', the
    ASCII file will be 'myfile.html'. The file will be overwritten without
    warning. If there is an active region,[5] only the region will be exported.
    If the selected region is a single tree,[6] the tree head will become the
    document title. If the tree head entry has, or inherits, an EXPORT_FILE_
    NAME property, that name will be used for the export.

C-c C-e b
    Export as HTML file and immediately open it with a browser.

---

[5] This requires transient-mark-mode be turned on.

[6] To select the current subtree, use C-c @.

`C-c C-e H`
> Export to a temporary buffer. Do not create a file.

`C-c C-e R`
> Export the active region to a temporary buffer. With a prefix argument, do not produce the file header and footer, but just the plain HTML section for the region. This is good for cut-and-paste operations.

`C-c C-e v h`
`C-c C-e v b`
`C-c C-e v H`
`C-c C-e v R`
> Export only the visible part of the document.

`M-x org-export-region-as-html`
> Convert the region to HTML under the assumption that it was Org-mode syntax before. This is a global command that can be invoked in any buffer.

`M-x org-replace-region-by-HTML`
> Replace the active region (assumed to be in Org-mode syntax) by HTML code.

In the exported version, the first 3 outline levels will become headlines, defining a general document structure. Additional levels will be exported as itemized lists. If you want that transition to occur at a different level, specify it with a numeric prefix argument. For example,

> `C-2 C-c C-e b`

creates two levels of headings and does the rest as items.

12.5.2 Quoting HTML tags

Plain '<' and '>' are always transformed to '<' and '>' in HTML export. If you want to include simple HTML tags which should be interpreted as such, mark them with '@' as in '@bold text@'. Note that this really works only for simple tags. For more extensive HTML that should be copied verbatim to the exported file use either

> `#+HTML: Literal HTML code for export`

or

> `#+BEGIN_HTML`
> `All lines between these markers are exported literally`
> `#+END_HTML`

12.5.3 Links in HTML export

Internal links (see Section 4.2 [Internal links], page 31) will continue to work in HTML. This includes automatic links created by radio targets (see Section 4.2.1 [Radio targets], page 32). Links to external files will still work if the target file is on the same *relative* path as the published Org file. Links to other '.org' files will be translated into HTML links under the assumption that an HTML version also exists of the linked file, at the same relative path. 'id:' links can then be used to jump to specific entries across files. For information related to linking files while publishing them to a publishing directory see Section 13.1.6 [Publishing links], page 158.

If you want to specify attributes for links, you can do so using a special #+ATTR_HTML line to define attributes that will be added to the <a> or <img> tags. Here is an example that sets title and style attributes for a link:

```
#+ATTR_HTML: title="The Org-mode homepage" style="color:red;"
[[http://orgmode.org]]
```

12.5.4 Tables

Org-mode tables are exported to HTML using the table tag defined in org-export-html-table-tag. The default setting makes tables without cell borders and frame. If you would like to change this for individual tables, place something like the following before the table:

```
#+CAPTION: This is a table with lines around and between cells
#+ATTR_HTML: border="2" rules="all" frame="all"
```

12.5.5 Images in HTML export

HTML export can inline images given as links in the Org file, and it can make an image the clickable part of a link. By default,[7] images are inlined if a link does not have a description. So '[[file:myimg.jpg]]' will be inlined, while '[[file:myimg.jpg][the image]]' will just produce a link 'the image' that points to the image. If the description part itself is a file: link or a http: URL pointing to an image, this image will be inlined and activated so that clicking on the image will activate the link. For example, to include a thumbnail that will link to a high resolution version of the image, you could use:

```
[[file:highres.jpg][file:thumb.jpg]]
```

If you need to add attributes to an inlined image, use a #+ATTR_HTML. In the example below we specify the alt and title attributes to support text viewers and accessibility, and align it to the right.

```
#+CAPTION: A black cat stalking a spider
#+ATTR_HTML: alt="cat/spider image" title="Action!" align="right"
[[./img/a.jpg]]
```

and you could use http addresses just as well.

---

[7] But see the variable org-export-html-inline-images.

12.5.6 Math formatting in HTML export

LaTeX math snippets (see Section 11.7.3 [LaTeX fragments], page 130) can be displayed in two different ways on HTML pages. The default is to use the MathJax system (http://www.mathjax.org) which should work out of the box with Org mode installation because http://orgmode.org serves 'MathJax' for Org-mode users for small applications and for testing purposes. **If you plan to use this regularly or on pages with significant page views, you should install MathJax on your own server in order to limit the load of our server.** To configure 'MathJax', use the variable org-export-html-mathjax-options or insert something like the following into the buffer:

    #+MATHJAX: align:"left" mathml:t path:"/MathJax/MathJax.js"

See the docstring of the variable org-export-html-mathjax-options for the meaning of the parameters in this line.

If you prefer, you can also request that LaTeX fragments are processed into small images that will be inserted into the browser page. Before the availability of MathJax, this was the default method for Org files. This method requires that the 'dvipng' program is available on your system. You can still get this processing with

    #+OPTIONS: LaTeX:dvipng

12.5.7 Text areas in HTML export

An alternative way to publish literal code examples in HTML is to use text areas, where the example can even be edited before pasting it into an application. It is triggered by a -t switch at an example or src block. Using this switch disables any options for syntax and label highlighting, and line numbering, which may be present. You may also use -h and -w switches to specify the height and width of the text area, which default to the number of lines in the example, and 80, respectively. For example

    #+BEGIN_EXAMPLE -t -w 40
    (defun org-xor (a b)
      "Exclusive or."
      (if a (not b) b))
    #+END_EXAMPLE

12.5.8 CSS support

You can also give style information for the exported file. The HTML exporter assigns the following special CSS classes[8] to appropriate parts of the document—your style specifications may change these, in addition to any of the standard classes like for headlines, tables, etc.

p.author	author information, including email
p.date	publishing date
p.creator	creator info, about org-mode version

---

[8] If the classes on TODO keywords and tags lead to conflicts, use the variables org-export-html-todo-kwd-class-prefix and org-export-html-tag-class-prefix to make them unique.

`.title`	document title
`.todo`	TODO keywords, all not-done states
`.done`	the DONE keywords, all states that count as done
`.WAITING`	each TODO keyword also uses a class named after itself
`.timestamp`	timestamp
`.timestamp-kwd`	keyword associated with a timestamp, like SCHEDULED
`.timestamp-wrapper`	span around keyword plus timestamp
`.tag`	tag in a headline
`._HOME`	each tag uses itself as a class, "@" replaced by "_"
`.target`	target for links
`.linenr`	the line number in a code example
`.code-highlighted`	for highlighting referenced code lines
`div.outline-N`	div for outline level N (headline plus text))
`div.outline-text-N`	extra div for text at outline level N
`.section-number-N`	section number in headlines, different for each level
`div.figure`	how to format an inlined image
`pre.src`	formatted source code
`pre.example`	normal example
`p.verse`	verse paragraph
`div.footnotes`	footnote section headline
`p.footnote`	footnote definition paragraph, containing a footnote
`.footref`	a footnote reference number (always a <sup>)
`.footnum`	footnote number in footnote definition (always <sup>)

Each exported file contains a compact default style that defines these classes in a basic way.[9] You may overwrite these settings, or add to them by using the variables `org-export-html-style` (for Org-wide settings) and `org-export-html-style-extra` (for more fine-grained settings, like file-local settings). To set the latter variable individually for each file, you can use

```
#+STYLE: <link rel="stylesheet" type="text/css" \(10)
          href="stylesheet.css" />
```

For longer style definitions, you can use several such lines. You could also directly write a <style> </style> section in this way, without referring to an external file.

---

[9] This style is defined in the constant `org-export-html-style-default`, which you should not modify. To turn inclusion of these defaults off, customize `org-export-html-style-include-default`

[10] Please note that the STYLE definition must be on a single line—it is wrapped here only because of formatting constraints.

In order to add styles to a subtree, use the :HTML_CONTAINER_CLASS: property to assign a class to the tree. In order to specify CSS styles for a particular headline, you can use the id specified in a :CUSTOM_ID: property.

12.5.9 JavaScript supported display of web pages

Sebastian Rose has written a JavaScript program especially designed to enhance the web viewing experience of HTML files created with Org. This program allows you to view large files in two different ways. The first one is an *Info*-like mode where each section is displayed separately and navigation can be done with the n and p keys (and some other keys as well, press ? for an overview of the available keys). The second view type is a *folding* view much like Org provides inside Emacs. The script is available at http://orgmode.org/org-info.js and you can find the documentation for it at http://orgmode.org/worg/code/org-info-js/. We host the script at our site, but if you use it a lot, you might not want to be dependent on orgmode.org and prefer to install a local copy on your own web server.

To use the script, you need to make sure that the 'org-jsinfo.el' module gets loaded. It should be loaded by default, but you can try M-x customize-variable (RET) org-modules (RET) to convince yourself that this is indeed the case. All it then takes to make use of the program is adding a single line to the Org file:

    #+INFOJS_OPT: view:info toc:nil

If this line is found, the HTML header will automatically contain the code needed to invoke the script. Using the line above, you can set the following viewing options:

path:
> The path to the script. The default is to grab the script from http://orgmode.org/org-info.js, but you might want to have a local copy and use a path like '../scripts/org-info.js'.

view:
> Initial view when website is first shown. Possible values are:

> | info | Info-like interface with one section per page. |
> | overview | Folding interface, initially showing only top-level. |
> | content | Folding interface, starting with all headlines visible. |
> | showall | Folding interface, all headlines and text visible. |

sdepth:
> Maximum headline level that will still become an independent section for info and folding modes. The default is taken from org-export-headline-levels (= the H switch in #+OPTIONS). If this is smaller than in org-export-headline-levels, each info/folding section can still contain child headlines.

toc:
> Should the table of contents *initially* be visible? Even when nil, you can always get to the "toc" with i.

tdepth:
> The depth of the table of contents. The defaults are taken from the variables `org-export-headline-levels` and `org-export-with-toc`.

ftoc:
> Does the CSS of the page specify a fixed position for the "toc"? If yes, the toc will never be displayed as a section.

ltoc:
> Should there be short contents (children) in each section? Make this above if the section should be above initial text.

mouse:
> Headings are highlighted when the mouse is over them. Should be 'underline' (default) or a background color like '#cccccc'.

buttons:
> Should view-toggle buttons be everywhere? When `nil` (the default), only one such button will be present.

You can choose default values for these options by customizing the variable `org-infojs-options`. If you always want to apply the script to your pages, configure the variable `org-export-html-use-infojs`.

12.6 LATEX and PDF export

Org-mode contains a LATEX exporter written by Bastien Guerry. With further processing,[11] this backend is also used to produce PDF output. Since the LATEX output uses 'hyperref' to implement links and cross references, the PDF output file will be fully linked.

12.6.1 LATEX export commands

C-c C-e l
> Export as LATEX file 'myfile.tex'. For an Org file 'myfile.org', the ASCII file will be 'myfile.tex'. The file will be overwritten without warning. If there is an active region,[12] only the region will be exported. If the selected region is a single tree,[13] the tree head will become the document title. If the tree head entry has or inherits an EXPORT_FILE_NAME property, that name will be used for the export.

C-c C-e L
> Export to a temporary buffer. Do not create a file.

---

[11] The default LATEX output is designed for processing with pdftex or latex. It includes packages that are not compatible with xetex and possibly luatex. See the variables `org-export-latex-default-packages-alist` and `org-export-latex-packages-alist`.

[12] This requires transient-mark-mode be turned on.

[13] To select the current subtree, use C-c @.

`C-c C-e v l`

`C-c C-e v L`

> Export only the visible part of the document.

`M-x org-export-region-as-latex`

> Convert the region to LaTeX under the assumption that it was Org-mode syntax before. This is a global command that can be invoked in any buffer.

`M-x org-replace-region-by-latex`

> Replace the active region (assumed to be in Org-mode syntax) by LaTeX code.

`C-c C-e p`

> Export as LaTeX and then process to PDF.

`C-c C-e d`

> Export as LaTeX and then process to PDF, then open the resulting PDF file.

In the exported version, the first 3 outline levels will become headlines, defining a general document structure. Additional levels will be exported as description lists. The exporter can ignore them or convert them to a custom string depending on `org-latex-low-levels`.

If you want that transition to occur at a different level, specify it with a numeric prefix argument. For example,

`C-2 C-c C-e l`

creates two levels of headings and does the rest as items.

12.6.2 Header and sectioning structure

By default, the LaTeX output uses the class `article`.

You can change this globally by setting a different value for `org-export-latex-default-class` or locally by adding an option like `#+LaTeX_CLASS: myclass` in your file, or with a `:LaTeX_CLASS:` property that applies when exporting a region containing only this (sub)tree. The class must be listed in `org-export-latex-classes`. This variable defines a header template for each class,[14] and allows you to define the sectioning structure for each class. You can also define your own classes there. `#+LaTeX_CLASS_OPTIONS` or a `LaTeX_CLASS_OPTIONS` property can specify the options for the `\documentclass` macro. You can also use `#+LATEX_HEADER: \usepackage{xyz}` to add lines to the header. See the docstring of `org-export-latex-classes` for more information.

---

[14] Into which the values of `org-export-latex-default-packages-alist` and `org-export-latex-packages-alist` are spliced.

12.6.3 Quoting LATEX code

Embedded LATEX as described in Section 11.7 [Embedded LaTeX], page 129, will be correctly inserted into the LATEX file. This includes simple macros like '\ref{LABEL}' to create a cross reference to a figure. Furthermore, you can add special code that should only be present in LATEX export with the following constructs:

```
#+LaTeX: Literal LaTeX code for export
```

or

```
#+BEGIN_LaTeX
All lines between these markers are exported literally
#+END_LaTeX
```

12.6.4 Tables in LATEX export

For LATEX export of a table, you can specify a label and a caption (see Section 11.2 [Images and tables], page 125). You can also use the ATTR_LaTeX line to request a longtable environment for the table, so that it may span several pages, or provide the multicolumn keyword that will make the table span the page in a multicolumn environment (table* environment). Finally, you can set the alignment string:

```
#+CAPTION: A long table
#+LABEL: tbl:long
#+ATTR_LaTeX: longtable align=l|lp{3cm}r|l
| ..... | ..... |
| ..... | ..... |
```

12.6.5 Images in LATEX export

Images that are linked to without a description part in the link, like '[[file:img.jpg]]' or '[[./img.jpg]]' will be inserted into the PDF output file resulting from LATEX processing. Org will use an \includegraphics macro to insert the image. If you have specified a caption and/or a label as described in Section 11.2 [Images and tables], page 125, the figure will be wrapped into a figure environment and thus become a floating element. You can use an #+ATTR_LaTeX: line to specify the various options that can be used in the optional argument of the \includegraphics macro. To modify the placement option of the figure environment, add something like 'placement=[h!]' to the Attributes.

If you would like to let text flow around the image, add the word 'wrap' to the #+ATTR_LaTeX: line, which will make the figure occupy the left half of the page. To fine-tune, the placement field will be the set of additional arguments needed by the wrapfigure environment. Note that if you change the size of the image, you need to use compatible settings for \includegraphics and wrapfigure.

```
#+CAPTION:  The black-body emission of the disk around HR 4049
#+LABEL:    fig:SED-HR4049
#+ATTR_LaTeX: width=5cm,angle=90
[[./img/sed-hr4049.pdf]]
```

```
#+ATTR_LaTeX: width=0.38\textwidth wrap \(15)
              placement={r}{0.4\textwidth}
[[./img/hst.png]]
```

If you need references to a label created in this way, write '\ref{fig:SED-HR4049}' just like in LaTeX.

12.6.6 Beamer class export

The LaTeX class 'beamer' allows production of high quality presentations using LaTeX and pdf processing. Org-mode has special support for turning an Org-mode file or tree into a 'beamer' presentation.

When the LaTeX class for the current buffer (as set with #+LaTeX_CLASS: beamer) or subtree (set with a LaTeX_CLASS property) is beamer, a special export mode will turn the file or tree into a beamer presentation. Any tree with not-too-deep level nesting should in principle be exportable as a beamer presentation. By default, the top-level entries (or the first level below the selected subtree heading) will be turned into frames, and the outline structure below this level will become itemize lists. You can also configure the variable org-beamer-frame-level to a different level—then the hierarchy above frames will produce the sectioning structure of the presentation.

A template for useful in-buffer settings or properties can be inserted into the buffer with M-x org-insert-beamer-options-template. Among other things, this will install a column view format which is very handy for editing special properties used by beamer.

You can influence the structure of the presentation using the following properties:

BEAMER_env

> The environment that should be used to format this entry. Valid environments are defined in the constant org-beamer-environments-default, and you can define more in org-beamer-environments-extra. If this property is set, the entry will also get a :B_environment: tag to make this visible. This tag has no semantic meaning, it is only a visual aid.

BEAMER_envargs

> The beamer-special arguments that should be used for the environment, like [t] or [<+->] of <2-3>. If the BEAMER_col property is also set, something like C[t] can be added here as well to set an options argument for the implied columns environment. c[t] will set an option for the implied column environment.

BEAMER_col

> The width of a column that should start with this entry. If this property is set, the entry will also get a :BMCOL: property to make this visible. Also this tag is only a visual aid. When this is a plain number, it will be interpreted as a fraction of \textwidth. Otherwise it will be assumed

---

(15) Please note that the ATTR_LaTeX definition must be on a single line—it is wrapped here only because of formatting constraints.

that you have specified the units, like '3cm'. The first such property in a frame will start a columns environment to surround the columns. This environment is closed when an entry has a BEAMER_col property with value 0 or 1, or automatically at the end of the frame.

BEAMER_extra

Additional commands that should be inserted after the environment has been opened. For example, when creating a frame, this can be used to specify transitions.

Frames will automatically receive a fragile option if they contain source code that uses the verbatim environment. Special 'beamer' specific code can be inserted using #+BEAMER: and #+BEGIN_beamer...#+end_beamer constructs, similar to other export backends, but with the difference that #+LaTeX: stuff will be included in the presentation as well.

Outline nodes with BEAMER_env property value 'note' or 'noteNH' will be formatted as beamer notes, i,e, they will be wrapped into \note{...}. The former will include the heading as part of the note text, the latter will ignore the heading of that node. To simplify note generation, it is actually enough to mark the note with a *tag* (either :B_note: or :B_noteNH:) instead of creating the BEAMER_env property.

You can turn on a special minor mode org-beamer-mode for editing support with

> #+STARTUP: beamer

C-c C-b

In org-beamer-mode, this key offers fast selection of a beamer environment or the BEAMER_col property.

Column view provides a great way to set the environment of a node and other important parameters. Make sure you are using a COLUMN format that is geared toward this special purpose. The command M-x org-insert-beamer-options-template defines such a format.

Here is a simple example Org document that is intended for beamer export.

```
#+LaTeX_CLASS: beamer
#+TITLE: Example Presentation
#+AUTHOR: Carsten Dominik
#+LaTeX_CLASS_OPTIONS: [presentation]
#+BEAMER_FRAME_LEVEL: 2
#+BEAMER_HEADER_EXTRA: \usetheme{Madrid}\usecolortheme{default}
#+COLUMNS: %35ITEM %10BEAMER_env(Env) %10BEAMER_envargs(Args) \(16)
          %4BEAMER_col(Col) %8BEAMER_extra(Ex)

* This is the first structural section

** Frame 1 \\ with a subtitle
```

---

(16) Please note that the COLUMNS definition must be on a single line—it is wrapped here only because of formatting constraints.

```
*** Thanks to Eric Fraga                          :BMCOL:B_block:
    :PROPERTIES:
    :BEAMER_env: block
    :BEAMER_envargs: C[t]
    :BEAMER_col: 0.5
    :END:
    for the first viable beamer setup in Org
*** Thanks to everyone else                       :BMCOL:B_block:
    :PROPERTIES:
    :BEAMER_col: 0.5
    :BEAMER_env: block
    :BEAMER_envargs: <2->
    :END:
    for contributing to the discussion
**** This will be formatted as a beamer note            :B_note:
** Frame 2 \\ where we will not use columns
*** Request                                           :B_block:
    Please test this stuff!
    :PROPERTIES:
    :BEAMER_env: block
    :END:
```

For more information, see the documentation on Worg.

12.7 DocBook export

Org contains a DocBook exporter written by Baoqiu Cui. Once an Org file is exported to DocBook format, it can be further processed to produce other formats, including PDF, HTML, man pages, etc., using many available DocBook tools and stylesheets.

Currently DocBook exporter only supports DocBook V5.0.

12.7.1 DocBook export commands

C-c C-e D
   Export as DocBook file. For an Org file, 'myfile.org', the DocBook XML file will be 'myfile.xml'. The file will be overwritten without warning. If there is an active region,[17] only the region will be exported. If the selected region is a single tree,[18] the tree head will become the document title. If the tree head entry has, or inherits, an EXPORT_FILE_NAME property, that name will be used for the export.

C-c C-e V
   Export as DocBook file, process to PDF, then open the resulting PDF file.

---

[17] This requires transient-mark-mode to be turned on
[18] To select the current subtree, use C-c @.

Note that, in order to produce PDF output based on exported DocBook file, you need to have XSLT processor and XSL-FO processor software installed on your system. Check variables `org-export-docbook-xslt-proc-command` and `org-export-docbook-xsl-fo-proc-command`.

The stylesheet argument `%s` in variable `org-export-docbook-xslt-proc-command` is replaced by the value of variable `org-export-docbook-xslt-stylesheet`, which needs to be set by the user. You can also overrule this global setting on a per-file basis by adding an in-buffer setting `#+XSLT:` to the Org file.

C-c C-e v D
Export only the visible part of the document.

12.7.2 Quoting DocBook code

You can quote DocBook code in Org files and copy it verbatim into exported DocBook file with the following constructs:

```
#+DOCBOOK: Literal DocBook code for export
```

or

```
#+BEGIN_DOCBOOK
All lines between these markers are exported by DocBook
exporter literally.
#+END_DOCBOOK
```

For example, you can use the following lines to include a DocBook warning admonition. As to what this warning says, you should pay attention to the document context when quoting DocBook code in Org files. You may make exported DocBook XML files invalid by not quoting DocBook code correctly.

```
#+BEGIN_DOCBOOK
<warning>
  <para>You should know what you are doing when quoting
  DocBook XML code in your Org file. Invalid DocBook XML may
  be generated by DocBook exporter if you are not
  careful!</para>
</warning>
#+END_DOCBOOK
```

12.7.3 Recursive sections

DocBook exporter exports Org files as articles using the `article` element in DocBook. Recursive sections, i.e., `section` elements, are used in exported articles. Top level headlines in Org files are exported as top level sections, and lower level headlines are exported as nested sections. The entire structure of Org files will be exported completely, no matter how many nested levels of headlines there are.

Using recursive sections makes it easy to port and reuse exported DocBook code in other DocBook document types like `book` or `set`.

12.7.4 Tables in DocBook export

Tables in Org files are exported as HTML tables, which have been supported since DocBook V4.3.

If a table does not have a caption, an informal table is generated using the `informaltable` element; otherwise, a formal table will be generated using the `table` element.

12.7.5 Images in DocBook export

Images that are linked to without a description part in the link, like '`[[file:img.jpg]]`' or '`[[./img.jpg]]`', will be exported to DocBook using `mediaobject` elements. Each `mediaobject` element contains an `imageobject` that wraps an `imagedata` element. If you have specified a caption for an image as described in Section 11.2 [Images and tables], page 125, a `caption` element will be added in `mediaobject`. If a label is also specified, it will be exported as an `xml:id` attribute of the `mediaobject` element.

Image attributes supported by the `imagedata` element, like `align` or `width`, can be specified in two ways: you can either customize variable `org-export-docbook-default-image-attributes` or use the `#+ATTR_DOCBOOK:` line. Attributes specified in variable `org-export-docbook-default-image-attributes` are applied to all inline images in the Org file to be exported (unless they are overridden by image attributes specified in `#+ATTR_DOCBOOK:` lines).

The `#+ATTR_DOCBOOK:` line can be used to specify additional image attributes or override default image attributes for individual images. If the same attribute appears in both the `#+ATTR_DOCBOOK:` line and variable `org-export-docbook-default-image-attributes`, the former takes precedence. Here is an example about how image attributes can be set:

```
#+CAPTION:    The logo of Org-mode
#+LABEL:      unicorn-svg
#+ATTR_DOCBOOK: scalefit="1" width="100%" depth="100%"
[[./img/org-mode-unicorn.svg]]
```

By default, DocBook exporter recognizes the following image file types: 'jpeg', 'jpg', 'png', 'gif', and 'svg'. You can customize variable `org-export-docbook-inline-image-extensions` to add more types to this list as long as DocBook supports them.

12.7.6 Special characters in DocBook export

Special characters that are written in TeX-like syntax, such as `\alpha`, `\Gamma`, and `\Zeta`, are supported by DocBook exporter. These characters are rewritten to XML entities, like `&alpha;`, `&Gamma;`, and `&Zeta;`, based on the list saved in variable `org-entities`. As long as the generated DocBook file includes the corresponding entities, these special characters are recognized.

You can customize variable `org-export-docbook-doctype` to include the entities you need. For example, you can set variable `org-export-docbook-doctype` to the following value to recognize all special characters included in XHTML entities:

```
"<!DOCTYPE article [
<!ENTITY % xhtml1-symbol PUBLIC
\"-//W3C//ENTITIES Symbol for HTML//EN//XML\"
\"http://www.w3.org/2003/entities/2007/xhtml1-symbol.ent\"
>
%xhtml1-symbol;
]>
"
```

12.8 TaskJuggler export

TaskJuggler (http://www.taskjuggler.org/) is a project management tool. It provides an optimizing scheduler that computes your project time lines and resource assignments based on the project outline and the constraints that you have provided.

The TaskJuggler exporter is a bit different from other exporters, such as the HTML and LaTeX exporters for example, in that it does not export all the nodes of a document or strictly follow the order of the nodes in the document.

Instead the TaskJuggler exporter looks for a tree that defines the tasks and a optionally tree that defines the resources for this project. It then creates a TaskJuggler file based on these trees and the attributes defined in all the nodes.

12.8.1 TaskJuggler export commands

C-c C-e j
> Export as TaskJuggler file.

C-c C-e J
> Export as TaskJuggler file and then open the file with TaskJugglerUI.

12.8.2 Tasks

Create your tasks as you usually do with Org-mode. Assign efforts to each task using properties (it's easiest to do this in the column view). You should end up with something similar to the example by Peter Jones.[19] Now mark the top node of your tasks with a tag named :taskjuggler_project: (or whatever you customized org-export-taskjuggler-project-tag to). You are now ready to export the project plan with C-c C-e J which will export the project plan and open a Gantt chart in TaskJugglerUI.

---

[19] http://www.contextualdevelopment.com/static/artifacts/articles/2008/project-planning/project-planning.org.

12.8.3 Resources

Next you can define resources and assign those to work on specific tasks. You can group your resources hierarchically. Tag the top node of the resources with :taskjuggler_resource: (or whatever you customized org-export-taskjuggler-resource-tag to). You can optionally assign an identifier (named 'resource_id') to the resources (using the standard Org properties commands, see Section 7.1 [Property syntax], page 59) or you can let the exporter generate identifiers automatically (the exporter picks the first word of the headline as the identifier as long as it is unique—see the documentation of org-taskjuggler-get-unique-id). Using that identifier you can then allocate resources to tasks. This is again done with the 'allocate' property on the tasks. Do this in column view or when on the task type C-c C-x p allocate (RET) <resource_id> (RET).

Once the allocations are done you can again export to TaskJuggler and check in the Resource Allocation Graph which person is working on what task at what time.

12.8.4 Export of properties

The exporter also takes TODO state information into consideration, i.e., if a task is marked as done it will have the corresponding attribute in TaskJuggler ('complete 100'). Also it will export any property on a task resource or resource node which is known to TaskJuggler, such as 'limits', 'vacation', 'shift', 'booking', 'efficiency', 'journalentry', 'rate' for resources or 'account', 'start', 'note', 'duration', 'end', 'journalentry', 'milestone', 'reference', 'responsible', 'scheduling', etc for tasks.

12.8.5 Dependencies

The exporter will handle dependencies that are defined in the tasks either with the 'ORDERED' attribute (see Section 5.2.7 [TODO dependencies], page 45), with the 'BLOCKER' attribute (see 'org-depend.el') or alternatively with a 'depends' attribute. Both the 'BLOCKER' and the 'depends' attribute can be either 'previous-sibling' or a reference to an identifier (named 'task_id') which is defined for another task in the project. 'BLOCKER' and the 'depends' attribute can define multiple dependencies separated by either space or comma. You can also specify optional attributes on the dependency by simply appending it. The following examples should illustrate this:

```
* Preparation
  :PROPERTIES:
  :task_id:  preparation
  :ORDERED:  t
  :END:
* Training material
  :PROPERTIES:
  :task_id:  training_material
  :ORDERED:  t
  :END:
** Markup Guidelines
```

```
:PROPERTIES:
:Effort:    2.0
:END:
** Workflow Guidelines
:PROPERTIES:
:Effort:    2.0
:END:
* Presentation
:PROPERTIES:
:Effort:    2.0
:BLOCKER:   training_material { gapduration 1d } preparation
:END:
```

12.8.6 Reports

TaskJuggler can produce many kinds of reports (e.g., Gantt chart, resource allocation, etc). The user defines what kind of reports should be generated for a project in the TaskJuggler file. The exporter will automatically insert some default reports in the file. These defaults are defined in `org-export-taskjuggler-default-reports`. They can be modified using customize along with a number of other options. For a more complete list, see `M-x customize-group` RET `org-export-taskjuggler` RET.

For more information and examples see the Org-taskjuggler tutorial at `http://orgmode.org/worg/org-tutorials/org-taskjuggler.php`.

12.9 Freemind export

The Freemind exporter was written by Lennart Borgman.

`C-c C-e m`
    Export as Freemind mind map 'myfile.mm'.

12.10 XOXO export

Org-mode contains an exporter that produces XOXO-style output. Currently, this exporter only handles the general outline structure and does not interpret any additional Org-mode features.

`C-c C-e x`
    Export as XOXO file 'myfile.html'.

`C-c C-e v x`
    Export only the visible part of the document.

12.11 iCalendar export

Some people use Org-mode for keeping track of projects, but still prefer a standard calendar application for anniversaries and appointments. In this case it can be useful to show deadlines and other time-stamped items in Org files in the calendar application. Org-mode can export calendar information in the standard iCalendar format. If you also want to have TODO entries included in the export, configure the variable `org-icalendar-include-todo`. Plain timestamps are exported as VEVENT, and TODO items as VTODO. It will also create events from deadlines that are in non-TODO items. Deadlines and scheduling dates in TODO items will be used to set the start and due dates for the TODO entry.[20] As categories, it will use the tags locally defined in the heading, and the file/tree category.[21] See the variable `org-icalendar-alarm-time` for a way to assign alarms to entries with a time.

The iCalendar standard requires each entry to have a globally unique identifier (UID). Org creates these identifiers during export. If you set the variable `org-icalendar-store-UID`, the UID will be stored in the `:ID:` property of the entry and re-used next time you report this entry. Since a single entry can give rise to multiple iCalendar entries (as a timestamp, a deadline, a scheduled item, and as a TODO item), Org adds prefixes to the UID, depending on what triggered the inclusion of the entry. In this way the UID remains unique, but a synchronization program can still figure out from which entry all the different instances originate.

`C-c C-e i`

Create iCalendar entries for the current file and store them in the same directory, using a file extension '.ics'.

`C-c C-e I`

Like C-c C-e i, but do this for all files in `org-agenda-files`. For each of these files, a separate iCalendar file will be written.

`C-c C-e c`

Create a single large iCalendar file from all files in `org-agenda-files` and write it to the file given by `org-combined-agenda-icalendar-file`.

The export will honor SUMMARY, DESCRIPTION and LOCATION[22] properties if the selected entries have them. If not, the summary will be derived from the headline, and the description from the body (limited to `org-icalendar-include-body` characters).

How this calendar is best read and updated, depends on the application you are using. The FAQ covers this issue.

---

[20] See the variables `org-icalendar-use-deadline` and `org-icalendar-use-scheduled`.

[21] To add inherited tags or the TODO state, configure the variable `org-icalendar-categories`.

[22] The LOCATION property can be inherited from higher in the hierarchy if you configure `org-use-property-inheritance` accordingly.

13 Publishing

Org includes a publishing management system that allows you to configure automatic HTML conversion of *projects* composed of interlinked org files. You can also configure Org to automatically upload your exported HTML pages and related attachments, such as images and source code files, to a web server.

You can also use Org to convert files into PDF, or even combine HTML and PDF conversion so that files are available in both formats on the server.

Publishing has been contributed to Org by David O'Toole.

13.1 Configuration

Publishing needs significant configuration to specify files, destination and many other properties of a project.

13.1.1 The variable `org-publish-project-alist`

Publishing is configured almost entirely through setting the value of one variable, called `org-publish-project-alist`. Each element of the list configures one project, and may be in one of the two following forms:

> ("project-name" :property value :property value ...)

i.e., a well-formed property list with alternating keys and values

> or

> ("project-name" :components ("project-name" "project-name" ...))

In both cases, projects are configured by specifying property values. A project defines the set of files that will be published, as well as the publishing configuration to use when publishing those files. When a project takes the second form listed above, the individual members of the :components property are taken to be sub-projects, which group together files requiring different publishing options. When you publish such a "meta-project", all the components will also be published, in the sequence given.

13.1.2 Sources and destinations for files

Most properties are optional, but some should always be set. In particular, Org needs to know where to look for source files, and where to put published files.

`:base-directory`
> Directory containing publishing source files

`:publishing-directory`
> Directory where output files will be published. You can directly publish to a webserver using a file name syntax appropriate for the Emacs 'tramp' package. Or you can publish to a local directory and use external tools to upload your website (see Section 13.2 [Uploading files], page 160).

`:preparation-function`
>   Function or list of functions to be called before starting the publishing process, for example, to run make for updating files to be published. The project property list is scoped into this call as the variable `project-plist`.

`:completion-function`
>   Function or list of functions called after finishing the publishing process, for example, to change permissions of the resulting files. The project property list is scoped into this call as the variable `project-plist`.

13.1.3 Selecting files

By default, all files with extension '`.org`' in the base directory are considered part of the project. This can be modified by setting the properties

`:base-extension`
>   Extension (without the dot!) of source files. This actually is a regular expression. Set this to the symbol any if you want to get all files in `:base-directory`, even without extension.

`:exclude`
>   Regular expression to match file names that should not be published, even though they have been selected on the basis of their extension.

`:include`
>   List of files to be included regardless of `:base-extension` and `:exclude`.

13.1.4 Publishing action

Publishing means that a file is copied to the destination directory and possibly transformed in the process. The default transformation is to export Org files as HTML files, and this is done by the function `org-publish-org-to-html` which calls the HTML exporter (see Section 12.5 [HTML export], page 136). But you also can publish your content as PDF files using `org-publish-org-to-pdf`, or as ascii, latin1 or utf8 encoded files using the corresponding functions. If you want to publish the Org file itself, but with *archived, commented,* and *tag-excluded* trees removed, use `org-publish-org-to-org` and set the parameters `:plain-source` and/or `:htmlized-source`. This will produce '`file.org`' and '`file.org.html`' in the publishing directory.[1] Other files like images only need to be copied to the publishing destination; for this you may use `org-publish-attachment`. For non-Org files, you always need to specify the publishing function:

`:publishing-function`
>   Function executing the publication of a file. This may also be a list of functions, which will all be called in turn.

---

[1] '`file-source.org`' and '`file-source.org.html`' if source and publishing directories are equal. Note that with this kind of setup, you need to add `:exclude "-source\\.org"` to the project definition in `org-publish-project-alist` to prevent the published source files from being considered as new org files the next time the project is published.

`:plain-source`
> Non-nil means, publish plain source.

`:htmlized-source`
> Non-nil means, publish htmlized source.

The function must accept three arguments: a property list containing at least a `:publishing-directory` property, the name of the file to be published, and the path to the publishing directory of the output file. It should take the specified file, make the necessary transformation (if any) and place the result into the destination folder.

13.1.5 Options for the HTML/LATEX exporters

The property list can be used to set many export options for the HTML and LATEX exporters. In most cases, these properties correspond to user variables in Org. The table below lists these properties along with the variable they belong to. See the documentation string for the respective variable for details.

`:link-up`	`org-export-html-link-up`
`:link-home`	`org-export-html-link-home`
`:language`	`org-export-default-language`
`:customtime`	`org-display-custom-times`
`:headline-levels`	`org-export-headline-levels`
`:section-numbers`	`org-export-with-section-numbers`
`:section-number-format`	`org-export-section-number-format`
`:table-of-contents`	`org-export-with-toc`
`:preserve-breaks`	`org-export-preserve-breaks`
`:archived-trees`	`org-export-with-archived-trees`
`:emphasize`	`org-export-with-emphasize`
`:sub-superscript`	`org-export-with-sub-superscripts`
`:special-strings`	`org-export-with-special-strings`
`:footnotes`	`org-export-with-footnotes`
`:drawers`	`org-export-with-drawers`
`:tags`	`org-export-with-tags`
`:todo-keywords`	`org-export-with-todo-keywords`
`:priority`	`org-export-with-priority`
`:TeX-macros`	`org-export-with-TeX-macros`
`:LaTeX-fragments`	`org-export-with-LaTeX-fragments`
`:latex-listings`	`org-export-latex-listings`
`:skip-before-1st-heading`	`org-export-skip-text-before-1st-heading`
`:fixed-width`	`org-export-with-fixed-width`
`:timestamps`	`org-export-with-timestamps`
`:author-info`	`org-export-author-info`
`:email-info`	`org-export-email-info`
`:creator-info`	`org-export-creator-info`
`:tables`	`org-export-with-tables`
`:table-auto-headline`	`org-export-highlight-first-table-line`
`:style-include-default`	`org-export-html-style-include-default`
`:style`	`org-export-html-style`
`:style-extra`	`org-export-html-style-extra`

`:convert-org-links`	`org-export-html-link-org-files-as-html`
`:inline-images`	`org-export-html-inline-images`
`:html-extension`	`org-export-html-extension`
`:xml-declaration`	`org-export-html-xml-declaration`
`:html-table-tag`	`org-export-html-table-tag`
`:expand-quoted-html`	`org-export-html-expand`
`:timestamp`	`org-export-html-with-timestamp`
`:publishing-directory`	`org-export-publishing-directory`
`:preamble`	`org-export-html-preamble`
`:postamble`	`org-export-html-postamble`
`:auto-preamble`	`org-export-html-auto-preamble`
`:auto-postamble`	`org-export-html-auto-postamble`
`:author`	`user-full-name`
`:email`	`user-mail-address : addr;addr;..`
`:select-tags`	`org-export-select-tags`
`:exclude-tags`	`org-export-exclude-tags`
`:latex-image-options`	`org-export-latex-image-default-option`

Most of the `org-export-with-*` variables have the same effect in both HTML and LaTeX exporters, except for `:TeX-macros` and `:LaTeX-fragments`, respectively nil and t in the LaTeX export.

When a property is given a value in `org-publish-project-alist`, its setting overrides the value of the corresponding user variable (if any) during publishing. Options set within a file (see Section 12.2 [Export options], page 133), however, override everything.

13.1.6 Links between published files

To create a link from one Org file to another, you would use something like '`[[file:foo.org][The foo]]`' or simply '`file:foo.org`.' (see Chapter 4 [Hyperlinks], page 31). When published, this link becomes a link to '`foo.html`'. In this way, you can interlink the pages of your "org web" project and the links will work as expected when you publish them to HTML. If you also publish the Org source file and want to link to that, use an `http:` link instead of a `file:` link, because `file:` links are converted to link to the corresponding '`html`' file.

You may also link to related files, such as images. Provided you are careful with relative file names, and provided you have also configured Org to upload the related files, these links will work too. See Section 13.3.2 [Complex example], page 161, for an example of this usage.

Sometimes an Org file to be published may contain links that are only valid in your production environment, but not in the publishing location. In this case, use the property

> `:link-validation-function`   Function to validate links

to define a function for checking link validity. This function must accept two arguments, the file name and a directory relative to which the file name is interpreted in the production environment. If this function returns nil, then the HTML generator will only insert a description into the HTML file, but no link. One option for this function is `org-publish-validate-link` which checks if the given file is part of any project in `org-publish-project-alist`.

13.1.7 Generating a sitemap

The following properties may be used to control publishing of a map of files for a given project.

:auto-sitemap
> When non-nil, publish a sitemap during org-publish-current-project or org-publish-all.

:sitemap-filename
> Filename for output of sitemap. Defaults to 'sitemap.org' (which becomes 'sitemap.html').

:sitemap-title
> Title of sitemap page. Defaults to name of file.

:sitemap-function
> Plug-in function to use for generation of the sitemap. Defaults to org-publish-org-sitemap, which generates a plain list of links to all files in the project.

:sitemap-sort-folders
> Where folders should appear in the sitemap. Set this to first (default) or last to display folders first or last, respectively. Any other value will mix files and folders.

:sitemap-alphabetically
> The site map is normally sorted alphabetically. Set this explicitly to nil to turn off sorting.

:sitemap-ignore-case
> Should sorting be case-sensitive? Default nil.

13.1.8 Generating an index

Org-mode can generate an index across the files of a publishing project.

:makeindex
> When non-nil, generate in index in the file 'theindex.org' and publish it as 'theindex.html'.

The file will be create when first publishing a project with the :makeindex set. The file only contains a statement #+include: "theindex.inc". You can then built around this include statement by adding a title, style information etc.

13.2 Uploading files

For those people already utilizing third party sync tools such as rsync or
unison, it might be preferable not to use the built in *remote* publishing facilities of Org-mode which rely heavily on Tramp. Tramp, while very useful and
powerful, tends not to be so efficient for multiple file transfer and has been
known to cause problems under heavy usage.

Specialized synchronization utilities offer several advantages. In addition to
timestamp comparison, they also do content and permissions/attribute checks.
For this reason you might prefer to publish your web to a local directory (possibly even *in place* with your Org files) and then use 'unison' or 'rsync' to do
the synchronization with the remote host.

Since Unison (for example) can be configured as to which files to transfer
to a certain remote destination, it can greatly simplify the project publishing
definition. Simply keep all files in the correct location, process your Org files
with org-publish and let the synchronization tool do the rest. You do not
need, in this scenario, to include attachments such as 'jpg', 'css' or 'gif' files
in the project definition since the 3rd party tool syncs them.

Publishing to a local directory is also much faster than to a remote one,
so that you can afford more easily to republish entire projects. If you set org-
publish-use-timestamps-flag to nil, you gain the main benefit of re-including
any changed external files such as source example files you might include with
#+INCLUDE. The timestamp mechanism in Org is not smart enough to detect if
included files have been modified.

13.3 Sample configuration

Below we provide two example configurations. The first one is a simple
project publishing only a set of Org files. The second example is more complex,
with a multi-component project.

13.3.1 Example: simple publishing configuration

This example publishes a set of Org files to the 'public_html' directory on
the local machine.

```
(setq org-publish-project-alist
 '(("org"
    :base-directory "~/org/"
    :publishing-directory "~/public_html"
    :section-numbers nil
    :table-of-contents nil
    :style "<link rel=\"stylesheet\"
        href=\"../other/mystyle.css\"
        type=\"text/css\"/>")))
```

13.3.2 Example: complex publishing configuration

This more complicated example publishes an entire website, including Org files converted to HTML, image files, Emacs Lisp source code, and style sheets. The publishing directory is remote and private files are excluded.

To ensure that links are preserved, care should be taken to replicate your directory structure on the web server, and to use relative file paths. For example, if your Org files are kept in '~/org' and your publishable images in '~/images', you would link to an image with

```
file:../images/myimage.png
```

On the web server, the relative path to the image should be the same. You can accomplish this by setting up an "images" folder in the right place on the web server, and publishing images to it.

```
(setq org-publish-project-alist
 '(("orgfiles"
      :base-directory "~/org/"
      :base-extension "org"
      :publishing-directory "/ssh:user@host:~/html/notebook/"
      :publishing-function org-publish-org-to-html
      :exclude "PrivatePage.org"     ;; regexp
      :headline-levels 3
      :section-numbers nil
      :table-of-contents nil
      :style "<link rel=\"stylesheet\"
              href=\"../other/mystyle.css\" type=\"text/css\"/>"
      :auto-preamble t
      :auto-postamble nil)

    ("images"
     :base-directory "~/images/"
     :base-extension "jpg\\|gif\\|png"
     :publishing-directory "/ssh:user@host:~/html/images/"
     :publishing-function org-publish-attachment)

    ("other"
     :base-directory "~/other/"
     :base-extension "css\\|el"
     :publishing-directory "/ssh:user@host:~/html/other/"
     :publishing-function org-publish-attachment)
    ("website" :components ("orgfiles" "images" "other")))))
```

13.4 Triggering publication

Once properly configured, Org can publish with the following commands:

C-c C-e C

Prompt for a specific project and publish all files that belong to it.

C-c C-e P

Publish the project containing the current file.

C-c C-e F

Publish only the current file.

C-c C-e E

Publish every project.

Org uses timestamps to track when a file has changed. The above functions normally only publish changed files. You can override this and force publishing of all files by giving a prefix argument to any of the commands above, or by customizing the variable org-publish-use-timestamps-flag. This may be necessary in particular if files include other files via #+SETUPFILE: or #+INCLUDE:.

14 Working with source code

Source code can be included in Org-mode documents using a 'src' block, e.g.,

```
#+BEGIN_SRC emacs-lisp
(defun org-xor (a b)
  "Exclusive or."
  (if a (not b) b))
#+END_SRC
```

Org-mode provides a number of features for working with live source code, including editing of code blocks in their native major-mode, evaluation of code blocks, converting code blocks into source files (known as *tangling* in literate programming), and exporting code blocks and their results in several formats. This functionality was contributed by Eric Schulte and Dan Davison, and was originally named Org-babel.

The following sections describe Org-mode's code block handling facilities.

14.1 Structure of code blocks

The structure of code blocks is as follows:

```
#+srcname: <name>
#+begin_src <language> <switches> <header arguments>
  <body>
#+end_src
```

code blocks can also be embedded in text as so called inline code blocks as

```
src_<language>{<body>}
```

or

```
src_<language>[<header arguments>]{<body>}
```

<name>

> This name is associated with the code block. This is similar to the '#+tblname' lines that can be used to name tables in Org-mode files. Referencing the name of a code block makes it possible to evaluate the block from other places in the file, other files, or from Org-mode table formulas (see Chapter 15 [The spreadsheet], page 185).

<language>

> The language of the code in the block.

<switches>

> Switches controlling exportation of the code block (see switches discussion in Section 11.3 [Literal examples], page 126)

<header arguments>

> Optional header arguments control many aspects of evaluation, export and tangling of code blocks. See the Section 14.8 [Header arguments], page 167 section. Header arguments can also be set on a per-buffer or per-subtree basis using properties.

```
<body>
```
    The source code.

14.2 Editing source code

Use C-c ' to edit the current code block. This brings up a language major-mode edit buffer containing the body of the code block. Saving this buffer will write the new contents back to the Org buffer. Use C-c ' again to exit.

The org-src-mode minor mode will be active in the edit buffer. The following variables can be used to configure the behavior of the edit buffer. See also the customization group org-edit-structure for further configuration options.

org-src-lang-modes
    If an Emacs major-mode named <lang>-mode exists, where <lang> is the language named in the header line of the code block, then the edit buffer will be placed in that major-mode. This variable can be used to map arbitrary language names to existing major modes.

org-src-window-setup
    Controls the way Emacs windows are rearranged when the edit buffer is created.

org-src-preserve-indentation
    This variable is especially useful for tangling languages such as Python, in which whitespace indentation in the output is critical.

org-src-ask-before-returning-to-edit-buffer
    By default, Org will ask before returning to an open edit buffer. Set this variable to nil to switch without asking.

14.3 Exporting code blocks

It is possible to export the *contents* of code blocks, the *results* of code block evaluation, *neither*, or *both*. For most languages, the default exports the contents of code blocks. However, for some languages (e.g., ditaa) the default exports the results of code block evaluation. For information on exporting code block bodies, see Section 11.3 [Literal examples], page 126.

The :exports header argument can be used to specify export behavior:

Header arguments:

:exports code
    The default in most languages. The body of the code block is exported, as described in Section 11.3 [Literal examples], page 126.

:exports results
    The code block will be evaluated and the results will be placed in the Org-mode buffer for export, either updating previous results of the code block located anywhere in the buffer or, if no previous results exist, placing the results immediately after the code block. The body of the code block will not be exported.

`:exports both`

> Both the code block and its results will be exported.

`:exports none`

> Neither the code block nor its results will be exported.

It is possible to inhibit the evaluation of code blocks during export. Setting the `org-export-babel-evaluate` variable to `nil` will ensure that no code blocks are evaluated as part of the export process. This can be useful in situations where potentially untrusted Org-mode files are exported in an automated fashion, for example when Org-mode is used as the markup language for a wiki.

14.4 Extracting source code

Creating pure source code files by extracting code from source blocks is referred to as "tangling"—a term adopted from the literate programming community. During "tangling" of code blocks their bodies are expanded using `org-babel-expand-src-block` which can expand both variable and "noweb" style references (see Section 14.10 [Noweb reference syntax], page 182).

Header arguments

`:tangle no`

> The default. The code block is not included in the tangled output.

`:tangle yes`

> Include the code block in the tangled output. The output file name is the name of the org file with the extension '`.org`' replaced by the extension for the block language.

`:tangle filename`

> Include the code block in the tangled output to file '`filename`'.

Functions

`org-babel-tangle`

> Tangle the current file. Bound to `C-c C-v t`.

`org-babel-tangle-file`

> Choose a file to tangle. Bound to `C-c C-v f`.

Hooks

`org-babel-post-tangle-hook`

> This hook is run from within code files tangled by `org-babel-tangle`. Example applications could include post-processing, compilation or evaluation of tangled code files.

14.5 Evaluating code blocks

Code blocks can be evaluated[1] and the results placed in the Org-mode
buffer. By default, evaluation is only turned on for emacs-lisp code blocks,
however support exists for evaluating blocks in many languages. See Section 14.7
[Languages], page 167 for a list of supported languages. See Section 14.1 [Struc-
ture of code blocks], page 163 for information on the syntax used to define a
code block.

There are a number of ways to evaluate code blocks. The simplest is to press
C-c C-c or C-c C-v e with the point on a code block.[2] This will call the org-
babel-execute-src-block function to evaluate the block and insert its results
into the Org-mode buffer.

It is also possible to evaluate named code blocks from anywhere in an Org-
mode buffer or an Org-mode table. #+call (or synonymously #+function or
#+lob) lines can be used to remotely execute code blocks located in the current
Org-mode buffer or in the "Library of Babel" (see Section 14.6 [Library of
Babel], page 166). These lines use the following syntax.

```
#+call: <name>(<arguments>) <header arguments>
#+function: <name>(<arguments>) <header arguments>
#+lob: <name>(<arguments>) <header arguments>
```

<name>
> The name of the code block to be evaluated.

<arguments>
> Arguments specified in this section will be passed to the code block.

<header arguments>
> Header arguments can be placed after the function invocation. See Sec-
> tion 14.8 [Header arguments], page 167 for more information on header
> arguments.

14.6 Library of Babel

The "Library of Babel" is a library of code blocks that can be called from
any Org-mode file. The library is housed in an Org-mode file located in the
'contrib' directory of Org-mode. Org-mode users can deposit functions they
believe to be generally useful in the library.

Code blocks defined in the "Library of Babel" can be called remotely as if they
were in the current Org-mode buffer (see Section 14.5 [Evaluating code blocks],
page 166 for information on the syntax of remote code block evaluation).

Code blocks located in any Org-mode file can be loaded into the "Library of
Babel" with the org-babel-lob-ingest function, bound to C-c C-v i.

---

[1] Whenever code is evaluated there is a potential for that code to do harm. Org-mode
provides a number of safeguards to ensure that it only evaluates code with explicit
confirmation from the user. For information on these safeguards (and on how to
disable them) see Section 16.4 [Code evaluation security], page 199.

[2] The org-babel-no-eval-on-ctrl-c-ctrl-c variable can be used to remove code
evaluation from the C-c C-c key binding.

14.7 Languages

Language	Identifier	Language	Identifier
Asymptote	asymptote	Objective Caml	ocaml
C	c	Octave	octave
C++	C++	Oz	oz
Clojure	clojure	Perl	perl
CSS	css	Python	python
ditaa	ditaa	R	R
Graphviz	dot	Ruby	ruby
Emacs Lisp	emacs-lisp	Sass	sass
gnuplot	gnuplot	GNU Screen	screen
Haskell	haskell	shell	sh
LaTeX	latex	SQL	sql
MATLAB	matlab	SQLite	sqlite
Mscgen	mscgen		

Language-specific documentation is available for some languages. If available, it can be found at http://orgmode.org/worg/org-contrib/babel/languages.

The org-babel-load-languages controls which languages are enabled for evaluation (by default only emacs-lisp is enabled). This variable can be set using the customization interface or by adding code like the following to your emacs configuration.

The following disables emacs-lisp evaluation and enables evaluation of R code blocks.

```
(org-babel-do-load-languages
 'org-babel-load-languages
 '((emacs-lisp . nil)
   (R . t)))
```

It is also possible to enable support for a language by loading the related elisp file with require.

The following adds support for evaluating clojure code blocks.

```
(require 'ob-clojure)
```

14.8 Header arguments

Code block functionality can be configured with header arguments. This section provides an overview of the use of header arguments, and then describes each header argument in detail.

14.8.1 Using header arguments

The values of header arguments can be set in six different ways, each more specific (and having higher priority) than the last.

System-wide header arguments

System-wide values of header arguments can be specified by customizing the
`org-babel-default-header-args` variable:

```
:session    => "none"
:results    => "replace"
:exports    => "code"
:cache      => "no"
:noweb      => "no"
```

For example, the following example could be used to set the default value
of :noweb header arguments to yes. This would have the effect of expanding
:noweb references by default when evaluating source code blocks.

```
(setq org-babel-default-header-args
(cons '(:noweb . "yes")
(assq-delete-all :noweb org-babel-default-header-args)))
```

Language-specific header arguments

Each language can define its own set of default header arguments. See the language-specific documentation available online at
http://orgmode.org/worg/org-contrib/babel.

Buffer-wide header arguments

Buffer-wide header arguments may be specified through the use of a special
line placed anywhere in an Org-mode file. The line consists of the #+BABEL:
keyword followed by a series of header arguments which may be specified using
the standard header argument syntax.

For example the following would set session to *R*, and results to silent
for every code block in the buffer, ensuring that all execution took place in the
same session, and no results would be inserted into the buffer.

```
#+BABEL: :session *R* :results silent
```

Header arguments in Org-mode properties

Header arguments are also read from Org-mode properties (see Section 7.1
[Property syntax], page 59), which can be set on a buffer-wide or per-heading
basis. An example of setting a header argument for all code blocks in a buffer
is

```
#+property: tangle yes
```

When properties are used to set default header arguments, they are looked
up with inheritance, so the value of the :cache header argument will default to
yes in all code blocks in the subtree rooted at the following heading:

```
* outline header
:PROPERTIES:
:cache:     yes
:END:
```

Properties defined in this way override the properties set in org-babel-default-header-args. It is convenient to use the org-set-property function bound to C-c C-x p to set properties in Org-mode documents.

Code block specific header arguments

The most common way to assign values to header arguments is at the code block level. This can be done by listing a sequence of header arguments and their values as part of the #+begin_src line. Properties set in this way override both the values of org-babel-default-header-args and header arguments specified as properties. In the following example, the :results header argument is set to silent, meaning the results of execution will not be inserted in the buffer, and the :exports header argument is set to code, meaning only the body of the code block will be preserved on export to HTML or LaTeX.

```
#+source: factorial
#+begin_src haskell :results silent :exports code :var n=0
fac 0 = 1
fac n = n * fac (n-1)
#+end_src
```

Similarly, it is possible to set header arguments for inline code blocks:

```
src_haskell[:exports both]{fac 5}
```

Header arguments in function calls

At the most specific level, header arguments for "Library of Babel" or function call lines can be set as shown below:

```
#+call: factorial(n=5) :exports results
```

14.8.2 Specific header arguments

The following header arguments are defined:

14.8.2.1 :var

The :var header argument is used to pass arguments to code blocks. The specifics of how arguments are included in a code block vary by language; these are addressed in the language-specific documentation. However, the syntax used to specify arguments is the same across all languages. The values passed to arguments can be literal values, values from org-mode tables and literal example blocks, or the results of other code blocks.

These values can be indexed in a manner similar to arrays—see the "indexable variable values" heading below.

The following syntax is used to pass arguments to code blocks using the :var header argument.

```
:var name=assign
```

where assign can take one of the following forms

- literal value either a string "string" or a number 9.
- reference a table name:

```
#+tblname: example-table
| 1 |
| 2 |
| 3 |
| 4 |

#+source: table-length
#+begin_src emacs-lisp :var table=example-table
(length table)
#+end_src

#+results: table-length
: 4
```

a code block name, as assigned by #+srcname:, followed by parentheses:

```
#+begin_src emacs-lisp :var length=table-length()
(* 2 length)
#+end_src

#+results:
: 8
```

In addition, an argument can be passed to the code block referenced by
:var. The argument is passed within the parentheses following the code
block name:

```
#+source: double
#+begin_src emacs-lisp :var input=8
(* 2 input)
#+end_src

#+results: double
: 16

#+source: squared
#+begin_src emacs-lisp :var input=double(input=1)
(* input input)
#+end_src

#+results: squared
: 4
```

Alternate argument syntax

It is also possible to specify arguments in a potentially more natural way using the #+source: line of a code block. As in the following example arguments can be packed inside of parenthesis, separated by commas, following the source name.

```
#+source: double(input=0, x=2)
#+begin_src emacs-lisp
(* 2 (+ input x))
#+end_src
```

Indexable variable values

It is possible to reference portions of variable values by "indexing" into the variables. Indexes are 0 based with negative values counting back from the end. If an index is separated by ,s then each subsequent section will index into the next deepest nesting or dimension of the value. The following example assigns the last cell of the first row the table example-table to the variable data:

```
#+results: example-table
| 1 | a |
| 2 | b |
| 3 | c |
| 4 | d |

#+begin_src emacs-lisp :var data=example-table[0,-1]
  data
#+end_src

#+results:
: a
```

Ranges of variable values can be referenced using two integers separated by a :, in which case the entire inclusive range is referenced. For example the following assigns the middle three rows of example-table to data.

```
#+results: example-table
| 1 | a |
| 2 | b |
| 3 | c |
| 4 | d |
| 5 | 3 |

#+begin_src emacs-lisp :var data=example-table[1:3]
  data
#+end_src

#+results:
| 2 | b |
| 3 | c |
| 4 | d |
```

Additionally, an empty index, or the single character *, are both interpreted to mean the entire range and as such are equivalent to 0:-1, as shown in the following example in which the entire first column is referenced.

```
#+results: example-table
| 1 | a |
| 2 | b |
| 3 | c |
| 4 | d |

#+begin_src emacs-lisp :var data=example-table[,0]
  data
#+end_src

#+results:
| 1 | 2 | 3 | 4 |
```

It is possible to index into the results of code blocks as well as tables. Any number of dimensions can be indexed. Dimensions are separated from one another by commas, as shown in the following example.

```
#+source: 3D
#+begin_src emacs-lisp
  '(((1  2  3)  (4  5  6)  (7  8  9))
    ((10 11 12) (13 14 15) (16 17 18))
    ((19 20 21) (22 23 24) (25 26 27)))
#+end_src

#+begin_src emacs-lisp :var data=3D[1,,1]
  data
#+end_src

#+results:
| 11 | 14 | 17 |
```

14.8.2.2 :results

There are three classes of :results header argument. Only one option of each type may be supplied per code block.

collection

> header arguments specify how the results should be collected from the code block

type

> header arguments specify what type of result the code block will return—which has implications for how they will be inserted into the Org-mode buffer

handling

> header arguments specify how the results of evaluating the code block should be handled.

Collection

The following options are mutually exclusive, and specify how the results should be collected from the code block.

value

> This is the default. The result is the value of the last statement in the code block. This header argument places the evaluation in functional mode. Note that in some languages, e.g., Python, use of this result type requires that a `return` statement be included in the body of the source code block. E.g., `:results value`.

output

> The result is the collection of everything printed to STDOUT during the execution of the code block. This header argument places the evaluation in scripting mode. E.g., `:results output`.

Type

The following options are mutually exclusive and specify what type of results the code block will return. By default, results are inserted as either a table or scalar depending on their value.

table, vector

> The results should be interpreted as an Org-mode table. If a single value is returned, it will be converted into a table with one row and one column. E.g., `:results value table`.

scalar, verbatim

> The results should be interpreted literally—they will not be converted into a table. The results will be inserted into the Org-mode buffer as quoted text. E.g., `:results value verbatim`.

file

> The results will be interpreted as the path to a file, and will be inserted into the Org-mode buffer as a file link. E.g., `:results value file`.

raw, org

> The results are interpreted as raw Org-mode code and are inserted directly into the buffer. If the results look like a table they will be aligned as such by Org-mode. E.g., `:results value raw`.

html

> Results are assumed to be HTML and will be enclosed in a `begin_html` block. E.g., `:results value html`.

latex

> Results assumed to be LaTeX and are enclosed in a `begin_latex` block. E.g., `:results value latex`.

code

> Result are assumed to be parseable code and are enclosed in a code block. E.g., `:results value code`.

pp   The result is converted to pretty-printed code and is enclosed in a code
     block. This option currently supports Emacs Lisp, Python, and Ruby.
     E.g., :results value pp.

Handling

The following results options indicate what happens with the results once
they are collected.

silent
> The results will be echoed in the minibuffer but will not be inserted into
> the Org-mode buffer. E.g., :results output silent.

replace
> The default value. Any existing results will be removed, and the new results
> will be inserted into the Org-mode buffer in their place. E.g., :results
> output replace.

append
> If there are pre-existing results of the code block then the new results will
> be appended to the existing results. Otherwise the new results will be
> inserted as with replace.

prepend
> If there are pre-existing results of the code block then the new results will
> be prepended to the existing results. Otherwise the new results will be
> inserted as with replace.

14.8.2.3   :file

The header argument :file is used to specify a path for file output. An
Org-mode style file: link is inserted into the buffer as the result (see Sec-
tion 4.1 [Link format], page 31). Common examples are graphical output from
R, gnuplot, ditaa and LaTeX code blocks.

Note that for some languages, including R, gnuplot, LaTeX and ditaa, graphical output is sent to the specified file without the file being referenced explicitly
in the code block. See the documentation for the individual languages for details. In contrast, general purpose languages such as Python and Ruby require
that the code explicitly create output corresponding to the path indicated by
:file.

14.8.2.4   :dir and remote execution

While the :file header argument can be used to specify the path to the
output file, :dir specifies the default directory during code block execution. If
it is absent, then the directory associated with the current buffer is used. In
other words, supplying :dir path temporarily has the same effect as changing
the current directory with M-x cd path, and then not supplying :dir. Under the
surface, :dir simply sets the value of the Emacs variable default-directory.

When using :dir, you should supply a relative path for file output (e.g.,
:file myfile.jpg or :file results/myfile.jpg) in which case that path will
be interpreted relative to the default directory.

In other words, if you want your plot to go into a folder called 'Work' in your home directory, you could use

```
#+begin_src R :file myplot.png :dir ~/Work
matplot(matrix(rnorm(100), 10), type="l")
#+end_src
```

Remote execution

A directory on a remote machine can be specified using tramp file syntax, in which case the code will be evaluated on the remote machine. An example is

```
#+begin_src R :file plot.png :dir /dand@example.edu:
plot(1:10, main=system("hostname", intern=TRUE))
#+end_src
```

Text results will be returned to the local Org-mode buffer as usual, and file output will be created on the remote machine with relative paths interpreted relative to the remote directory. An Org-mode link to the remote file will be created.

So, in the above example a plot will be created on the remote machine, and a link of the following form will be inserted in the org buffer:

```
[[file:/scp:dand@example.edu:/home/dand/plot.png][plot.png]]
```

Most of this functionality follows immediately from the fact that :dir sets the value of the Emacs variable default-directory, thanks to tramp. Those using XEmacs, or GNU Emacs prior to version 23 may need to install tramp separately in order for these features to work correctly.

Further points

- If :dir is used in conjunction with :session, although it will determine the starting directory for a new session as expected, no attempt is currently made to alter the directory associated with an existing session.

- :dir should typically not be used to create files during export with :exports results or :exports both. The reason is that, in order to retain portability of exported material between machines, during export links inserted into the buffer will *not* be expanded against default directory. Therefore, if default-directory is altered using :dir, it is probable that the file will be created in a location to which the link does not point.

14.8.2.5 :exports

The :exports header argument specifies what should be included in HTML or LaTeX exports of the Org-mode file.

code
> The default. The body of code is included into the exported file. E.g., :exports code.

results
> The result of evaluating the code is included in the exported file. E.g., :exports results.

both
> Both the code and results are included in the exported file. E.g., `:exports both`.

none
> Nothing is included in the exported file. E.g., `:exports none`.

14.8.2.6 `:tangle`

The `:tangle` header argument specifies whether or not the code block should be included in tangled extraction of source code files.

yes
> The code block is exported to a source code file named after the basename (name w/o extension) of the Org-mode file. E.g., `:tangle yes`.

no   The default. The code block is not exported to a source code file. E.g., `:tangle no`.

other
> Any other string passed to the `:tangle` header argument is interpreted as a file basename to which the block will be exported. E.g., `:tangle basename`.

14.8.2.7 `:comments`

By default code blocks are tangled to source-code files without any insertion of comments beyond those which may already exist in the body of the code block. The `:comments` header argument can be set as follows to control the insertion of extra comments into the tangled code file.

no   The default. No extra comments are inserted during tangling.

link
> The code block is wrapped in comments which contain pointers back to the original Org file from which the code was tangled.

yes
> A synonym for "link" to maintain backwards compatibility.

org
> Include text from the org-mode file as a comment.
>
> The text is picked from the leading context of the tangled code and is limited by the nearest headline or source block as the case may be.

both
> Turns on both the "link" and "org" comment options.

14.8.2.8 `:no-expand`

By default, code blocks are expanded with `org-babel-expand-src-block` during tangling. This has the effect of assigning values to variables specified with `:var` (see Section 14.8.2.1 [var], page 169), and of replacing "noweb" references (see Section 14.10 [Noweb reference syntax], page 182) with their targets. The `:no-expand` header argument can be used to turn off this behavior.

14.8.2.9 :session

The :session header argument starts a session for an interpreted language where state is preserved.

By default, a session is not started.

A string passed to the :session header argument will give the session a name. This makes it possible to run concurrent sessions for each interpreted language.

14.8.2.10 :noweb

The :noweb header argument controls expansion of "noweb" style (see Section 14.10 [Noweb reference syntax], page 182) references in a code block. This header argument can have one of three values: yes no or tangle.

yes
> All "noweb" syntax references in the body of the code block will be expanded before the block is evaluated, tangled or exported.

no   The default. No "noweb" syntax specific action is taken on evaluating code blocks, However, noweb references will still be expanded during tangling.

tangle
> All "noweb" syntax references in the body of the code block will be expanded before the block is tangled, however "noweb" references will not be expanded when the block is evaluated or exported.

Noweb prefix lines

Noweb insertions are now placed behind the line prefix of the <<reference>>. This behavior is illustrated in the following example. Because the <<example>> noweb reference appears behind the SQL comment syntax, each line of the expanded noweb reference will be commented.

This code block:

```
-- <<example>>
```

expands to:

```
-- this is the
-- multi-line body of example
```

Note that noweb replacement text that does not contain any newlines will not be affected by this change, so it is still possible to use inline noweb references.

14.8.2.11 :cache

The :cache header argument controls the use of in-buffer caching of the results of evaluating code blocks. It can be used to avoid re-evaluating unchanged code blocks. This header argument can have one of two values: yes or no.

no   The default. No caching takes place, and the code block will be evaluated every time it is called.

yes

Every time the code block is run a SHA1 hash of the code and arguments passed to the block will be generated. This hash is packed into the #+results: line and will be checked on subsequent executions of the code block. If the code block has not changed since the last time it was evaluated, it will not be re-evaluated.

14.8.2.12 :hlines

Tables are frequently represented with one or more horizontal lines, or hlines. The :hlines argument to a code block accepts the values yes or no, with a default value of no.

no   Strips horizontal lines from the input table. In most languages this is the desired effect because an hline symbol is interpreted as an unbound variable and raises an error. Setting :hlines no or relying on the default value yields the following results.

```
#+tblname: many-cols
| a | b | c |
|---+---+---|
| d | e | f |
|---+---+---|
| g | h | i |

#+source: echo-table
#+begin_src python :var tab=many-cols
  return tab
#+end_src

#+results: echo-table
| a | b | c |
| d | e | f |
| g | h | i |
```

yes

Leaves hlines in the table. Setting :hlines yes has this effect.

```
#+tblname: many-cols
| a | b | c |
|---+---+---|
| d | e | f |
|---+---+---|
| g | h | i |

#+source: echo-table
#+begin_src python :var tab=many-cols :hlines yes
  return tab
#+end_src

#+results: echo-table
```

```
| a | b | c |
|---+---+---|
| d | e | f |
|---+---+---|
| g | h | i |
```

14.8.2.13 :colnames

The :colnames header argument accepts the values yes, no, or nil for unassigned. The default value is nil.

nil

> If an input table looks like it has column names (because its second row is an hline), then the column names will be removed from the table before processing, then reapplied to the results.
>
> ```
> #+tblname: less-cols
> | a |
> |---|
> | b |
> | c |
>
> #+srcname: echo-table-again
> #+begin_src python :var tab=less-cols
>   return [[val + '*' for val in row] for row in tab]
> #+end_src
>
> #+results: echo-table-again
> | a   |
> |-----|
> | b*  |
> | c*  |
> ```

no   No column name pre-processing takes place

yes

> Column names are removed and reapplied as with nil even if the table does not "look like" it has column names (i.e., the second row is not an hline)

14.8.2.14 :rownames

The :rownames header argument can take on the values yes or no, with a default value of no.

no   No row name pre-processing will take place.

yes

> The first column of the table is removed from the table before processing, and is then reapplied to the results.

```
#+tblname: with-rownames
| one | 1 | 2 | 3 | 4 |  5 |
| two | 6 | 7 | 8 | 9 | 10 |

#+srcname: echo-table-once-again
#+begin_src python :var tab=with-rownames :rownames yes
  return [[val + 10 for val in row] for row in tab]
#+end_src

#+results: echo-table-once-again
| one | 11 | 12 | 13 | 14 | 15 |
| two | 16 | 17 | 18 | 19 | 20 |
```

14.8.2.15 :shebang

Setting the :shebang header argument to a string value (e.g., :shebang "#!/bin/bash") causes the string to be inserted as the first line of any tangled file holding the code block, and the file permissions of the tangled file are set to make it executable.

14.8.2.16 :eval

The :eval header argument can be used to limit the evaluation of specific code blocks. :eval accepts two arguments "never" and "query". :eval never will ensure that a code block is never evaluated, this can be useful for protecting against the evaluation of dangerous code blocks. :eval query will require a query for every execution of a code block regardless of the value of the org-confirm-babel-evaluate variable.

14.9 Results of evaluation

The way in which results are handled depends on whether a session is invoked, as well as on whether :results value or :results output is used. The following table shows the possibilities:

	Non-session	Session
:results value	value of last expression	value of last expression
:results output	contents of STDOUT	concatenation of interpreter output

Note: With :results value, the result in both :session and non-session is returned to Org-mode as a table (a one- or two-dimensional vector of strings or numbers) when appropriate.

14.9.1 Non-session

14.9.1.1 :results value

This is the default. Internally, the value is obtained by wrapping the code in a function definition in the external language, and evaluating that function. Therefore, code should be written as if it were the body of such a function. In particular, note that Python does not automatically return a value from a function unless a return statement is present, and so a 'return' statement will usually be required in Python.

This is the only one of the four evaluation contexts in which the code is automatically wrapped in a function definition.

14.9.1.2 :results output

The code is passed to the interpreter as an external process, and the contents of the standard output stream are returned as text. (In certain languages this also contains the error output stream; this is an area for future work.)

14.9.2 Session

14.9.2.1 :results value

The code is passed to the interpreter running as an interactive Emacs inferior process. The result returned is the result of the last evaluation performed by the interpreter. (This is obtained in a language-specific manner: the value of the variable _ in Python and Ruby, and the value of .Last.value in R).

14.9.2.2 :results output

The code is passed to the interpreter running as an interactive Emacs inferior process. The result returned is the concatenation of the sequence of (text) output from the interactive interpreter. Notice that this is not necessarily the same as what would be sent to STDOUT if the same code were passed to a non-interactive interpreter running as an external process. For example, compare the following two blocks:

```
#+begin_src python :results output
print "hello"
2
print "bye"
#+end_src

#+resname:
: hello
: bye
```

In non-session mode, the '2' is not printed and does not appear.

```
#+begin_src python :results output :session
print "hello"
2
print "bye"
#+end_src
```

```
#+resname:
: hello
: 2
: bye
```

But in :session mode, the interactive interpreter receives input '2' and prints out its value, '2'. (Indeed, the other print statements are unnecessary here).

14.10 Noweb reference syntax

The "noweb" (see http://www.cs.tufts.edu/~nr/noweb/) Literate Programming system allows named blocks of code to be referenced by using the familiar Noweb syntax:

    `<<code-block-name>>`

When a code block is tangled or evaluated, whether or not "noweb" references are expanded depends upon the value of the :noweb header argument. If :noweb yes, then a Noweb reference is expanded before evaluation. If :noweb no, the default, then the reference is not expanded before evaluation.

Note: the default value, :noweb no, was chosen to ensure that correct code is not broken in a language, such as Ruby, where <<arg>> is a syntactically valid construct. If <<arg>> is not syntactically valid in languages that you use, then please consider setting the default value.

14.11 Key bindings and useful functions

Many common Org-mode key sequences are re-bound depending on the context.

Within a code block, the following key bindings are active:

```
C-c C-c              org-babel-execute-src-block
C-c C-o              org-babel-open-src-block-result
C-up                 org-babel-load-in-session
M-down               org-babel-pop-to-session
```

In an Org-mode buffer, the following key bindings are active:

```
C-c C-v a   or   C-c C-v C-a      org-babel-sha1-hash
C-c C-v b   or   C-c C-v C-b      org-babel-execute-buffer
C-c C-v f   or   C-c C-v C-f      org-babel-tangle-file
C-c C-v g                         org-babel-goto-named-source-block
C-c C-v h                         org-babel-describe-bindings
C-c C-v l   or   C-c C-v C-l      org-babel-lob-ingest
C-c C-v p   or   C-c C-v C-p      org-babel-expand-src-block
C-c C-v s   or   C-c C-v C-s      org-babel-execute-subtree
C-c C-v t   or   C-c C-v C-t      org-babel-tangle
C-c C-v z   or   C-c C-v C-z      org-babel-switch-to-session
```

14.12 Batch execution

It is possible to call functions from the command line. This shell script calls org-babel-tangle on every one of its arguments.

Be sure to adjust the paths to fit your system.

```
#!/bin/sh
# -*- mode: shell-script -*-
#
# tangle files with org-mode
#
DIR=`pwd`
FILES=""
ORGINSTALL="~/src/org/lisp/org-install.el"

# wrap each argument in the code required to call tangle on it
for i in $@; do
        FILES="$FILES \"$i\""
done

emacs -Q --batch -l $ORGINSTALL \
--eval "(progn
(add-to-list 'load-path (expand-file-name \"~/src/org/lisp/\"))
(add-to-list 'load-path (expand-file-name
                        \"~/src/org/contrib/lisp/\"))
(require 'org)(require 'org-exp)
(require 'ob)(require 'ob-tangle)
(mapc (lambda (file)
        (find-file (expand-file-name file \"$DIR\"))
        (org-babel-tangle)
        (kill-buffer)) '($FILES)))" 2>&1 |grep tangled
```

15 The spreadsheet

This chapter describes the spreadsheet capabilities of Org mode tables (see Chapter 3 [Tables], page 23).

15.1 References

To compute fields in the table from other fields, formulas must reference other fields or ranges. In Org, fields can be referenced by name, by absolute coordinates, and by relative coordinates. To find out what the coordinates of a field are, press C-c ? in that field, or press C-c } to toggle the display of a grid.

Field references

Formulas can reference the value of another field in two ways. Like in any other spreadsheet, you may reference fields with a letter/number combination like B3, meaning the 2nd field in the 3rd row.

Org also uses another, more general operator that looks like this:

    `@row$column`

Column references can be absolute like '1', '2',...'N', or relative to the current column like '+1' or '-2'.

The row specification only counts data lines and ignores horizontal separator lines (hlines). You can use absolute row numbers '1'...'N', and row numbers relative to the current row like '+3' or '-1'. Or specify the row relative to one of the hlines: 'I' refers to the first hline,[1] 'II' to the second, etc. '-I' refers to the first such line above the current line, '+I' to the first such line below the current line. You can also write 'III+2' which is the second data line after the third hline in the table.

'0' refers to the current row and column. Also, if you omit either the column or the row part of the reference, the current row/column is implied.

Org's references with *unsigned* numbers are fixed references in the sense that if you use the same reference in the formula for two different fields, the same field will be referenced each time. Org's references with *signed* numbers are floating references because the same reference operator can reference different fields depending on the field being calculated by the formula.

As a special case, references like '$LR5' and '$LR12' can be used to refer in a stable way to the 5th and 12th field in the last row of the table.

Here are a few examples:

---

[1] Note that only hlines are counted that *separate* table lines. If the table starts with a hline above the header, it does not count.

@2$3	2nd row, 3rd column
C2	same as previous
$5	column 5 in the current row
E&	same as previous
@2	current column, row 2
@-1$-3	the field one row up, three columns to the left
@-I$2	field just under hline above current row, column 2

Range references

You may reference a rectangular range of fields by specifying two field references connected by two dots '..'. If both fields are in the current row, you may simply use '$2..$7', but if at least one field is in a different row, you need to use the general @row$column format at least for the first field (i.e the reference must start with '@' in order to be interpreted correctly). Examples:

$1..$3	First three fields in the current row.
$P..$Q	Range, using column names (see under Advanced)
@2$1..@4$3	6 fields between these two fields.
A2..C4	Same as above.
@-1$-2..@-1	3 numbers from the column to the left, 2 up to current row

Range references return a vector of values that can be fed into Calc vector functions. Empty fields in ranges are normally suppressed, so that the vector contains only the non-empty fields (but see the 'E' mode switch below). If there are no non-empty fields, '[0]' is returned to avoid syntax errors in formulas.

Field coordinates in formulas

For Calc formulas and Lisp formulas @# and $# can be used to get the row or column number of the field where the formula result goes. The traditional Lisp formula equivalents are org-table-current-dline and org-table-current-column. Examples:

if(@# % 2, $#, string(""))	column number on odd lines only
$3 = remote(FOO, @@#$2)	copy column 2 from table FOO into column 3 of the current table

For the second example, table FOO must have at least as many rows as the current table. Note that this is inefficient[2] for large number of rows.

---

[2] The computation time scales as $O(N^2)$ because table FOO is parsed for each field to be copied.

Named references

'$name' is interpreted as the name of a column, parameter or constant. Constants are defined globally through the variable org-table-formula-constants, and locally (for the file) through a line like

    #+CONSTANTS: c=299792458. pi=3.14 eps=2.4e-6

Also properties (see Chapter 7 [Properties and Columns], page 59) can be used as constants in table formulas: for a property ':Xyz:' use the name '$PROP_Xyz', and the property will be searched in the current outline entry and in the hierarchy above it. If you have the 'constants.el' package, it will also be used to resolve constants, including natural constants like '$h' for Planck's constant, and units like '$km' for kilometers.[3] Column names and parameters can be specified in special table lines. These are described below, see Section 15.8 [Advanced features], page 192. All names must start with a letter, and further consist of letters and numbers.

Remote references

You may also reference constants, fields and ranges from a different table, either in the current file or even in a different file. The syntax is

    remote(NAME-OR-ID,REF)

where NAME can be the name of a table in the current file as set by a #+TBLNAME: NAME line before the table. It can also be the ID of an entry, even in a different file, and the reference then refers to the first table in that entry. REF is an absolute field or range reference as described above for example @3$3 or $somename, valid in the referenced table.

15.2 Formula syntax for Calc

A formula can be any algebraic expression understood by the Emacs 'Calc' package. **Note that 'calc' has the non-standard convention that '/' has lower precedence than '*', so that 'a/b*c' is interpreted as 'a/(b*c)'.** Before evaluation by calc-eval (see section "Calling Calc from Your Lisp Programs" in *GNU Emacs Calc Manual*), variable substitution takes place according to the rules described above. The range vectors can be directly fed into the Calc vector functions like 'vmean' and 'vsum'.

A formula can contain an optional mode string after a semicolon. This string consists of flags to influence Calc and other modes during execution. By default, Org uses the standard Calc modes (precision 12, angular units degrees, fraction and symbolic modes off). The display format, however, has been changed to (float 8) to keep tables compact. The default settings can be configured using the variable org-calc-default-modes.

p20   set the internal Calc calculation precision to 20 digits

---

[3] 'constants.el' can supply the values of constants in two different unit systems, SI and cgs. Which one is used depends on the value of the variable constants-unit-system. You can use the #+STARTUP options constSI and constcgs to set this value for the current buffer.

n3 s3 e2 f4	Normal, scientific, engineering, or fixed format of the result of Calc passed back to Org. Calc formatting is unlimited in precision as long as the Calc calculation precision is greater.
D R	angle modes: degrees, radians
F S	fraction and symbolic modes
N	interpret all fields as numbers, use 0 for non-numbers
T	force text interpretation
E	keep empty fields in ranges
L	literal

Unless you use large integer numbers or high-precision-calculation and -display for floating point numbers you may alternatively provide a printf format specifier to reformat the Calc result after it has been passed back to Org instead of letting Calc already do the formatting.[4] A few examples:

$1+$2	Sum of first and second field
$1+$2;%.2f	Same, format result to two decimals
exp($2)+exp($1)	Math functions can be used
$0;%.1f	Reformat current cell to 1 decimal
($3-32)*5/9	Degrees F -> C conversion
$c/$1/$cm	Hz -> cm conversion, using 'constants.el'
tan($1);Dp3s1	Compute in degrees, precision 3, display SCI 1
sin($1);Dp3%.1e	Same, but use printf specifier for display
vmean($2..$7)	Compute column range mean, using vector function
vmean($2..$7);EN	Same, but treat empty fields as 0
taylor($3,x=7,2)	Taylor series of $3, at x=7, second degree

Calc also contains a complete set of logical operations. For example

| if($1<20,teen,string("")) | "teen" if age $1 less than 20, else empty |

15.3 Emacs Lisp forms as formulas

It is also possible to write a formula in Emacs Lisp; this can be useful for string manipulation and control structures, if Calc's functionality is not enough. If a formula starts with a single-quote followed by an opening parenthesis, then it is evaluated as a Lisp form. The evaluation should return either a string or a number. Just as with 'calc' formulas, you can specify modes and a printf format after a semicolon. With Emacs Lisp forms, you need to be conscious about the way field references are interpolated into the form. By default, a reference will be interpolated as a Lisp string (in double-quotes) containing the field. If you provide the 'N' mode switch, all referenced elements will be numbers (non-number fields will be zero) and interpolated as Lisp numbers, without quotes. If you provide the 'L' flag, all fields will be interpolated literally, without quotes.

---

[4] The printf reformatting is limited in precision because the value passed to it is converted into an integer or double. The integer is limited in size by truncating the signed value to 32 bits. The double is limited in precision to 64 bits overall which leaves approximately 16 significant decimal digits.

I.e., if you want a reference to be interpreted as a string by the Lisp form, enclose the reference operator itself in double-quotes, like "$3". Ranges are inserted as space-separated fields, so you can embed them in list or vector syntax. Here are a few examples—note how the 'N' mode is used when we do computations in Lisp:

Swap the first two characters of the content of column 1
```
'(concat (substring $1 1 2) (substring $1 0 1)
         (substring $1 2))
```
Add columns 1 and 2, equivalent to Calc's $1+$2
```
'(+ $1 $2);N
```
Compute the sum of columns 1-4, like Calc's vsum($1..$4)
```
'(apply '+ '($1..$4));N
```

15.4 Field formulas

To assign a formula to a particular field, type it directly into the field, preceded by ':=', for example ':=$1+$2'. When you press (TAB) or (RET) or C-c C-c with the cursor still in the field, the formula will be stored as the formula for this field, evaluated, and the current field replaced with the result.

Formulas are stored in a special line starting with '#+TBLFM:' directly below the table. If you type the equation in the 4th field of the 3rd data line in the table, the formula will look like '@3$4=$1+$2'. When inserting/deleting/swapping column and rows with the appropriate commands, *absolute references* (but not relative ones) in stored formulas are modified in order to still reference the same field. Of course this is not true if you edit the table structure with normal editing commands—then you must fix the equations yourself. The left-hand side of a formula may also be a named field (see Section 15.8 [Advanced features], page 192), or a last-row reference like '$LR3'.

Instead of typing an equation into the field, you may also use the following command

C-u C-c =

Install a new formula for the current field. The command prompts for a formula with default taken from the '#+TBLFM:' line, applies it to the current field, and stores it.

15.5 Column formulas

Often in a table, the same formula should be used for all fields in a particular column. Instead of having to copy the formula to all fields in that column, Org allows you to assign a single formula to an entire column. If the table contains horizontal separator hlines, everything before the first such line is considered part of the table *header* and will not be modified by column formulas.

To assign a formula to a column, type it directly into any field in the column, preceded by an equal sign, like '=$1+$2'. When you press (TAB) or (RET) or C-c C-c with the cursor still in the field, the formula will be stored as the formula for the current column, evaluated and the current field replaced with the result. If the field contains only '=', the previously stored formula for this column is used. For each column, Org will only remember the most recently used formula. In the '#+TBLFM:' line, column formulas will look like '$4=$1+$2'. The left-hand side of a column formula cannot currently be the name of column, it must be the numeric column reference.

Instead of typing an equation into the field, you may also use the following command:

C-c =

> Install a new formula for the current column and replace current field with the result of the formula. The command prompts for a formula, with default taken from the '#+TBLFM' line, applies it to the current field and stores it. With a numeric prefix argument(e.g., C-5 C-c =) the command will apply it to that many consecutive fields in the current column.

15.6 Editing and debugging formulas

You can edit individual formulas in the minibuffer or directly in the field. Org can also prepare a special buffer with all active formulas of a table. When offering a formula for editing, Org converts references to the standard format (like B3 or D&) if possible. If you prefer to only work with the internal format (like @3$2 or $4), configure the variable org-table-use-standard-references.

C-c =
C-u C-c =

> Edit the formula associated with the current column/field in the minibuffer. See Section 15.5 [Column formulas], page 189, and Section 15.4 [Field formulas], page 189.

C-u C-u C-c =

> Re-insert the active formula (either a field formula, or a column formula) into the current field, so that you can edit it directly in the field. The advantage over editing in the minibuffer is that you can use the command C-c ?.

C-c ?

> While editing a formula in a table field, highlight the field(s) referenced by the reference at the cursor position in the formula.

C-c }

> Toggle the display of row and column numbers for a table, using overlays. These are updated each time the table is aligned; you can force it with C-c C-c.

C-c {

> Toggle the formula debugger on and off. See below.

C-c '

> Edit all formulas for the current table in a special buffer, where the formulas will be displayed one per line. If the current field has an active formula, the cursor in the formula editor will mark it. While inside the special buffer, Org will automatically highlight any field or range reference at the cursor

position. You may edit, remove and add formulas, and use the following
commands:

`C-c C-c`
`C-x C-s`

> Exit the formula editor and store the modified formulas. With `C-u`
> prefix, also apply the new formulas to the entire table.

`C-c C-q`

> Exit the formula editor without installing changes.

`C-c C-r`

> Toggle all references in the formula editor between standard (like B3)
> and internal (like @3$2).

(TAB)

> Pretty-print or indent Lisp formula at point. When in a line contain-
> ing a Lisp formula, format the formula according to Emacs Lisp rules.
> Another (TAB) collapses the formula back again. In the open formula,
> (TAB) re-indents just like in Emacs Lisp mode.

M-(TAB)

> Complete Lisp symbols, just like in Emacs Lisp mode.

S-(up)/(down)/(left)/(right)

> Shift the reference at point. For example, if the reference is B3 and
> you press S-(right), it will become C3. This also works for relative
> references and for hline references.

M-S-(up)/(down)

> Move the test line for column formulas in the Org buffer up and down.

M-(up)/(down)

> Scroll the window displaying the table.

`C-c }`

> Turn the coordinate grid in the table on and off.

Making a table field blank does not remove the formula associated with the
field, because that is stored in a different line (the '#+TBLFM' line)—during the
next recalculation the field will be filled again. To remove a formula from a
field, you have to give an empty reply when prompted for the formula, or to
edit the '#+TBLFM' line.

You may edit the '#+TBLFM' directly and re-apply the changed equations with
`C-c C-c` in that line or with the normal recalculation commands in the table.

Debugging formulas

When the evaluation of a formula leads to an error, the field content becomes
the string '#ERROR'. If you would like see what is going on during variable
substitution and calculation in order to find a bug, turn on formula debugging
in the Tbl menu and repeat the calculation, for example by pressing `C-u C-u`
`C-c =` (RET) in a field. Detailed information will be displayed.

15.7 Updating the table

Recalculation of a table is normally not automatic, but needs to be triggered by a command. See Section 15.8 [Advanced features], page 192, for a way to make recalculation at least semi-automatic.

In order to recalculate a line of a table or the entire table, use the following commands:

C-c *

> Recalculate the current row by first applying the stored column formulas from left to right, and all field formulas in the current row.

C-u C-c *
C-u C-c C-c

> Recompute the entire table, line by line. Any lines before the first hline are left alone, assuming that these are part of the table header.

C-u C-u C-c *
C-u C-u C-c C-c

> Iterate the table by recomputing it until no further changes occur. This may be necessary if some computed fields use the value of other fields that are computed *later* in the calculation sequence.

M-x org-table-recalculate-buffer-tables

> Recompute all tables in the current buffer.

M-x org-table-iterate-buffer-tables

> Iterate all tables in the current buffer, in order to converge table-to-table dependencies.

15.8 Advanced features

If you want the recalculation of fields to happen automatically, or if you want to be able to assign *names* to fields and columns, you need to reserve the first column of the table for special marking characters.

C-#

> Rotate the calculation mark in first column through the states ' ', '#', '*', '!', '$'. When there is an active region, change all marks in the region.

Here is an example of a table that collects exam results of students and makes use of these features:

```
|---+----------+--------+--------+--------+-------+------|
|   | Student  | Prob 1 | Prob 2 | Prob 3 | Total | Note |
|---+----------+--------+--------+--------+-------+------|
| ! |          |   P1   |   P2   |   P3   |  Tot  |      |
| # | Maximum  |   10   |   15   |   25   |    50 | 10.0 |
| ^ |          |   m1   |   m2   |   m3   |  mt   |      |
|---+----------+--------+--------+--------+-------+------|
| # | Peter    |   10   |    8   |   23   |    41 |  8.2 |
| # | Sam      |    2   |    4   |    3   |     9 |  1.8 |
|---+----------+--------+--------+--------+-------+------|
|   | Average  |        |        |        |       | 29.7 |
| ^ |          |        |        |        |       | at   |
| $ | max=50   |        |        |        |       |      |
|---+----------+--------+--------+--------+-------+------|
```
#+TBLFM: $6=vsum($P1..$P3)::$7=10*$Tot/$max;%.1f::$at=vmean(@-I I..@-I);%.1f

Important: please note that for these special tables, recalculating the table with C-u C-c * will only affect rows that are marked '#' or '*', and fields that have a formula assigned to the field itself. The column formulas are not applied in rows with empty first field.

The marking characters have the following meaning:

'!' The fields in this line define names for the columns, so that you may refer to a column as '$Tot' instead of '$6'.

'^' This row defines names for the fields *above* the row. With such a definition, any formula in the table may use '$m1' to refer to the value '10'. Also, if you assign a formula to a names field, it will be stored as '$name=...'.

'_' Similar to '^', but defines names for the fields in the row *below*.

'$' Fields in this row can define *parameters* for formulas. For example, if a field in a '$' row contains 'max=50', then formulas in this table can refer to the value 50 using '$max'. Parameters work exactly like constants, only that they can be defined on a per-table basis.

'#' Fields in this row are automatically recalculated when pressing (TAB) or (RET) or S-(TAB) in this row. Also, this row is selected for a global recalculation with C-u C-c *. Unmarked lines will be left alone by this command.

'*' Selects this line for global recalculation with C-u C-c *, but not for automatic recalculation. Use this when automatic recalculation slows down editing too much.

'' Unmarked lines are exempt from recalculation with C-u C-c *. All lines that should be recalculated should be marked with '#' or '*'.

'/' Do not export this line. Useful for lines that contain the narrowing '<N>' markers or column group markers.

Finally, just to whet your appetite for what can be done with the fantastic 'calc.el' package, here is a table that computes the Taylor series of degree n at location x for a couple of functions.

```
|---+------------+---+-----+------------------------------------|
|   | Func       | n | x   | Result                             |
|---+------------+---+-----+------------------------------------|
| # | exp(x)     | 1 | x   | 1 + x                              |
| # | exp(x)     | 2 | x   | 1 + x + x^2 / 2                    |
| # | exp(x)     | 3 | x   | 1 + x + x^2 / 2 + x^3 / 6          |
| # | x^2+sqrt(x)| 2 | x=0 | x*(0.5 / 0) + x^2 (2 - 0.25 / 0) / 2 |
| # | x^2+sqrt(x)| 2 | x=1 | 2 + 2.5 x - 2.5 + 0.875 (x - 1)^2 |
| * | tan(x)     | 3 | x   | 0.0175 x + 1.77e-6 x^3             |
|---+------------+---+-----+------------------------------------|
#+TBLFM: $5=taylor($2,$4,$3);n3
```

15.9 Org-Plot

Org-Plot can produce 2D and 3D graphs of information stored in org tables using 'Gnuplot'[5] and 'gnuplot-mode'[6]. To see this in action, ensure that you have both Gnuplot and Gnuplot mode installed on your system, then call org-plot/gnuplot on the following table.

```
#+PLOT: title:"Citas" ind:1 deps:(3) type:2d with:histograms \[7]
        set:"yrange [0:]"
| Sede       | Max cites | H-index |
|------------+-----------+---------|
| Chile      |    257.72 |   21.39 |
| Leeds      |    165.77 |   19.68 |
| Sao Paolo  |     71.00 |   11.50 |
| Stockholm  |    134.19 |   14.33 |
| Morelia    |    257.56 |   17.67 |
```

Notice that Org Plot is smart enough to apply the table's headers as labels. Further control over the labels, type, content, and appearance of plots can be exercised through the #+PLOT: lines preceding a table. See below for a complete list of Org-plot options. For more information and examples see the Org-plot tutorial at http://orgmode.org/worg/org-tutorials/org-plot.php.

---

[5] http://www.gnuplot.info/

[6] http://cars9.uchicago.edu/~ravel/software/gnuplot-mode.html

[7] Please note that the PLOT definition must be on a single line—it is wrapped here only because of formatting constraints.

Plot Options

`set`

> Specify any gnuplot option to be set when graphing.

`title`

> Specify the title of the plot.

`ind`

> Specify which column of the table to use as the x axis.

`deps`

> Specify the columns to graph as a Lisp style list, surrounded by parentheses and separated by spaces for example dep:(3 4) to graph the third and fourth columns (defaults to graphing all other columns aside from the ind column).

`type`

> Specify whether the plot will be 2d, 3d, or grid.

`with`

> Specify a with option to be inserted for every col being plotted (e.g., lines, points, boxes, impulses, etc...). Defaults to lines.

`file`

> If you want to plot to a file, specify "path/to/desired/output-file".

`labels`

> List of labels to be used for the deps (defaults to the column headers if they exist).

`line`

> Specify an entire line to be inserted in the Gnuplot script.

`map`

> When plotting 3d or grid types, set this to t to graph a flat mapping rather than a 3d slope.

`timefmt`

> Specify format of Org-mode timestamps as they will be parsed by Gnuplot. Defaults to '%Y-%m-%d-%H:%M:%S'.

`script`

> If you want total control, you can specify a script file (place the file name between double-quotes) which will be used to plot. Before plotting, every instance of $datafile in the specified script will be replaced with the path to the generated data file. Note: even if you set this option, you may still want to specify the plot type, as that can impact the content of the data file.

16 Miscellaneous

16.1 Completion

Emacs would not be Emacs without completion, and Org-mode uses it whenever it makes sense. If you prefer an *iswitchb-* or *ido*-like interface for some of the completion prompts, you can specify your preference by setting at most one of the variables org-completion-use-iswitchb org-completion-use-ido.

Org supports in-buffer completion. This type of completion does not make use of the minibuffer. You simply type a few letters into the buffer and use the key to complete text right there.

M-(TAB)
    Complete word at point

- At the beginning of a headline, complete TODO keywords.
- After '\', complete TEX symbols supported by the exporter.
- After '*', complete headlines in the current buffer so that they can be used in search links like '[[*find this headline]]'.
- After ':' in a headline, complete tags. The list of tags is taken from the variable org-tag-alist (possibly set through the '#+TAGS' in-buffer option, see Section 6.2 [Setting tags], page 56), or it is created dynamically from all tags used in the current buffer.
- After ':' and not in a headline, complete property keys. The list of keys is constructed dynamically from all keys used in the current buffer.
- After '[', complete link abbreviations (see Section 4.6 [Link abbreviations], page 38).
- After '#+', complete the special keywords like 'TYP_TODO' or 'OPTIONS' which set file-specific options for Org-mode. When the option keyword is already complete, pressing M-(TAB) again will insert example settings for this keyword.
- In the line after '#+STARTUP: ', complete startup keywords, i.e., valid keys for this line.
- Elsewhere, complete dictionary words using Ispell.

16.2 Easy Templates

Org-mode supports insertion of empty structural elements (like #+BEGIN_SRC and #+END_SRC pairs) with just a few key strokes. This is achieved through a native template expansion mechanism. Note that Emacs has several other template mechanisms which could be used in a similar way, for example 'yasnippet'.

To insert a structural element, type a '<', followed by a template selector and (TAB). Completion takes effect only when the above keystrokes are typed on a line by itself.

The following template selectors are currently supported.

s	#+begin_src ... #+end_src
e	#+begin_example ... #+end_example
q	#+begin_quote ... #+end_quote
v	#+begin_verse ... #+end_verse
c	#+begin_center ... #+end_center
l	#+begin_latex ... #+end_latex
L	#+latex:
h	#+begin_html ... #+end_html
H	#+html:
a	#+begin_ascii ... #+end_ascii
A	#+ascii:
i	#+include: line

For example, on an empty line, typing "<e" and then pressing TAB, will expand into a complete EXAMPLE template.

You can install additional templates by customizing the variable org-structure-template-alist. See the docstring of the variable for additional details.

16.3 Speed keys

Single keys can be made to execute commands when the cursor is at the beginning of a headline, i.e., before the first star. Configure the variable org-use-speed-commands to activate this feature. There is a pre-defined list of commands, and you can add more such commands using the variable org-speed-commands-user. Speed keys do not only speed up navigation and other commands, but they also provide an alternative way to execute commands bound to keys that are not or not easily available on a TTY, or on a small mobile device with a limited keyboard.

To see which commands are available, activate the feature and press ? with the cursor at the beginning of a headline.

16.4 Code evaluation and security issues

Org provides tools to work with the code snippets, including evaluating them.

Running code on your machine always comes with a security risk. Badly written or malicious code can be executed on purpose or by accident. Org has default settings which will only evaluate such code if you give explicit permission to do so, and as a casual user of these features you should leave these precautions intact.

For people who regularly work with such code, the confirmation prompts can become annoying, and you might want to turn them off. This can be done, but you must be aware of the risks that are involved.

Code evaluation can happen under the following circumstances:

Source code blocks
> Source code blocks can be evaluated during export, or when pressing C-c C-c in the block. The most important thing to realize here is that Org mode files which contain code snippets are, in a certain sense, like executable files. So you should accept them and load them into Emacs only from trusted sources—just like you would do with a program you install on your computer.
>
> Make sure you know what you are doing before customizing the variables which take off the default security brakes.

org-confirm-babel-evaluate   User Option
> When set to t user is queried before code block evaluation

Following shell *and* elisp *links*
> Org has two link types that can directly evaluate code (see Section 4.3 [External links], page 32). These links can be problematic because the code to be evaluated is not visible.

org-confirm-shell-link-function   User Option
> Function to queries user about shell link execution.

org-confirm-elisp-link-function   User Option
> Functions to query user for Emacs Lisp link execution.

Formulas in tables
> Formulas in tables (see Chapter 15 [The spreadsheet], page 185) are code that is evaluated either by the *calc* interpreter, or by the *Emacs Lisp* interpreter.

16.5 Customization

There are more than 180 variables that can be used to customize Org. For the sake of compactness of the manual, I am not describing the variables here. A structured overview of customization variables is available with M-x org-customize. Or select Browse Org Group from the Org->Customization menu. Many settings can also be activated on a per-file basis, by putting special lines into the buffer (see Section 16.6 [In-buffer settings], page 200).

16.6 Summary of in-buffer settings

Org-mode uses special lines in the buffer to define settings on a per-file basis. These lines start with a '#+' followed by a keyword, a colon, and then individual words defining a setting. Several setting words can be in the same line, but you can also have multiple repeated lines for the same keyword. While these settings are described throughout the manual, here is a summary. After changing any of those lines in the buffer, press C-c C-c with the cursor still in the line to activate the changes immediately. Otherwise they become effective only when the file is visited again in a new Emacs session.

#+ARCHIVE: %s_done::
> This line sets the archive location for the agenda file. It applies for all subsequent lines until the next '#+ARCHIVE' line, or the end of the file. The first such line also applies to any entries before it. The corresponding variable is org-archive-location.

#+CATEGORY:
> This line sets the category for the agenda file. The category applies for all subsequent lines until the next '#+CATEGORY' line, or the end of the file. The first such line also applies to any entries before it.

#+COLUMNS: %25ITEM .....
> Set the default format for columns view. This format applies when columns view is invoked in locations where no COLUMNS property applies.

#+CONSTANTS: name1=value1 ...
> Set file-local values for constants to be used in table formulas. This line sets the local variable org-table-formula-constants-local. The global version of this variable is org-table-formula-constants.

#+FILETAGS: :tag1:tag2:tag3:
> Set tags that can be inherited by any entry in the file, including the top-level entries.

#+DRAWERS: NAME1 .....
> Set the file-local set of drawers. The corresponding global variable is org-drawers.

#+LINK: linkword replace
> These lines (several are allowed) specify link abbreviations. See Section 4.6 [Link abbreviations], page 38. The corresponding variable is org-link-abbrev-alist.

#+PRIORITIES: highest lowest default
> This line sets the limits and the default for the priorities. All three must be either letters A-Z or numbers 0-9. The highest priority must have a lower ASCII number than the lowest priority.

#+PROPERTY: Property_Name Value
> This line sets a default inheritance value for entries in the current buffer, most useful for specifying the allowed values of a property.

#+SETUPFILE: file

> This line defines a file that holds more in-buffer setup. Normally this is entirely ignored. Only when the buffer is parsed for option-setting lines (i.e., when starting Org-mode for a file, when pressing C-c C-c in a settings line, or when exporting), then the contents of this file are parsed as if they had been included in the buffer. In particular, the file can be any other Org-mode file with internal setup. You can visit the file the cursor is in the line with C-c '.

#+STARTUP:

> This line sets options to be used at startup of Org-mode, when an Org file is being visited.

> The first set of options deals with the initial visibility of the outline tree. The corresponding variable for global default settings is org-startup-folded, with a default value t, which means overview.

overview	top-level headlines only
content	all headlines
showall	no folding of any entries
showeverything	show even drawer contents

> Dynamic virtual indentation is controlled by the variable org-startup-indented[1]

indent	start with org-indent-mode turned on
noindent	start with org-indent-mode turned off

> Then there are options for aligning tables upon visiting a file. This is useful in files containing narrowed table columns. The corresponding variable is org-startup-align-all-tables, with a default value nil.

align	align all tables
noalign	don't align tables on startup

> When visiting a file, inline images can be automatically displayed. The corresponding variable is org-startup-with-inline-images, with a default value nil to avoid delays when visiting a file.

inlineimages	show inline images
noinlineimages	don't show inline images on startup

> Logging the closing and reopening of TODO items and clock intervals can be configured using these options (see variables org-log-done, org-log-note-clock-out and org-log-repeat)

logdone	record a timestamp when an item is marked DONE
lognotedone	record timestamp and a note when DONE
nologdone	don't record when items are marked DONE
logrepeat	record a time when reinstating a repeating item

---

[1] Emacs 23 and Org-mode 6.29 are required

lognoterepeat	record a note when reinstating a repeating item
nologrepeat	do not record when reinstating repeating item
lognoteclock-out	record a note when clocking out
nolognoteclock-out	don't record a note when clocking out
logreschedule	record a timestamp when scheduling time changes
lognotereschedule	record a note when scheduling time changes
nologreschedule	do not record when a scheduling date changes
logredeadline	record a timestamp when deadline changes
lognoteredeadline	record a note when deadline changes
nologredeadline	do not record when a deadline date changes
logrefile	record a timestamp when refiling
lognoterefile	record a note when refiling
nologrefile	do not record when refiling

Here are the options for hiding leading stars in outline headings, and for indenting outlines. The corresponding variables are org-hide-leading-stars and org-odd-levels-only, both with a default setting nil (meaning showstars and oddeven).

hidestars	make all but one of the stars starting a headline invisible.
showstars	show all stars starting a headline
indent	virtual indentation according to outline level
noindent	no virtual indentation according to outline level
odd	allow only odd outline levels (1,3,...)
oddeven	allow all outline levels

To turn on custom format overlays over timestamps (variables org-put-time-stamp-overlays and org-time-stamp-overlay-formats), use

| customtime | overlay custom time format |

The following options influence the table spreadsheet (variable constants-unit-system).

| constcgs | 'constants.el' should use the c-g-s unit system |
| constSI | 'constants.el' should use the SI unit system |

To influence footnote settings, use the following keywords. The corresponding variables are org-footnote-define-inline, org-footnote-auto-label, and org-footnote-auto-adjust.

fninline	define footnotes inline
fnnoinline	define footnotes in separate section
fnlocal	define footnotes near first reference, but not inline
fnprompt	prompt for footnote labels
fnauto	create [fn:1]-like labels automatically (default)

    `fnconfirm`   offer automatic label for editing or confirmation
    `fnplain`   create [1]-like labels automatically
    `fnadjust`   automatically renumber and sort footnotes
    `nofnadjust`   do not renumber and sort automatically

To hide blocks on startup, use these keywords. The corresponding variable is `org-hide-block-startup`.

    `hideblocks`   Hide all begin/end blocks on startup
    `nohideblocks`   Do not hide blocks on startup

The display of entities as UTF-8 characters is governed by the variable `org-pretty-entities` and the keywords

    `entitiespretty`   Show entities as UTF-8 characters where possible
    `entitiesplain`   Leave entities plain

`#+TAGS: TAG1(c1) TAG2(c2)`
> These lines (several such lines are allowed) specify the valid tags in this file, and (potentially) the corresponding *fast tag selection* keys. The corresponding variable is `org-tag-alist`.

`#+TBLFM:`
> This line contains the formulas for the table directly above the line.

`#+TITLE:`, `#+AUTHOR:`, `#+EMAIL:`, `#+LANGUAGE:`, `#+TEXT:`, `#+DATE:`,
`#+OPTIONS:`, `#+BIND:`, `#+XSLT:`,
`#+DESCRIPTION:`, `#+KEYWORDS:`,
`#+LATEX_HEADER:`, `#+STYLE:`, `#+LINK_UP:`, `#+LINK_HOME:`,
`#+EXPORT_SELECT_TAGS:`, `#+EXPORT_EXCLUDE_TAGS:`
> These lines provide settings for exporting files. For more details see Section 12.2 [Export options], page 133.

`#+TODO:` `#+SEQ_TODO:` `#+TYP_TODO:`
> These lines set the TODO keywords and their interpretation in the current file. The corresponding variable is `org-todo-keywords`.

16.7 The very busy C-c C-c key

The key `C-c C-c` has many purposes in Org, which are all mentioned scattered throughout this manual. One specific function of this key is to add *tags* to a headline (see Chapter 6 [Tags], page 55). In many other circumstances it means something like *"Hey Org, look here and update according to what you see here"*. Here is a summary of what this means in different contexts.

- If there are highlights in the buffer from the creation of a sparse tree, or from clock display, remove these highlights.

- If the cursor is in one of the special `#+KEYWORD` lines, this triggers scanning the buffer for these lines and updating the information.

- If the cursor is inside a table, realign the table. This command works even if the automatic table editor has been turned off.

- If the cursor is on a `#+TBLFM` line, re-apply the formulas to the entire table.

- If the current buffer is a capture buffer, close the note and file it. With a prefix argument, file it, without further interaction, to the default location.
- If the cursor is on a <<<target>>>, update radio targets and corresponding links in this buffer.
- If the cursor is in a property line or at the start or end of a property drawer, offer property commands.
- If the cursor is at a footnote reference, go to the corresponding definition, and vice versa.
- If the cursor is on a statistics cookie, update it.
- If the cursor is in a plain list item with a checkbox, toggle the status of the checkbox.
- If the cursor is on a numbered item in a plain list, renumber the ordered list.
- If the cursor is on the #+BEGIN line of a dynamic block, the block is updated.

16.8 A cleaner outline view

Some people find it noisy and distracting that the Org headlines start with a potentially large number of stars, and that text below the headlines is not indented. While this is no problem when writing a *book-like* document where the outline headings are really section headings, in a more *list-oriented* outline, indented structure is a lot cleaner:

```
* Top level headline        |  * Top level headline
** Second level             |    * Second level
*** 3rd level               |      * 3rd level
some text                   |      some text
*** 3rd level               |      * 3rd level
more text                   |      more text
* Another top level headline|  * Another top level headline
```

If you are using at least Emacs 23.2[2] and version 6.29 of Org, this kind of view can be achieved dynamically at display time using org-indent-mode. In this minor mode, all lines are prefixed for display with the necessary amount of space.[3] Also headlines are prefixed with additional stars, so that the amount of indentation shifts by two[4] spaces per level. All headline stars but the last one are made invisible using the org-hide face[5]—see below under '2.' for more information on how this works. You can turn on org-indent-mode for all

---

[2] Emacs 23.1 can actually crash with org-indent-mode

[3] org-indent-mode also sets the wrap-prefix property, such that visual-line-mode (or purely setting word-wrap) wraps long lines (including headlines) correctly indented.

[4] See the variable org-indent-indentation-per-level.

[5] Turning on org-indent-mode sets org-hide-leading-stars to t and org-adapt-indentation to nil.

files by customizing the variable `org-startup-indented`, or you can turn it on for individual files using

```
#+STARTUP: indent
```

If you want a similar effect in an earlier version of Emacs and/or Org, or if you want the indentation to be hard space characters so that the plain text file looks as similar as possible to the Emacs display, Org supports you in the following way:

1. *Indentation of text below headlines*
   You may indent text below each headline to make the left boundary line up with the headline, like

   ```
   *** 3rd level
       more text, now indented
   ```

   Org supports this with paragraph filling, line wrapping, and structure editing,[6] preserving or adapting the indentation as appropriate.

2. *Hiding leading stars*
   You can modify the display in such a way that all leading stars become invisible. To do this in a global way, configure the variable `org-hide-leading-stars` or change this on a per-file basis with

   ```
   #+STARTUP: hidestars
   #+STARTUP: showstars
   ```

   With hidden stars, the tree becomes:

   ```
   * Top level headline
    * Second level
     * 3rd level
     ...
   ```

   The leading stars are not truly replaced by whitespace, they are only fontified with the face org-hide that uses the background color as font color. If you are not using either white or black background, you may have to customize this face to get the wanted effect. Another possibility is to set this font such that the extra stars are *almost* invisible, for example using the color grey90 on a white background.

3. Things become cleaner still if you skip all the even levels and use only odd levels 1, 3, 5..., effectively adding two stars to go from one outline level to the next.[7] In this way we get the outline view shown at the beginning of this section. In order to make the structure editing and export commands handle this convention correctly, configure the variable `org-odd-levels-only`, or set this on a per-file basis with one of the following lines:

   ```
   #+STARTUP: odd
   #+STARTUP: oddeven
   ```

   You can convert an Org file from single-star-per-level to the double-star-per-level convention with M-x org-convert-to-odd-levels RET in that file. The reverse operation is M-x org-convert-to-oddeven-levels.

---

[6] See also the variable `org-adapt-indentation`.

[7] When you need to specify a level for a property search or refile targets, 'LEVEL=2' will correspond to 3 stars, etc.

16.9 Using Org on a tty

Because Org contains a large number of commands, by default many of Org's core commands are bound to keys that are generally not accessible on a tty, such as the cursor keys (`left`, `right`, `up`, `down`), `TAB` and `RET`, in particular when used together with modifiers like `Meta` and/or `Shift`. To access these commands on a tty when special keys are unavailable, the following alternative bindings can be used. The tty bindings below will likely be more cumbersome; you may find for some of the bindings below that a customized workaround suits you better. For example, changing a timestamp is really only fun with S-`cursor` keys, whereas on a tty you would rather use C-c . to re-insert the timestamp.

Default	Alternative 1	Speed key	Alternative 2
S-`TAB`	C-u `TAB`	c	
M-`left`	C-c C-x l	l	`Esc` `left`
M-S-`left`	C-c C-x L	L	
M-`right`	C-c C-x r	r	`Esc` `right`
M-S-`right`	C-c C-x R	R	
M-`up`	C-c C-x u		`Esc` `up`
M-S-`up`	C-c C-x U	U	
M-`down`	C-c C-x d		`Esc` `down`
M-S-`down`	C-c C-x D	D	
S-`RET`	C-c C-x c		
M-`RET`	C-c C-x m		`Esc` `RET`
M-S-`RET`	C-c C-x M		
S-`left`	C-c `left`		
S-`right`	C-c `right`		
S-`up`	C-c `up`		
S-`down`	C-c `down`		
C-S-`left`	C-c C-x `left`		
C-S-`right`	C-c C-x `right`		

16.10 Interaction with other packages

Org lives in the world of GNU Emacs and interacts in various ways with other code out there.

16.10.1 Packages that Org cooperates with

'calc.el' by Dave Gillespie

Org uses the Calc package for implementing spreadsheet functionality in its tables (see Chapter 15 [The spreadsheet], page 185). Org checks for the availability of Calc by looking for the function calc-eval which will have been autoloaded during setup if Calc has been installed properly. As of Emacs 22, Calc is part of the Emacs distribution. Another possibility for interaction between the two packages is using Calc for embedded calculations. See section "Embedded Mode" in *GNU Emacs Calc Manual*.

'constants.el' by Carsten Dominik
   In a table formula (see Chapter 15 [The spreadsheet], page 185), it is possible to use names for natural constants or units. Instead of defining your own constants in the variable org-table-formula-constants, install the 'constants' package which defines a large number of constants and units, and lets you use unit prefixes like 'M' for 'Mega', etc. You will need version 2.0 of this package, available at http://www.astro.uva.nl/~dominik/Tools. Org checks for the function constants-get, which has to be autoloaded in your setup. See the installation instructions in the file 'constants.el'.

'cdlatex.el' by Carsten Dominik
   Org-mode can make use of the CDLaTeX package to efficiently enter LaTeX fragments into Org files. See Section 11.7.5 [CDLaTeX mode], page 132.

'imenu.el' by Ake Stenhoff and Lars Lindberg
   Imenu allows menu access to an index of items in a file. Org-mode supports Imenu—all you need to do to get the index is the following:

```
(add-hook 'org-mode-hook
          (lambda () (imenu-add-to-menubar "Imenu")))
```

   By default the index is two levels deep—you can modify the depth using the option org-imenu-depth.

'remember.el' by John Wiegley
   Org used to use this package for capture, but no longer does.

'speedbar.el' by Eric M. Ludlam
   Speedbar is a package that creates a special frame displaying files and index items in files. Org-mode supports Speedbar and allows you to drill into Org files directly from the Speedbar. It also allows you to restrict the scope of agenda commands to a file or a subtree by using the command < in the Speedbar frame.

'table.el' by Takaaki Ota
   Complex ASCII tables with automatic line wrapping, column- and row-spanning, and alignment can be created using the Emacs table package by Takaaki Ota (http://sourceforge.net/projects/table, and also part of Emacs 22). Org-mode will recognize these tables and export them properly. Because of interference with other Org-mode functionality, you unfortunately cannot edit these tables directly in the buffer. Instead, you need to use the command C-c ' to edit them, similar to source code snippets.

C-c '
   Edit a 'table.el' table. Works when the cursor is in a table.el table.

C-c ~
> Insert a 'table.el' table. If there is already a table at point, this
> command converts it between the 'table.el' format and the Org-
> mode format. See the documentation string of the command org-
> convert-table for the restrictions under which this is possible.

'table.el' is part of Emacs since Emacs 22.

'footnote.el' by Steven L. Baur
> Org-mode recognizes numerical footnotes as provided by this package.
> However, Org-mode also has its own footnote support (see Section 2.10
> [Footnotes], page 20), which makes using 'footnote.el' unnecessary.

16.10.2 Packages that lead to conflicts with Org-mode

In Emacs 23, shift-selection-mode is on by default, meaning that cursor
motions combined with the shift key should start or enlarge regions. This
conflicts with the use of S-(cursor) commands in Org to change timestamps, TODO keywords, priorities, and item bullet types if the cursor is
at such a location. By default, S-(cursor) commands outside special contexts don't do anything, but you can customize the variable org-support-
shift-select. Org-mode then tries to accommodate shift selection by (i)
using it outside of the special contexts where special commands apply, and
by (ii) extending an existing active region even if the cursor moves across
a special context.

'CUA.el' by Kim. F. Storm
> Key bindings in Org conflict with the S-<cursor> keys used by CUA mode
> (as well as pc-select-mode and s-region-mode) to select and extend the
> region. In fact, Emacs 23 has this built-in in the form of shift-selection-
> mode, see previous paragraph. If you are using Emacs 23, you probably
> don't want to use another package for this purpose. However, if you prefer
> to leave these keys to a different package while working in Org-mode, con-
> figure the variable org-replace-disputed-keys. When set, Org will move
> the following key bindings in Org files, and in the agenda buffer (but not
> during date selection).

S-UP	⇒	M-p	S-DOWN	⇒	M-n
S-LEFT	⇒	M--	S-RIGHT	⇒	M-+
C-S-LEFT	⇒	M-S--	C-S-RIGHT	⇒	M-S-+

Yes, these are unfortunately more difficult to remember. If you want to
have other replacement keys, look at the variable org-disputed-keys.

'yasnippet.el'
> The way Org-mode binds the TAB key (binding to [tab] instead of "\t")
> overrules YASnippet's access to this key. The following code fixed this
> problem:

```
(add-hook 'org-mode-hook
          (lambda ()
            (org-set-local 'yas/trigger-key [tab])
            (define-key yas/keymap [tab]
              'yas/next-field-group)))
```

'windmove.el' by Hovav Shacham

This package also uses the S-<cursor> keys, so everything written in the paragraph above about CUA mode also applies here. If you want make the windmove function active in locations where Org-mode does not have special functionality on S-(cursor), add this to your configuration:

```
;; Make windmove work in org-mode:
(add-hook 'org-shiftup-final-hook 'windmove-up)
(add-hook 'org-shiftleft-final-hook 'windmove-left)
(add-hook 'org-shiftdown-final-hook 'windmove-down)
(add-hook 'org-shiftright-final-hook 'windmove-right)
```

'viper.el' by Michael Kifer

Viper uses C-c / and therefore makes this key not access the corresponding Org-mode command org-sparse-tree. You need to find another key for this command, or override the key in viper-vi-global-user-map with

```
(define-key viper-vi-global-user-map "C-c /"
  'org-sparse-tree)
```

Appendix A Hacking

This appendix covers some aspects where users can extend the functionality of Org.

A.1 Hooks

Org has a large number of hook variables that can be used to add functionality. This appendix about hacking is going to illustrate the use of some of them. A complete list of all hooks with documentation is maintained by the Worg project and can be found at orgmode.org[1].

A.2 Add-on packages

A large number of add-on packages have been written by various authors. These packages are not part of Emacs, but they are distributed as contributed packages with the separate release available at the Org-mode home page at http://orgmode.org. The list of contributed packages, along with documentation about each package, is maintained by the Worg project at http://orgmode.org/worg/org-contrib/.

A.3 Adding hyperlink types

Org has a large number of hyperlink types built-in (see Chapter 4 [Hyperlinks], page 31). If you would like to add new link types, Org provides an interface for doing so. Let's look at an example file, 'org-man.el', that will add support for creating links like '[[man:printf][The printf manpage]]' to show Unix manual pages inside Emacs:

```
;;; org-man.el - Support for links to manpages in Org

(require 'org)

(org-add-link-type "man" 'org-man-open)
(add-hook 'org-store-link-functions 'org-man-store-link)

(defcustom org-man-command 'man
  "The Emacs command to be used to display a man page."
  :group 'org-link
  :type '(choice (const man) (const woman)))

(defun org-man-open (path)
  "Visit the manpage on PATH.
PATH should be a topic that can be thrown at the man command."
  (funcall org-man-command path))
```

---

[1] http://orgmode.org/worg/org-configs/org-hooks.php

```
(defun org-man-store-link ()
  "Store a link to a manpage."
  (when (memq major-mode '(Man-mode woman-mode))
    ;; This is a man page, we do make this link
    (let* ((page (org-man-get-page-name))
           (link (concat "man:" page))
           (description (format "Manpage for %s" page)))
      (org-store-link-props
       :type "man"
       :link link
       :description description))))

(defun org-man-get-page-name ()
  "Extract the page name from the buffer name."
  ;; This works for both 'Man-mode' and 'woman-mode'.
  (if (string-match " \\(\\S-+\\)\\*" (buffer-name))
      (match-string 1 (buffer-name))
    (error "Cannot create link to this man page")))

(provide 'org-man)

;;; org-man.el ends here
```

You would activate this new link type in '.emacs' with

```
(require 'org-man)
```

Let's go through the file and see what it does.

1. It does (require 'org) to make sure that 'org.el' has been loaded.

2. The next line calls org-add-link-type to define a new link type with prefix 'man'. The call also contains the name of a function that will be called to follow such a link.

3. The next line adds a function to org-store-link-functions, in order to allow the command C-c l to record a useful link in a buffer displaying a man page.

   The rest of the file defines the necessary variables and functions. First there is a customization variable that determines which Emacs command should be used to display man pages. There are two options, man and woman. Then the function to follow a link is defined. It gets the link path as an argument—in this case the link path is just a topic for the manual command. The function calls the value of org-man-command to display the man page.

   Finally the function org-man-store-link is defined. When you try to store a link with C-c l, this function will be called to try to make a link. The function must first decide if it is supposed to create the link for this buffer type; we do this by checking the value of the variable major-mode. If not, the function must exit and return the value nil. If yes, the link is created by getting the manual topic from the buffer name and prefixing it with the string 'man:'. Then it must call the command org-store-link-props and set the :type and :link properties. Optionally you can also set the :description property to provide a default for the link description when the link is later inserted into an Org buffer with C-c C-l.

When it makes sense for your new link type, you may also define a function org-PREFIX-complete-link that implements special (e.g., completion) support for inserting such a link with C-c C-l. Such a function should not accept any arguments, and return the full link with prefix.

A.4 Context-sensitive commands

Org has several commands that act differently depending on context. The most important example it the C-c C-c (see Section 16.7 [The very busy C-c C-c key], page 203). Also the M-cursor and M-S-cursor keys have this property.

Add-ons can tap into this functionality by providing a function that detects special context for that add-on and executes functionality appropriate for the context. Here is an example from Dan Davison's 'org-R.el' which allows you to evaluate commands based on the 'R' programming language .[2] For this package, special contexts are lines that start with #+R: or #+RR:.

```
(defun org-R-apply-maybe ()
  "Detect if this is context for org-R and execute R commands."
  (if (save-excursion
        (beginning-of-line 1)
        (looking-at "#\\+RR?:"))
      (progn (call-interactively 'org-R-apply)
             t) ;; to signal that we took action
    nil)) ;; to signal that we did not

(add-hook 'org-ctrl-c-ctrl-c-hook 'org-R-apply-maybe)
```

The function first checks if the cursor is in such a line. If that is the case, org-R-apply is called and the function returns t to signal that action was taken, and C-c C-c will stop looking for other contexts. If the function finds it should do nothing locally, it returns nil so that other, similar functions can have a try.

A.5 Tables and lists in arbitrary syntax

Since Orgtbl mode can be used as a minor mode in arbitrary buffers, a frequent feature request has been to make it work with native tables in specific languages, for example LATEX. However, this is extremely hard to do in a general way, would lead to a customization nightmare, and would take away much of the simplicity of the Orgtbl-mode table editor.

This appendix describes a different approach. We keep the Orgtbl mode table in its native format (the *source table*), and use a custom function to *translate* the table to the correct syntax, and to *install* it in the right location (the *target table*). This puts the burden of writing conversion functions on the user, but it allows for a very flexible system.

---

[2] 'org-R.el' has been replaced by the org-mode functionality described in Chapter 14 [Working With Source Code], page 163 and is now obsolete.

Bastien added the ability to do the same with lists, in Orgstruct mode. You can use Org's facilities to edit and structure lists by turning `orgstruct-mode` on, then locally exporting such lists in another format (HTML, LATEX or Texinfo.)

A.5.1 Radio tables

To define the location of the target table, you first need to create two lines that are comments in the current mode, but contain magic words for Orgtbl mode to find. Orgtbl mode will insert the translated table between these lines, replacing whatever was there before. For example:

```
/* BEGIN RECEIVE ORGTBL table_name */
/* END RECEIVE ORGTBL table_name */
```

Just above the source table, we put a special line that tells Orgtbl mode how to translate this table and where to install it. For example:

```
#+ORGTBL: SEND table_name translation_function arguments....
```

`table_name` is the reference name for the table that is also used in the receiver lines. `translation_function` is the Lisp function that does the translation. Furthermore, the line can contain a list of arguments (alternating key and value) at the end. The arguments will be passed as a property list to the translation function for interpretation. A few standard parameters are already recognized and acted upon before the translation function is called:

`:skip N`

Skip the first N lines of the table. Hlines do count as separate lines for this parameter!

`:skipcols (n1 n2 ...)`

List of columns that should be skipped. If the table has a column with calculation marks, that column is automatically discarded as well. Please note that the translator function sees the table *after* the removal of these columns, the function never knows that there have been additional columns.

The one problem remaining is how to keep the source table in the buffer without disturbing the normal workings of the file, for example during compilation of a C file or processing of a LATEX file. There are a number of different solutions:

- The table could be placed in a block comment if that is supported by the language. For example, in C mode you could wrap the table between '/*' and '*/' lines.

- Sometimes it is possible to put the table after some kind of *END* statement, for example '\bye' in TEX and '\end{document}' in LATEX.

- You can just comment the table line-by-line whenever you want to process the file, and uncomment it whenever you need to edit the table. This only sounds tedious—the command `M-x orgtbl-toggle-comment` makes this comment-toggling very easy, in particular if you bind it to a key.

A.5.2 A LaTeX example of radio tables

The best way to wrap the source table in LaTeX is to use the comment environment provided by 'comment.sty'. It has to be activated by placing \usepackage{comment} into the document header. Orgtbl mode can insert a radio table skeleton[3] with the command M-x orgtbl-insert-radio-table. You will be prompted for a table name, let's say we use 'salesfigures'. You will then get the following template:

```
% BEGIN RECEIVE ORGTBL salesfigures
% END RECEIVE ORGTBL salesfigures
\begin{comment}
#+ORGTBL: SEND salesfigures orgtbl-to-latex
| | |
\end{comment}
```

The #+ORGTBL: SEND line tells Orgtbl mode to use the function orgtbl-to-latex to convert the table into LaTeX and to put it into the receiver location with name salesfigures. You may now fill in the table—feel free to use the spreadsheet features:[4]

```
% BEGIN RECEIVE ORGTBL salesfigures
% END RECEIVE ORGTBL salesfigures
\begin{comment}
#+ORGTBL: SEND salesfigures orgtbl-to-latex
| Month | Days | Nr sold | per day |
|-------+------+---------+---------|
| Jan   | 23 |      55 |     2.4 |
| Feb   | 21 |      16 |     0.8 |
| March | 22 |     278 |    12.6 |
#+TBLFM: $4=$3/$2;%.1f
% $ (optional extra dollar to keep font-lock happy, see footnote)
\end{comment}
```

When you are done, press C-c C-c in the table to get the converted table inserted between the two marker lines.

Now let's assume you want to make the table header by hand, because you want to control how columns are aligned, etc. In this case we make sure that the table translator skips the first 2 lines of the source table, and tell the command to work as a *splice*, i.e., to not produce header and footer commands of the target table:

---

[3] By default this works only for LaTeX, HTML, and Texinfo. Configure the variable orgtbl-radio-tables to install templates for other modes.

[4] If the '#+TBLFM' line contains an odd number of dollar characters, this may cause problems with font-lock in LaTeX mode. As shown in the example you can fix this by adding an extra line inside the comment environment that is used to balance the dollar expressions. If you are using AUCTeX with the font-latex library, a much better solution is to add the comment environment to the variable LaTeX-verbatim-environments.

```
\begin{tabular}{lrrr}
Month & \multicolumn{1}{c}{Days} & Nr.\ sold & per day\\
% BEGIN RECEIVE ORGTBL salesfigures
% END RECEIVE ORGTBL salesfigures
\end{tabular}
%
\begin{comment}
#+ORGTBL: SEND salesfigures orgtbl-to-latex :splice t :skip 2
| Month | Days | Nr sold | per day |
|-------+------+---------+---------|
| Jan   |   23 |      55 |     2.4 |
| Feb   |   21 |      16 |     0.8 |
| March |   22 |     278 |    12.6 |
#+TBLFM: $4=$3/$2;%.1f
\end{comment}
```

The LaTeX translator function `orgtbl-to-latex` is already part of Orgtbl mode. It uses a `tabular` environment to typeset the table and marks horizontal lines with `\hline`. Furthermore, it interprets the following parameters (see also see Section A.5.3 [Translator functions], page 217):

`:splice nil/t`

When set to t, return only table body lines, don't wrap them into a tabular environment. Default is nil.

`:fmt fmt`

A format to be used to wrap each field, it should contain %s for the original field value. For example, to wrap each field value in dollars, you could use `:fmt "$%s$"`. This may also be a property list with column numbers and formats. for example `:fmt (2 "$%s$" 4 "%s\\%%")`. A function of one argument can be used in place of the strings; the function must return a formatted string.

`:efmt efmt`

Use this format to print numbers with exponentials. The format should have %s twice for inserting mantissa and exponent, for example `"%s\\times10^{%s}"`. The default is `"%s\\,(%s)"`. This may also be a property list with column numbers and formats, for example `:efmt (2 "$%s\\times10^{%s}$" 4 "$%s\\cdot10^{%s}$")`. After efmt has been applied to a value, fmt will also be applied. Similar to fmt, functions of two arguments can be supplied instead of strings.

A.5.3 Translator functions

Orgtbl mode has several translator functions built-in: `orgtbl-to-csv` (comma-separated values), `orgtbl-to-tsv` (TAB-separated values) `orgtbl-to-latex`, `orgtbl-to-html`, and `orgtbl-to-texinfo`. Except for `orgtbl-to-html`,[5] these all use a generic translator, `orgtbl-to-generic`. For example, `orgtbl-to-latex` itself is a very short function that computes the column definitions for the tabular environment, defines a few field and line separators and then hands processing over to the generic translator. Here is the entire code:

```
(defun orgtbl-to-latex (table params)
  "Convert the Orgtbl mode TABLE to LaTeX."
  (let* ((alignment (mapconcat (lambda (x) (if x "r" "l"))
                               org-table-last-alignment ""))
         (params2
          (list
           :tstart (concat "\\begin{tabular}{" alignment "}")
           :tend "\\end{tabular}"
           :lstart "" :lend " \\\\" :sep " & "
           :efmt "%s\\,(%s)" :hline "\\hline")))
    (orgtbl-to-generic table
                       (org-combine-plists params2 params)))
```

As you can see, the properties passed into the function (variable *PARAMS*) are combined with the ones newly defined in the function (variable *PARAMS2*). The ones passed into the function (i.e., the ones set by the 'ORGTBL SEND' line) take precedence. So if you would like to use the LaTeX translator, but wanted the line endings to be '\\[2mm]' instead of the default '\\', you could just overrule the default with

```
#+ORGTBL: SEND test orgtbl-to-latex :lend " \\\\[2mm]"
```

For a new language, you can either write your own converter function in analogy with the LaTeX translator, or you can use the generic function directly. For example, if you have a language where a table is started with '!BTBL!', ended with '!ETBL!', and where table lines are started with '!BL!', ended with '!EL!', and where the field separator is a TAB, you could call the generic translator like this (on a single line!):

```
#+ORGTBL: SEND test orgtbl-to-generic
              :tstart "!BTBL!" :tend "!ETBL!"
              :lstart "!BL! " :lend " !EL!" :sep "\t"
```

Please check the documentation string of the function `orgtbl-to-generic` for a full list of parameters understood by that function, and remember that you can pass each of them into `orgtbl-to-latex`, `orgtbl-to-texinfo`, and any other function using the generic function.

Of course you can also write a completely new function doing complicated things the generic translator cannot do. A translator function takes two arguments. The first argument is the table, a list of lines, each line either the symbol

---

[5] The HTML translator uses the same code that produces tables during HTML export.

hline or a list of fields. The second argument is the property list containing
all parameters specified in the '#+ORGTBL: SEND' line. The function must return
a single string containing the formatted table. If you write a generally useful
translator, please post it on emacs-orgmode@gnu.org so that others can benefit
from your work.

A.5.4 Radio lists

Sending and receiving radio lists works exactly the same way as sending and
receiving radio tables (see Section A.5.1 [Radio tables], page 214). As for radio
tables, you can insert radio list templates in HTML, LaTeX and Texinfo modes
by calling org-list-insert-radio-list.

Here are the differences with radio tables:

— Orgstruct mode must be active.

— Use the ORGLST keyword instead of ORGTBL.

— The available translation functions for radio lists don't take parameters.

— C-c C-c will work when pressed on the first item of the list.

Here is a LaTeX example. Let's say that you have this in your LaTeX file:

```
% BEGIN RECEIVE ORGLST to-buy
% END RECEIVE ORGLST to-buy
\begin{comment}
#+ORGLST: SEND to-buy org-list-to-latex
- a new house
- a new computer
  + a new keyboard
  + a new mouse
- a new life
\end{comment}
```

Pressing 'C-c C-c' on a new house and will insert the converted LaTeX list
between the two marker lines.

A.6 Dynamic blocks

Org documents can contain *dynamic blocks*. These are specially marked regions that are updated by some user-written function. A good example for such
a block is the clock table inserted by the command C-c C-x C-r (see Section 8.4
[Clocking work time], page 76).

Dynamic blocks are enclosed by a BEGIN-END structure that assigns a name
to the block and can also specify parameters for the function producing the
content of the block.

```
#+BEGIN: myblock :parameter1 value1 :parameter2 value2 ...

#+END:
```

Dynamic blocks are updated with the following commands

C-c C-x C-u
    Update dynamic block at point.

```
C-u C-c C-x C-u
```
  Update all dynamic blocks in the current file.

Updating a dynamic block means to remove all the text between BEGIN and END, parse the BEGIN line for parameters and then call the specific writer function for this block to insert the new content. If you want to use the original content in the writer function, you can use the extra parameter :content.

For a block with name myblock, the writer function is org-dblock-write:myblock with as only parameter a property list with the parameters given in the begin line. Here is a trivial example of a block that keeps track of when the block update function was last run:

```
#+BEGIN: block-update-time :format "on %m/%d/%Y at %H:%M"

#+END:
```
The corresponding block writer function could look like this:

```
(defun org-dblock-write:block-update-time (params)
   (let ((fmt (or (plist-get params :format) "%d. %m. %Y")))
      (insert "Last block update at: "
            (format-time-string fmt (current-time)))))
```
If you want to make sure that all dynamic blocks are always up-to-date, you could add the function org-update-all-dblocks to a hook, for example before-save-hook. org-update-all-dblocks is written in a way such that it does nothing in buffers that are not in org-mode.

A.7 Special agenda views

Org provides a special hook that can be used to narrow down the selection made by these agenda views: todo, alltodo, tags, tags-todo, tags-tree. You may specify a function that is used at each match to verify if the match should indeed be part of the agenda view, and if not, how much should be skipped.

Let's say you want to produce a list of projects that contain a WAITING tag anywhere in the project tree. Let's further assume that you have marked all tree headings that define a project with the TODO keyword PROJECT. In this case you would run a TODO search for the keyword PROJECT, but skip the match unless there is a WAITING tag anywhere in the subtree belonging to the project line.

To achieve this, you must write a function that searches the subtree for the tag. If the tag is found, the function must return nil to indicate that this match should not be skipped. If there is no such tag, return the location of the end of the subtree, to indicate that search should continue from there.

```
(defun my-skip-unless-waiting ()
   "Skip trees that are not waiting"
   (let ((subtree-end (save-excursion (org-end-of-subtree t))))
      (if (re-search-forward ":waiting:" subtree-end t)
            nil           ; tag found, do not skip
         subtree-end)))   ; tag not found, continue after end of
                          subtree
```

Now you may use this function in an agenda custom command, for example
like this:

```
(org-add-agenda-custom-command
 '("b" todo "PROJECT"
   ((org-agenda-skip-function 'my-skip-unless-waiting)
    (org-agenda-overriding-header
     "Projects waiting for something: "))))
```

Note that this also binds `org-agenda-overriding-header` to get a meaningful header in the agenda view.

A general way to create custom searches is to base them on a search for
entries with a certain level limit. If you want to study all entries with your
custom search function, simply do a search for 'LEVEL>0',[6] and then use `org-agenda-skip-function` to select the entries you really want to have.

You may also put a Lisp form into `org-agenda-skip-function`. In particular,
you may use the functions `org-agenda-skip-entry-if` and `org-agenda-skip-subtree-if` in this form, for example:

`'(org-agenda-skip-entry-if 'scheduled)`
  Skip current entry if it has been scheduled.

`'(org-agenda-skip-entry-if 'notscheduled)`
  Skip current entry if it has not been scheduled.

`'(org-agenda-skip-entry-if 'deadline)`
  Skip current entry if it has a deadline.

`'(org-agenda-skip-entry-if 'scheduled 'deadline)`
  Skip current entry if it has a deadline, or if it is scheduled.

`'(org-agenda-skip-entry-if 'todo '("TODO" "WAITING"))`
  Skip current entry if the TODO keyword is TODO or WAITING.

`'(org-agenda-skip-entry-if 'todo 'done)`
  Skip current entry if the TODO keyword marks a DONE state.

`'(org-agenda-skip-entry-if 'timestamp)`
  Skip current entry if it has any timestamp, may also be deadline or scheduled.

`'(org-agenda-skip-entry 'regexp "regular expression")`
  Skip current entry if the regular expression matches in the entry.

`'(org-agenda-skip-entry 'notregexp "regular expression")`
  Skip current entry unless the regular expression matches.

`'(org-agenda-skip-subtree-if 'regexp "regular expression")`
  Same as above, but check and skip the entire subtree.

Therefore we could also have written the search for WAITING projects like
this, even without defining a special function:

---

[6] Note that, when using `org-odd-levels-only`, a level number corresponds to order
    in the hierarchy, not to the number of stars.

```
(org-add-agenda-custom-command
 '("b" todo "PROJECT"
   ((org-agenda-skip-function '(org-agenda-skip-subtree-if
                                'regexp ":waiting:"))
    (org-agenda-overriding-header
     "Projects waiting for something: "))))
```

A.8 Extracting agenda information

Org provides commands to access agenda information for the command line in Emacs batch mode. This extracted information can be sent directly to a printer, or it can be read by a program that does further processing of the data. The first of these commands is the function `org-batch-agenda`, that produces an agenda view and sends it as ASCII text to STDOUT. The command takes a single string as parameter. If the string has length 1, it is used as a key to one of the commands you have configured in `org-agenda-custom-commands`, basically any key you can use after C-c a. For example, to directly print the current TODO list, you could use

```
emacs -batch -l ~/.emacs -eval '(org-batch-agenda "t")' | lpr
```

If the parameter is a string with 2 or more characters, it is used as a tags/TODO match string. For example, to print your local shopping list (all items with the tag 'shop', but excluding the tag 'NewYork'), you could use

```
emacs -batch -l ~/.emacs                                          \
      -eval '(org-batch-agenda "+shop-NewYork")' | lpr
```

You may also modify parameters on the fly like this:

```
emacs -batch -l ~/.emacs                                          \
   -eval '(org-batch-agenda "a"                                   \
           org-agenda-ndays 30                                    \
           org-agenda-include-diary nil                           \
           org-agenda-files (quote ("~/org/project.org")))'       \
      | lpr
```

which will produce a 30-day agenda, fully restricted to the Org file '~/org/projects.org', not even including the diary.

If you want to process the agenda data in more sophisticated ways, you can use the command `org-batch-agenda-csv` to get a comma-separated list of values for each agenda item. Each line in the output will contain a number of fields separated by commas. The fields in a line are:

category
:   The category of the item

head
:   The headline, without TODO keyword, TAGS and PRIORITY

type
:   The type of the agenda entry, can be

todo	selected in TODO match
tagsmatch	selected in tags match

diary	imported from diary
deadline	a deadline
scheduled	scheduled
timestamp	appointment, selected by timestamp
closed	entry was closed on date
upcoming-deadline	warning about nearing deadline
past-scheduled	forwarded scheduled item
block	entry has date block including date

todo
>   The TODO keyword, if any

tags
>   All tags including inherited ones, separated by colons

date
>   The relevant date, like 2007-2-14

time
>   The time, like 15:00-16:50

extra
>   String with extra planning info

priority-l
>   The priority letter if any was given

priority-n
>   The computed numerical priority

Time and date will only be given if a timestamp (or deadline/scheduled) led to the selection of the item.

A CSV list like this is very easy to use in a post-processing script. For example, here is a Perl program that gets the TODO list from Emacs/Org and prints all the items, preceded by a checkbox:

```
#!/usr/bin/perl

# define the Emacs command to run
$cmd =
"emacs -batch -l ~/.emacs -eval '(org-batch-agenda-csv \"t\")'";

# run it and capture the output
$agenda = qx{$cmd 2>/dev/null};

# loop over all lines
foreach $line (split(/\n/,$agenda)) {
  # get the individual values
  ($category,$head,$type,$todo,$tags,$date,$time,$extra,
   $priority_l,$priority_n) = split(/,/,$line);
  # process and print
  print "[ ] $head\n";
}
```

A.9 Using the property API

Here is a description of the functions that can be used to work with properties.

org-entry-properties &optional pom which   *Function*
> Get all properties of the entry at point-or-marker POM.
> This includes the TODO keyword, the tags, time strings for deadline, sched-uled, and clocking, and any additional properties defined in the entry. The return value is an alist. Keys may occur multiple times if the property key was used several times.
> POM may also be nil, in which case the current entry is used. If WHICH is nil or 'all', get all properties. If WHICH is 'special' or 'standard', only get that subclass.

org-entry-get pom property &optional inherit   *Function*
> Get value of PROPERTY for entry at point-or-marker POM. By default, this only looks at properties defined locally in the entry. If INHERIT is non-nil and the entry does not have the property, then also check higher levels of the hierarchy. If INHERIT is the symbol selective, use inheritance if and only if the setting of org-use-property-inheritance selects PROPERTY for inheritance.

org-entry-delete pom property   *Function*
> Delete the property PROPERTY from entry at point-or-marker POM.

org-entry-put pom property value   *Function*
> Set PROPERTY to VALUE for entry at point-or-marker POM.

org-buffer-property-keys &optional include-specials   *Function*
> Get all property keys in the current buffer.

org-insert-property-drawer   *Function*
> Insert a property drawer at point.

org-entry-put-multivalued-property pom property &rest values   *Function*
> Set PROPERTY at point-or-marker POM to VALUES. VALUES should be a list of strings. They will be concatenated, with spaces as separators.

org-entry-get-multivalued-property pom property   *Function*
> Treat the value of the property PROPERTY as a whitespace-separated list of values and return the values as a list of strings.

org-entry-add-to-multivalued-property pom property value   *Function*
> Treat the value of the property PROPERTY as a whitespace-separated list of values and make sure that VALUE is in this list.

org-entry-remove-from-multivalued-property pom property   *Function*
    value
> Treat the value of the property PROPERTY as a whitespace-separated list of values and make sure that VALUE is *not* in this list.

`org-entry-member-in-multivalued-property` pom property value   Function
>   Treat the value of the property PROPERTY as a whitespace-separated list
>   of values and check if VALUE is in this list.

`org-property-allowed-value-functions`   User Option
>   Hook for functions supplying allowed values for a specific property. The
>   functions must take a single argument, the name of the property, and return
>   a flat list of allowed values. If ':ETC' is one of the values, use the values as
>   completion help, but allow also other values to be entered. The functions
>   must return `nil` if they are not responsible for this property.

A.10 Using the mapping API

Org has sophisticated mapping capabilities to find all entries satisfying certain
criteria. Internally, this functionality is used to produce agenda views, but there
is also an API that can be used to execute arbitrary functions for each or selected
entries. The main entry point for this API is:

`org-map-entries` func &optional match scope &rest skip   Function
>   Call FUNC at each headline selected by MATCH in SCOPE.
>
>   FUNC is a function or a Lisp form. The function will be called without
>   arguments, with the cursor positioned at the beginning of the headline. The
>   return values of all calls to the function will be collected and returned as a
>   list.
>
>   The call to FUNC will be wrapped into a save-excursion form, so FUNC does
>   not need to preserve point. After evaluation, the cursor will be moved to the
>   end of the line (presumably of the headline of the processed entry) and search
>   continues from there. Under some circumstances, this may not produce the
>   wanted results. For example, if you have removed (e.g., archived) the current
>   (sub)tree it could mean that the next entry will be skipped entirely. In such
>   cases, you can specify the position from where search should continue by
>   making FUNC set the variable 'org-map-continue-from' to the desired buffer
>   position.
>
>   MATCH is a tags/property/todo match as it is used in the agenda match
>   view. Only headlines that are matched by this query will be considered
>   during the iteration. When MATCH is nil or t, all headlines will be visited
>   by the iteration.
>
>   SCOPE determines the scope of this command. It can be any of:
>
>   nil   the current buffer, respecting the restriction if any
>   tree   the subtree started with the entry at point
>   file   the current buffer, without restriction
>   file-with-archives
>   the current buffer, and any archives associated with it
>   agenda all agenda files
>   agenda-with-archives
>   all agenda files with any archive files associated with them
>   (file1 file2 ...)
>   if this is a list, all files in the list will be scanned

The remaining args are treated as settings for the skipping facilities of the scanner. The following items can be given here:

archive   skip trees with the archive tag
comment   skip trees with the COMMENT keyword
function or Lisp form
            will be used as value for org-agenda-skip-function,
            so whenever the function returns t, FUNC
            will not be called for that entry and search will
            continue from the point where the function leaves it

The function given to that mapping routine can really do anything you like. It can use the property API (see Section A.9 [Using the property API], page 223) to gather more information about the entry, or in order to change metadata in the entry. Here are a couple of functions that might be handy:

org-todo &optional arg   Function
    Change the TODO state of the entry. See the docstring of the functions for the many possible values for the argument ARG.

org-priority &optional action   Function
    Change the priority of the entry. See the docstring of this function for the possible values for ACTION.

org-toggle-tag tag &optional onoff   Function
    Toggle the tag TAG in the current entry. Setting ONOFF to either on or off will not toggle tag, but ensure that it is either on or off.

org-promote   Function
    Promote the current entry.

org-demote   Function
    Demote the current entry.

Here is a simple example that will turn all entries in the current file with a tag TOMORROW into TODO entries with the keyword UPCOMING. Entries in comment trees and in archive trees will be ignored.

```
(org-map-entries
   '(org-todo "UPCOMING")
   "+TOMORROW" 'file 'archive 'comment)
```

The following example counts the number of entries with TODO keyword WAITING, in all agenda files.

```
(length (org-map-entries t "/+WAITING" 'agenda))
```

Appendix B MobileOrg

MobileOrg (http://mobileorg.ncogni.to/) is an application for the
iPhone/iPod Touch series of devices, developed by Richard Moreland.
MobileOrg offers offline viewing and capture support for an Org-mode system
rooted on a "real" computer. It does also allow you to record changes
to existing entries. Android users should check out MobileOrg Android
(http://wiki.github.com/matburt/mobileorg-android/) by Matt Jones.

This appendix describes the support Org has for creating agenda views in a
format that can be displayed by *MobileOrg*, and for integrating notes captured
and changes made by *MobileOrg* into the main system.

For changing tags and TODO states in MobileOrg, you should have set up
the customization variables org-todo-keywords and org-tags-alist to cover
all important tags and TODO keywords, even if individual files use only part of
these. MobileOrg will also offer you states and tags set up with in-buffer settings,
but it will understand the logistics of TODO state *sets* (see Section 5.2.5 [Per-
file keywords], page 44) and *mutually exclusive* tags (see Section 6.2 [Setting
tags], page 56) only for those set in these variables.

B.1 Setting up the staging area

MobileOrg needs to interact with Emacs through a directory on a server.
If you are using a public server, you should consider to encrypt the files that
are uploaded to the server. This can be done with Org-mode 7.02 and with
MobileOrg 1.5 (iPhone version), and you need an 'openssl' installation on your
system. To turn on encryption, set a password in *MobileOrg* and, on the Emacs
side, configure the variable org-mobile-use-encryption.[1]

The easiest way to create that directory is to use a free Dropbox.com
(http://dropbox.com) account.[2] When MobileOrg first connects to your
Dropbox, it will create a directory *MobileOrg* inside the Dropbox. After the
directory has been created, tell Emacs about it:

    (setq org-mobile-directory "~/Dropbox/MobileOrg")

Org-mode has commands to put files for *MobileOrg* into that directory, and
to read captured notes from there.

---

[1] If you can safely store the password in your Emacs setup, you might also want
to configure org-mobile-encryption-password. Please read the docstring of that
variable. Note that encryption will apply only to the contents of the '.org' files.
The file names themselves will remain visible.

[2] If you cannot use Dropbox, or if your version of MobileOrg does not
support it, you can use a webdav server. For more information,
check out the documentation of MobileOrg and also this FAQ entry
(http://orgmode.org/worg/org-faq.php#mobileorg_webdav).

B.2 Pushing to MobileOrg

This operation copies all files currently listed in `org-mobile-files` to the directory `org-mobile-directory`. By default this list contains all agenda files (as listed in `org-agenda-files`), but additional files can be included by customizing `org-mobiles-files`. File names will be staged with paths relative to `org-directory`, so all files should be inside this directory. The push operation also creates a special Org file 'agendas.org' with all custom agenda view defined by the user.[3] Finally, Org writes the file 'index.org', containing links to all other files. *MobileOrg* first reads this file from the server, and then downloads all agendas and Org files listed in it. To speed up the download, MobileOrg will only read files whose checksums[4] have changed.

B.3 Pulling from MobileOrg

When *MobileOrg* synchronizes with the server, it not only pulls the Org files for viewing. It also appends captured entries and pointers to flagged and changed entries to the file 'mobileorg.org' on the server. Org has a *pull* operation that integrates this information into an inbox file and operates on the pointers to flagged entries. Here is how it works:

1. Org moves all entries found in 'mobileorg.org'[5] and appends them to the file pointed to by the variable `org-mobile-inbox-for-pull`. Each captured entry and each editing event will be a top-level entry in the inbox file.

2. After moving the entries, Org will attempt to implement the changes made in *MobileOrg*. Some changes are applied directly and without user interaction. Examples are all changes to tags, TODO state, headline and body text that can be cleanly applied. Entries that have been flagged for further action will receive a tag `:FLAGGED:`, so that they can be easily found again. When there is a problem finding an entry or applying the change, the pointer entry will remain in the inbox and will be marked with an error message. You need to later resolve these issues by hand.

3. Org will then generate an agenda view with all flagged entries. The user should then go through these entries and do whatever actions are necessary. If a note has been stored while flagging an entry in *MobileOrg*, that note will be displayed in the echo area when the cursor is on the corresponding agenda line.

---

[3] While creating the agendas, Org-mode will force ID properties on all referenced entries, so that these entries can be uniquely identified if *MobileOrg* flags them for further action. If you do not want to get these properties in so many entries, you can set the variable `org-mobile-force-id-on-agenda-items` to nil. Org mode will then rely on outline paths, in the hope that these will be unique enough.

[4] stored automatically in the file 'checksums.dat'

[5] 'mobileorg.org' will be empty after this operation.

? Pressing ? in that special agenda will display the full flagging note in another window and also push it onto the kill ring. So you could use ? z C-y C-c C-c to store that flagging note as a normal note in the entry. Pressing ? twice in succession will offer to remove the :FLAGGED: tag along with the recorded flagging note (which is stored in a property). In this way you indicate that the intended processing for this flagged entry is finished.

If you are not able to process all flagged entries directly, you can always return to this agenda view[6] using C-c a ?.

---

[6] Note, however, that there is a subtle difference. The view created automatically by M-x org-mobile-pull (RET) is guaranteed to search all files that have been addressed by the last pull. This might include a file that is not currently in your list of agenda files. If you later use C-c a ? to regenerate the view, only the current agenda files will be searched.

Appendix C History and acknowledgments

Org was born in 2003, out of frustration over the user interface of the Emacs Outline mode. I was trying to organize my notes and projects, and using Emacs seemed to be the natural way to go. However, having to remember eleven different commands with two or three keys per command, only to hide and show parts of the outline tree, that seemed entirely unacceptable to me. Also, when using outlines to take notes, I constantly wanted to restructure the tree, organizing it parallel to my thoughts and plans. *Visibility cycling* and *structure editing* were originally implemented in the package 'outline-magic.el', but quickly moved to the more general 'org.el'. As this environment became comfortable for project planning, the next step was adding *TODO entries*, basic *timestamps*, and *table support*. These areas highlighted the two main goals that Org still has today: to be a new, outline-based, plain text mode with innovative and intuitive editing features, and to incorporate project planning functionality directly into a notes file.

Since the first release, literally thousands of emails to me or to emacs-orgmode@gnu.org have provided a constant stream of bug reports, feedback, new ideas, and sometimes patches and add-on code. Many thanks to everyone who has helped to improve this package. I am trying to keep here a list of the people who had significant influence in shaping one or more aspects of Org. The list may not be complete, if I have forgotten someone, please accept my apologies and let me know.

Before I get to this list, a few special mentions are in order:

Bastien Guerry
> Bastien has written a large number of extensions to Org (most of them integrated into the core by now), including the LaTeX exporter and the plain list parser. His support during the early days, when he basically acted as co-maintainer, was central to the success of this project. Bastien also invented Worg, helped establishing the Web presence of Org, and sponsors hosting costs for the orgmode.org website.

Eric Schulte and Dan Davison
> Eric and Dan are jointly responsible for the Org-babel system, which turns Org into a multi-language environment for evaluating code and doing literate programming and reproducible research.

John Wiegley
> John has also contributed a number of great ideas and patches directly to Org, including the attachment system ('org-attach.el'), integration with Apple Mail ('org-mac-message.el'), hierarchical dependencies of TODO items, habit tracking ('org-habits.el'), and encryption ('org-crypt.el'). Also, the capture system is really an extended copy of his great 'remember.el'.

Sebastian Rose

> Without Sebastian, the HTML/XHTML publishing of Org would be the pitiful work of an ignorant amateur. Sebastian has pushed this part of Org onto a much higher level. He also wrote 'org-info.js', a Java script for displaying webpages derived from Org using an Info-like or a folding interface with single-key navigation.

OK, now to the full list of contributions! Again, please let me know what I am missing here!

- *Russel Adams* came up with the idea for drawers.
- *Thomas Baumann* wrote 'org-bbdb.el' and 'org-mhe.el'.
- *Christophe Bataillon* created the great unicorn logo that we use on the Org-mode website.
- *Alex Bochannek* provided a patch for rounding timestamps.
- *Jan Böcker* wrote 'org-docview.el'.
- *Brad Bozarth* showed how to pull RSS feed data into Org-mode files.
- *Tom Breton* wrote 'org-choose.el'.
- *Charles Cave*'s suggestion sparked the implementation of templates for Remember, which are now templates for capture.
- *Pavel Chalmoviansky* influenced the agenda treatment of items with specified time.
- *Gregory Chernov* patched support for Lisp forms into table calculations and improved XEmacs compatibility, in particular by porting 'nouline.el' to XEmacs.
- *Sacha Chua* suggested copying some linking code from Planner.
- *Baoqiu Cui* contributed the DocBook exporter.
- *Eddward DeVilla* proposed and tested checkbox statistics. He also came up with the idea of properties, and that there should be an API for them.
- *Nick Dokos* tracked down several nasty bugs.
- *Kees Dullemond* used to edit projects lists directly in HTML and so inspired some of the early development, including HTML export. He also asked for a way to narrow wide table columns.
- *Thomas S. Dye* contributed documentation on Worg and helped integrating the Org-Babel documentation into the manual.
- *Christian Egli* converted the documentation into Texinfo format, patched CSS formatting into the HTML exporter, and inspired the agenda.
- *David Emery* provided a patch for custom CSS support in exported HTML agendas.
- *Nic Ferrier* contributed mailcap and XOXO support.
- *Miguel A. Figueroa-Villanueva* implemented hierarchical checkboxes.
- *John Foerch* figured out how to make incremental search show context around a match in a hidden outline tree.
- *Raimar Finken* wrote 'org-git-line.el'.

- *Mikael Fornius* works as a mailing list moderator.
- *Austin Frank* works as a mailing list moderator.
- *Niels Giesen* had the idea to automatically archive DONE trees.
- *Nicolas Goaziou* rewrote much of the plain list code.
- *Kai Grossjohann* pointed out key-binding conflicts with other packages.
- *Bernt Hansen* has driven much of the support for auto-repeating tasks, task state change logging, and the clocktable. His clear explanations have been critical when we started to adopt the Git version control system.
- *Manuel Hermenegildo* has contributed various ideas, small fixes and patches.
- *Phil Jackson* wrote 'org-irc.el'.
- *Scott Jaderholm* proposed footnotes, control over whitespace between folded entries, and column view for properties.
- *Matt Jones* wrote *MobileOrg Android*.
- *Tokuya Kameshima* wrote 'org-wl.el' and 'org-mew.el'.
- *Shidai Liu* ("Leo") asked for embedded LaTeX and tested it. He also provided frequent feedback and some patches.
- *Matt Lundin* has proposed last-row references for table formulas and named invisible anchors. He has also worked a lot on the FAQ.
- *David Maus* wrote 'org-atom.el', maintains the issues file for Org, and is a prolific contributor on the mailing list with competent replies, small fixes and patches.
- *Jason F. McBrayer* suggested agenda export to CSV format.
- *Max Mikhanosha* came up with the idea of refiling.
- *Dmitri Minaev* sent a patch to set priority limits on a per-file basis.
- *Stefan Monnier* provided a patch to keep the Emacs-Lisp compiler happy.
- *Richard Moreland* wrote *MobileOrg* for the iPhone.
- *Rick Moynihan* proposed allowing multiple TODO sequences in a file and being able to quickly restrict the agenda to a subtree.
- *Todd Neal* provided patches for links to Info files and Elisp forms.
- *Greg Newman* refreshed the unicorn logo into its current form.
- *Tim O'Callaghan* suggested in-file links, search options for general file links, and TAGS.
- *Osamu Okano* wrote 'orgcard2ref.pl', a Perl program to create a text version of the reference card.
- *Takeshi Okano* translated the manual and David O'Toole's tutorial into Japanese.
- *Oliver Oppitz* suggested multi-state TODO items.
- *Scott Otterson* sparked the introduction of descriptive text for links, among other things.

- *Pete Phillips* helped during the development of the TAGS feature, and provided frequent feedback.
- *Martin Pohlack* provided the code snippet to bundle character insertion into bundles of 20 for undo.
- *T.V. Raman* reported bugs and suggested improvements.
- *Matthias Rempe* (Oelde) provided ideas, Windows support, and quality control.
- *Paul Rivier* provided the basic implementation of named footnotes. He also acted as mailing list moderator for some time.
- *Kevin Rogers* contributed code to access VM files on remote hosts.
- *Frank Ruell* solved the mystery of the keymapp nil bug, a conflict with 'allout.el'.
- *Jason Riedy* generalized the send-receive mechanism for Orgtbl tables with extensive patches.
- *Philip Rooke* created the Org reference card, provided lots of feedback, developed and applied standards to the Org documentation.
- *Christian Schlauer* proposed angular brackets around links, among other things.
- *Paul Sexton* wrote 'org-ctags.el'.
- Linking to VM/BBDB/Gnus was first inspired by *Tom Shannon*'s 'organizer-mode.el'.
- *Ilya Shlyakhter* proposed the Archive Sibling, line numbering in literal examples, and remote highlighting for referenced code lines.
- *Stathis Sideris* wrote the 'ditaa.jar' ASCII to PNG converter that is now packaged into Org's 'contrib' directory.
- *Daniel Sinder* came up with the idea of internal archiving by locking sub-trees.
- *Dale Smith* proposed link abbreviations.
- *James TD Smith* has contributed a large number of patches for useful tweaks and features.
- *Adam Spiers* asked for global linking commands, inspired the link extension system, added support for mairix, and proposed the mapping API.
- *Ulf Stegemann* created the table to translate special symbols to HTML, LaTeX, UTF-8, Latin-1 and ASCII.
- *Andy Stewart* contributed code to 'org-w3m.el', to copy HTML content with links transformation to Org syntax.
- *David O'Toole* wrote 'org-publish.el' and drafted the manual chapter about publishing.
- *Stefan Vollmar* organized a video-recorded talk at the Max-Planck-Institute for Neurology. He also inspired the creation of a concept index for HTML export.
- *Jürgen Vollmer* contributed code generating the table of contents in HTML output.

- *Samuel Wales* has provided important feedback and bug reports.
- *Chris Wallace* provided a patch implementing the 'QUOTE' keyword.
- *David Wainberg* suggested archiving, and improvements to the linking system.
- *Carsten Wimmer* suggested some changes and helped fix a bug in linking to Gnus.
- *Roland Winkler* requested additional key bindings to make Org work on a tty.
- *Piotr Zielinski* wrote 'org-mouse.el', proposed agenda blocks and contributed various ideas and code snippets.

GNU Free Documentation License

Version 1.3, 3 November 2008

Copyright © 2000, 2001, 2002, 2007, 2008 Free Software Foundation, Inc.
http://fsf.org/

Everyone is permitted to copy and distribute verbatim copies of this license document, but changing it is
not allowed.

0. PREAMBLE

    The purpose of this License is to make a manual, textbook, or other functional and useful document *free* in the sense of freedom: to assure everyone the effective freedom to copy and redistribute it, with or without modifying it, either commercially or noncommercially. Secondarily, this License preserves for the author and publisher a way to get credit for their work, while not being considered responsible for modifications made by others.

    This License is a kind of "copyleft", which means that derivative works of the document must themselves be free in the same sense. It complements the GNU General Public License, which is a copyleft license designed for free software.

    We have designed this License in order to use it for manuals for free software, because free software needs free documentation: a free program should come with manuals providing the same freedoms that the software does. But this License is not limited to software manuals; it can be used for any textual work, regardless of subject matter or whether it is published as a printed book. We recommend this License principally for works whose purpose is instruction or reference.

1. APPLICABILITY AND DEFINITIONS

    This License applies to any manual or other work, in any medium, that contains a notice placed by the copyright holder saying it can be distributed under the terms of this License. Such a notice grants a world-wide, royalty-free license, unlimited in duration, to use that work under the conditions stated herein. The "Document", below, refers to any such manual or work. Any member of the public is a licensee, and is addressed as "you". You accept the license if you copy, modify or distribute the work in a way requiring permission under copyright law.

    A "Modified Version" of the Document means any work containing the Document or a portion of it, either copied verbatim, or with modifications and/or translated into another language.

    A "Secondary Section" is a named appendix or a front-matter section of the Document that deals exclusively with the relationship of the publishers or authors of the Document to the Document's overall subject (or to related matters) and contains nothing that could fall directly within that overall subject. (Thus, if the Document is in part a textbook of mathematics, a Secondary Section may not explain any mathematics.) The relationship could be a matter of historical connection with the subject or with related matters, or of legal, commercial, philosophical, ethical or political position regarding them.

    The "Invariant Sections" are certain Secondary Sections whose titles are designated, as being those of Invariant Sections, in the notice that says that the Document is released under this License. If a section does not fit the above definition of Secondary then it is not allowed to be designated as Invariant. The Document may contain zero Invariant Sections. If the Document does not identify any Invariant Sections then there are none.

    The "Cover Texts" are certain short passages of text that are listed, as Front-Cover Texts or Back-Cover Texts, in the notice that says that the Document is released under this License. A Front-Cover Text may be at most 5 words, and a Back-Cover Text may be at most 25 words.

A "Transparent" copy of the Document means a machine-readable copy, represented in a format whose specification is available to the general public, that is suitable for revising the document straightforwardly with generic text editors or (for images composed of pixels) generic paint programs or (for drawings) some widely available drawing editor, and that is suitable for input to text formatters or for automatic translation to a variety of formats suitable for input to text formatters. A copy made in an otherwise Transparent file format whose markup, or absence of markup, has been arranged to thwart or discourage subsequent modification by readers is not Transparent. An image format is not Transparent if used for any substantial amount of text. A copy that is not "Transparent" is called "Opaque".

Examples of suitable formats for Transparent copies include plain ASCII without markup, Texinfo input format, LaTeX input format, SGML or XML using a publicly available DTD, and standard-conforming simple HTML, PostScript or PDF designed for human modification. Examples of transparent image formats include PNG, XCF and JPG. Opaque formats include proprietary formats that can be read and edited only by proprietary word processors, SGML or XML for which the DTD and/or processing tools are not generally available, and the machine-generated HTML, PostScript or PDF produced by some word processors for output purposes only.

The "Title Page" means, for a printed book, the title page itself, plus such following pages as are needed to hold, legibly, the material this License requires to appear in the title page. For works in formats which do not have any title page as such, "Title Page" means the text near the most prominent appearance of the work's title, preceding the beginning of the body of the text.

The "publisher" means any person or entity that distributes copies of the Document to the public.

A section "Entitled XYZ" means a named subunit of the Document whose title either is precisely XYZ or contains XYZ in parentheses following text that translates XYZ in another language. (Here XYZ stands for a specific section name mentioned below, such as "Acknowledgements", "Dedications", "Endorsements", or "History".) To "Preserve the Title" of such a section when you modify the Document means that it remains a section "Entitled XYZ" according to this definition.

The Document may include Warranty Disclaimers next to the notice which states that this License applies to the Document. These Warranty Disclaimers are considered to be included by reference in this License, but only as regards disclaiming warranties: any other implication that these Warranty Disclaimers may have is void and has no effect on the meaning of this License.

2. VERBATIM COPYING

You may copy and distribute the Document in any medium, either commercially or noncommercially, provided that this License, the copyright notices, and the license notice saying this License applies to the Document are reproduced in all copies, and that you add no other conditions whatsoever to those of this License. You may not use technical measures to obstruct or control the reading or further copying of the copies you make or distribute. However, you may accept compensation in exchange for copies. If you distribute a large enough number of copies you must also follow the conditions in section 3.

You may also lend copies, under the same conditions stated above, and you may publicly display copies.

3. COPYING IN QUANTITY

If you publish printed copies (or copies in media that commonly have printed covers) of the Document, numbering more than 100, and the Document's license notice requires Cover Texts, you must enclose the copies in covers that carry, clearly and legibly, all these Cover Texts: Front-Cover Texts on the front cover, and Back-Cover Texts on the back cover. Both covers must also clearly and legibly identify you as the publisher of these copies. The front cover must present the full title with all words of the title equally prominent and visible. You may add other material on the covers in addition. Copying with changes limited to the covers, as long as they preserve the title of the Document and satisfy these conditions, can be treated as verbatim copying in other respects.

If the required texts for either cover are too voluminous to fit legibly, you should put the first ones listed (as many as fit reasonably) on the actual cover, and continue the rest onto adjacent pages.

If you publish or distribute Opaque copies of the Document numbering more than 100, you must either include a machine-readable Transparent copy along with each Opaque copy, or state in or with each Opaque copy a computer-network location from which the general network-using public has access to download using public-standard network protocols a complete Transparent copy of the Document, free of added material. If you use the latter option, you must take reasonably prudent steps, when you begin distribution of Opaque copies in quantity, to ensure that this Transparent copy will remain thus accessible at the stated location until at least one year after the last time you distribute an Opaque copy (directly or through your agents or retailers) of that edition to the public.

It is requested, but not required, that you contact the authors of the Document well before redistributing any large number of copies, to give them a chance to provide you with an updated version of the Document.

4. MODIFICATIONS

You may copy and distribute a Modified Version of the Document under the conditions of sections 2 and 3 above, provided that you release the Modified Version under precisely this License, with the Modified Version filling the role of the Document, thus licensing distribution and modification of the Modified Version to whoever possesses a copy of it. In addition, you must do these things in the Modified Version:

A. Use in the Title Page (and on the covers, if any) a title distinct from that of the Document, and from those of previous versions (which should, if there were any, be listed in the History section of the Document). You may use the same title as a previous version if the original publisher of that version gives permission.

B. List on the Title Page, as authors, one or more persons or entities responsible for authorship of the modifications in the Modified Version, together with at least five of the principal authors of the Document (all of its principal authors, if it has fewer than five), unless they release you from this requirement.

C. State on the Title page the name of the publisher of the Modified Version, as the publisher.

D. Preserve all the copyright notices of the Document.

E. Add an appropriate copyright notice for your modifications adjacent to the other copyright notices.

F. Include, immediately after the copyright notices, a license notice giving the public permission to use the Modified Version under the terms of this License, in the form shown in the Addendum below.

G. Preserve in that license notice the full lists of Invariant Sections and required Cover Texts given in the Document's license notice.

H. Include an unaltered copy of this License.

I. Preserve the section Entitled "History", Preserve its Title, and add to it an item stating at least the title, year, new authors, and publisher of the Modified Version as given on the Title Page. If there is no section Entitled "History" in the Document, create one stating the title, year, authors, and publisher of the Document as given on its Title Page, then add an item describing the Modified Version as stated in the previous sentence.

J. Preserve the network location, if any, given in the Document for public access to a Transparent copy of the Document, and likewise the network locations given in the Document for previous versions it was based on. These may be placed in the "History" section. You may omit a network location for a work that was published at least four years before the Document itself, or if the original publisher of the version it refers to gives permission.

K. For any section Entitled "Acknowledgements" or "Dedications", Preserve the Title of the section, and preserve in the section all the substance and tone of each of the contributor acknowledgements and/or dedications given therein.

L. Preserve all the Invariant Sections of the Document, unaltered in their text and in their titles. Section numbers or the equivalent are not considered part of the section titles.

M. Delete any section Entitled "Endorsements". Such a section may not be included in the Modified Version.

N. Do not retitle any existing section to be Entitled "Endorsements" or to conflict in title with any Invariant Section.

O. Preserve any Warranty Disclaimers.

If the Modified Version includes new front-matter sections or appendices that qualify as Secondary Sections and contain no material copied from the Document, you may at your option designate some or all of these sections as invariant. To do this, add their titles to the list of Invariant Sections in the Modified Version's license notice. These titles must be distinct from any other section titles.

You may add a section Entitled "Endorsements", provided it contains nothing but endorsements of your Modified Version by various parties—for example, statements of peer review or that the text has been approved by an organization as the authoritative definition of a standard.

You may add a passage of up to five words as a Front-Cover Text, and a passage of up to 25 words as a Back-Cover Text, to the end of the list of Cover Texts in the Modified Version. Only one passage of Front-Cover Text and one of Back-Cover Text may be added by (or through arrangements made by) any one entity. If the Document already includes a cover text for the same cover, previously added by you or by arrangement made by the same entity you are acting on behalf of, you may not add another; but you may replace the old one, on explicit permission from the previous publisher that added the old one.

The author(s) and publisher(s) of the Document do not by this License give permission to use their names for publicity for or to assert or imply endorsement of any Modified Version.

5. COMBINING DOCUMENTS

You may combine the Document with other documents released under this License, under the terms defined in section 4 above for modified versions, provided that you include in the combination all of the Invariant Sections of all of the original documents, unmodified, and list them all as Invariant Sections of your combined work in its license notice, and that you preserve all their Warranty Disclaimers.

The combined work need only contain one copy of this License, and multiple identical Invariant Sections may be replaced with a single copy. If there are multiple Invariant Sections with the same name but different contents, make the title of each such section unique by adding at the end of it, in parentheses, the name of the original author or publisher of that section if known, or else a unique number. Make the same adjustment to the section titles in the list of Invariant Sections in the license notice of the combined work.

In the combination, you must combine any sections Entitled "History" in the various original documents, forming one section Entitled "History"; likewise combine any sections Entitled "Acknowledgements", and any sections Entitled "Dedications". You must delete all sections Entitled "Endorsements."

6. COLLECTIONS OF DOCUMENTS

You may make a collection consisting of the Document and other documents released under this License, and replace the individual copies of this License in the various documents with a single copy that is included in the collection, provided that you follow the rules of this License for verbatim copying of each of the documents in all other respects.

You may extract a single document from such a collection, and distribute it individually under this License, provided you insert a copy of this License into the extracted document, and follow this License in all other respects regarding verbatim copying of that document.

7. AGGREGATION WITH INDEPENDENT WORKS

A compilation of the Document or its derivatives with other separate and independent documents or works, in or on a volume of a storage or distribution medium, is called an "aggregate" if the copyright resulting from the compilation is not used to limit the legal rights of the compilation's users beyond what the individual works permit. When the Document is included in an aggregate, this License does not apply to the other works in the aggregate which are not themselves derivative works of the Document.

If the Cover Text requirement of section 3 is applicable to these copies of the Document, then if the Document is less than one half of the entire aggregate, the Document's Cover Texts may be placed on covers that bracket the Document within the aggregate, or the electronic equivalent of covers if the Document is in electronic form. Otherwise they must appear on printed covers that bracket the whole aggregate.

8. TRANSLATION

Translation is considered a kind of modification, so you may distribute translations of the Document under the terms of section 4. Replacing Invariant Sections with translations requires special permission from their copyright holders, but you may include translations of some or all Invariant Sections in addition to the original versions of these Invariant Sections. You may include a translation of this License, and all the license notices in the Document, and any Warranty Disclaimers, provided that you also include the original English version of this License and the original versions of those notices and disclaimers. In case of a disagreement between the translation and the original version of this License or a notice or disclaimer, the original version will prevail.

If a section in the Document is Entitled "Acknowledgements", "Dedications", or "History", the requirement (section 4) to Preserve its Title (section 1) will typically require changing the actual title.

9. TERMINATION

You may not copy, modify, sublicense, or distribute the Document except as expressly provided under this License. Any attempt otherwise to copy, modify, sublicense, or distribute it is void, and will automatically terminate your rights under this License.

However, if you cease all violation of this License, then your license from a particular copyright holder is reinstated (a) provisionally, unless and until the copyright holder explicitly and finally terminates your license, and (b) permanently, if the copyright holder fails to notify you of the violation by some reasonable means prior to 60 days after the cessation.

Moreover, your license from a particular copyright holder is reinstated permanently if the copyright holder notifies you of the violation by some reasonable means, this is the first time you have received notice of violation of this License (for any work) from that copyright holder, and you cure the violation prior to 30 days after your receipt of the notice.

Termination of your rights under this section does not terminate the licenses of parties who have received copies or rights from you under this License. If your rights have been terminated and not permanently reinstated, receipt of a copy of some or all of the same material does not give you any rights to use it.

10. FUTURE REVISIONS OF THIS LICENSE

The Free Software Foundation may publish new, revised versions of the GNU Free Documentation License from time to time. Such new versions will be similar in spirit to the present version, but may differ in detail to address new problems or concerns. See http://www.gnu.org/copyleft/.

Each version of the License is given a distinguishing version number. If the Document specifies that a particular numbered version of this License "or any later version" applies to it, you have the option of following the terms and conditions either of that specified version or of any later version that has been published (not as a draft) by the Free Software Foundation. If the Document does not specify a version number of this License, you may choose any version ever published (not as a draft) by the Free Software Foundation. If the Document specifies that a proxy can decide which future versions of this License can be used, that proxy's public statement of acceptance of a version permanently authorizes you to choose that version for the Document.

11. RELICENSING

"Massive Multiauthor Collaboration Site" (or "MMC Site") means any World Wide
Web server that publishes copyrightable works and also provides prominent facilities
for anybody to edit those works. A public wiki that anybody can edit is an example
of such a server. A "Massive Multiauthor Collaboration" (or "MMC") contained in
the site means any set of copyrightable works thus published on the MMC site.

"CC-BY-SA" means the Creative Commons Attribution-Share Alike 3.0 license published by Creative Commons Corporation, a not-for-profit corporation with a principal
place of business in San Francisco, California, as well as future copyleft versions of
that license published by that same organization.

"Incorporate" means to publish or republish a Document, in whole or in part, as part
of another Document.

An MMC is "eligible for relicensing" if it is licensed under this License, and if all
works that were first published under this License somewhere other than this MMC,
and subsequently incorporated in whole or in part into the MMC, (1) had no cover
texts or invariant sections, and (2) were thus incorporated prior to November 1, 2008.

The operator of an MMC Site may republish an MMC contained in the site under
CC-BY-SA on the same site at any time before August 1, 2009, provided the MMC
is eligible for relicensing.

ADDENDUM: How to use this License for your documents

To use this License in a document you have written, include a copy of the License in the
document and put the following copyright and license notices just after the title page:

```
Copyright (C)  year  your name.
Permission is granted to copy, distribute and/or modify
this document under the terms of the GNU Free
Documentation License, Version 1.3 or any later version
published by the Free Software Foundation; with no
Invariant Sections, no Front-Cover Texts, and no
Back-Cover Texts.  A copy of the license is included in
the section entitled ''GNU Free Documentation License''.
```

If you have Invariant Sections, Front-Cover Texts and Back-Cover Texts, replace the
"with. . . Texts." line with this:

```
with the Invariant Sections being list their
titles, with the Front-Cover Texts being list, and
with the Back-Cover Texts being list.
```

If you have Invariant Sections without Cover Texts, or some other combination of the
three, merge those two alternatives to suit the situation.

If your document contains nontrivial examples of program code, we recommend releasing
these examples in parallel under your choice of free software license, such as the GNU General
Public License, to permit their use in free software.

History

This section gives the history of the modifications made to the manual by the publisher, as required by the GNU Free Documentation License.

10/2010 "The Org Manual" (original edition)
Carsten Dominik with contributions by David O'Toole, Bastien Guerry, Philip Rooke, Dan Davison, Eric Schulte, and Thomas Dye.
Publisher: Free Software Foundation.

11/2010 "Org Mode 7 Reference Manual"
Edited for publication by Brian Gough and Barry Gidden
Publisher: Network Theory Ltd.
Published under different title, as given above. Added publisher's preface. Minor modifications for publication as a printed book, reformatted examples to fit smaller page width. Added this "History" section.

The source code for the original version of this document is available from `http://orgmode.org/org-7.3.tar.gz`.

The source code for this version is available from `http://www.network-theory.co.uk/orgmode/manual/src/`. A complete set of differences can be obtained from the same location.

Other books from the publisher

Network Theory publishes books about free software under free documentation licenses. Our current catalogue includes the following titles:

- **The Perl Language Reference Manual** Larry Wall et al. (ISBN 978-1-906966-02-7) $39.95 (£29.95)

  This manual is a printed edition of the official Perl reference documentation from the Perl 5.12.1 distribution. It describes the syntax of Perl and its built-in datatypes, operators, functions, variables, regular expressions and diagnostic messages. For each copy of this manual sold $1 is donated to The Perl Foundation.

- **PostgreSQL Reference Manual: Volumes 1A, 1B, 2, 3** (ISBN 978-1-906966-04-1) $19.95 (£14.95), (ISBN 978-1-906966-05-8) $19.95 (£14.95), (ISBN 978-1-906966-06-5) $19.95 (£14.95), (ISBN 978-1-906966-07-2) $14.95 (£9.95)

  These manuals document the SQL language and commands of PostgreSQL 9.0, its client and server programming interfaces, and the configuration and maintenance of PostgreSQL servers. For each copy of these manuals sold, $1 is donated to the PostgreSQL project.

- **The XML 1.0 Standard (5th Edition)** W3C XML Working Group (ISBN 0954612094) $12.95 (£8.95)

  This manual is a printed edition of the Extensible Markup Language (XML) 1.0 standard from the World Wide Web Consortium. It also includes the Namespaces in XML 1.0 specification (Third Edition) and XML Information Set (Second Edition).

- **XML Path Language (XPath) 2.0 Standard** W3C XML Query and XSL Working Groups (ISBN 978-1-906966-01-0) $12.95 (£8.95)

  This manual is a printed edition of the XPath 2.0 standard from the World Wide Web Consortium.

- **GNU Bash Reference Manual** by Chet Ramey and Brian Fox (ISBN 0-9541617-7-7) $29.95 (£19.95)

  This manual is the definitive reference for GNU Bash, the standard GNU command-line interpreter. GNU Bash is a complete implementation of the POSIX.2 Bourne shell specification, with additional features from the C-shell and Korn shell. For each copy of this manual sold, $1 is donated to the Free Software Foundation.

- **An Introduction to Python** by Guido van Rossum and Fred L. Drake, Jr. (ISBN 0-9541617-6-9) $19.95 (£12.95)

This tutorial provides an introduction to Python, an easy to learn object oriented programming language. For each copy of this manual sold, $1 is donated to the Python Software Foundation.

- **Python Language Reference Manual** by Guido van Rossum and Fred L. Drake, Jr. (ISBN 0-9541617-8-5) $19.95 (£12.95)

  This manual is the official reference for the Python language itself. It describes the syntax of Python and its built-in datatypes in depth, This manual is suitable for readers who need to be familiar with the details and rules of the Python language and its object system. For each copy of this manual sold, $1 is donated to the Python Software Foundation.

- **An Introduction to GCC** by Brian J. Gough, foreword by Richard M. Stallman. (ISBN 0-9541617-9-3) $19.95 (£12.95)

  This manual provides a tutorial introduction to the GNU C and C++ compilers, gcc and g++. Many books teach the C and C++ languages, but this book explains how to use the compiler itself. Based on years of observation of questions posted on mailing lists, it guides the reader straight to the important options of GCC.

- **Valgrind 3.3** by J. Seward, N. Nethercote, J. Weidendorfer et al. (ISBN 0-9546120-5-1) $19.95 (£12.95)

  This manual describes how to use Valgrind, an award-winning suite of tools for debugging and profiling GNU/Linux programs. Valgrind detects memory and threading bugs automatically, avoiding hours of frustrating bug-hunting and making programs more stable. For each copy of this manual sold, $1 is donated to the Valgrind developers.

- **Comparing and Merging Files with GNU diff and patch** by David MacKenzie, Paul Eggert, and Richard Stallman (ISBN 0-9541617-5-0) $19.95 (£12.95)

  This manual describes how to compare and merge files using GNU diff and patch. It includes an extensive tutorial that guides the reader through all the options of the diff and patch commands. For each copy of this manual sold, $1 is donated to the Free Software Foundation.

- **Version Management with CVS** by Per Cederqvist et al. (ISBN 0-9541617-1-8) $29.95 (£19.95)

  This manual describes how to use CVS, the concurrent versioning system— one of the most widely-used source-code management systems available today. The manual provides tutorial examples for new users of CVS, as well as the definitive reference documentation for every CVS command and configuration option.

- **An Introduction to R** by W.N. Venables, D.M. Smith and the R Development Core Team (ISBN 0-9541617-4-2) $19.95 (£12.95)

This tutorial manual provides a comprehensive introduction to GNU R, a free software package for statistical computing and graphics.

- **GNU Scientific Library Reference Manual—Third Edition** by M. Galassi, et al (ISBN 0-9546120-7-8) $39.95 (£24.95)

  This reference manual is the definitive guide to the GNU Scientific Library (GSL), a numerical library for C and C++ programmers. The manual documents over 1,000 mathematical routines needed for solving problems in science and engineering. All the money raised from the sale of this book supports the development of the GNU Scientific Library.

- **GNU Octave Manual Version 3** by John W. Eaton et al. (ISBN 0-9546120-6-X) $39.95 (£24.95)

  This manual is the definitive guide to GNU Octave, an interactive environment for numerical computation with matrices and vectors. This edition covers version 3 of GNU Octave. For each copy sold $1 is donated to the GNU Octave Development Fund.

All titles are available for order from bookstores worldwide.

Sales of the manuals fund the development of more free software and documentation.

For details, visit the website `http://www.network-theory.co.uk/`. For questions or comments, please contact `sales@network-theory.co.uk`.

Key index

C

Command and function index

Variable index

This is not a complete index of variables and faces, only the ones that are mentioned in the manual. For a more complete list, use M-x org-customize (RET) and then click yourself through the tree.

Concept index

L

M

N

V

W

X

Y

CPSIA information can be obtained at www.ICGtesting.com
Printed in the USA
BVOW05s0403140414

350396BV00001B/106/P